COMPUTER SCIENCE, TECHNOLOGY AND APPLICATIONS

NATURE-INSPIRED COMPUTATION

COMPUTER SCIENCE, TECHNOLOGY AND APPLICATIONS

Additional books in this series can be found on Nova's website under the Series tab.

Additional e-books in this series can be found on Nova's website under the e-book tab.

COMPUTER SCIENCE, TECHNOLOGY AND APPLICATIONS

NATURE-INSPIRED COMPUTATION

MARIO D'ACUNTO

nova publishers
New York

Library of Congress Cataloging-in-Publication Data

Nature-inspired computation / editors, Mario D'Acunto (Consiglio Nazionale delle Ricerche, Istituto di Scienze e Tecnologie dell'Informazione and Istituto di Struttura della Materia and NanoICT Laboratory, Rome, Italy).
pages cm. -- (Computer science, technology and applications)
Includes index.
ISBN 978-1-63463-831-9 (hardcover)
1. Biocomputers. 2. Biocomplexity--Computer simulation. I. D'Acunto, Mario.
QA76.884.N38 2014
006.3'842--dc23
2015008471

Published by Nova Science Publishers, Inc. † New York

To Ovidio Salvetti

CONTENTS

PREFACE

Nature inspired computation is an old idea, first proposed in the early fifties by Alan Turing, one of the founders of the computer science. Turing suggested computational models of pattern formation in living systems based on systems of coupled reaction-diffusion equations giving rise to spatial patterns due to self-organization of substances in chemical concentrations.

Since the pioneering work by Turing, many optimization algorithms stimulated by real-world features have gained great popularity and impact in all scientific topics, thanks to their efficiency in solving nonlinear design problems. Nature-inspired computation has permeated into almost all areas of sciences, engineering and industries, from data mining to optimization, from computational intelligence to signal processing, from image analysis and vision systems to industrial applications, giving also the possibility to approach to wide multidisciplinary connections.

Nature is full of examples of computation and intelligence, complex systems and optimal solutions, so looking at natural systems, nature-inspired computation is a term that encompasses the entire range of the computational version of the process of extracting ideas from Nature to develop or improve computational systems, or using natural systems (like DNA, atoms, molecules, ant colony, reaction-diffusion systems, etc.) to perform computation. Just to give an example, any sensory systems that responds and adapts can naturally be viewed as an information device. Sensory systems can be characterized by fast response and slow adaption to varying environmental cues. As sensory adaptive systems map environmental changes to changes of their internal degrees of freedom, they can be regarded as computational devices manipulating information.

The book provides an introductory tour of the most popular nature inspired computational strategies. The book is subdivided in two parts, anyone briefly describing the inspiration and motivation by natural processes and phenomena, main players, design principles, scope of each branch, current trends and open problems. After an introductive description of some basic ideas underlying the nature-inspired computation, chapter 1, in the first part of the book, we focus the attention on the long tradition computing inspired by nature as Artificial and Spiking Neural Networks (chapter 2), Evolutionary and Genetic Algorithms (chapter 3), and Swarm Intelligence algorithms (chapter 4). In the second part, we present the emergent knowledge and technologies in Multiscale Nature processes (chapter 5), Quantum Computing and Quantum Cryptography (chapter 6), Encryption and Secure Communication system (chapter 7), Image processing and Vision systems (chapter 8), and finally on Nanophotonics Information (chapter 9).

Mario D'Acunto
Pisa, Italy

ACKNOWLEDGMENTS

I would like to thank Dr. Ovidio Salvetti (National Research Council of Italy, CNR, Institute of Information Science and Technologies, ISTI) for his encouragement and discussions throughout the preparation of this book. His suggestions were a valuable contribution and a great incentive to carry out this demanding work in the writing of this book. For the enormous contribution both scientifically and humanly that Ovidio gave me during these years of working together, the book is dedicated to him.

Furthermore, I would like to thank Dr. Makoto Naruse for useful discussions and activity that took place as part of the bilateral project CNR-JSPS "Fluctutation-phonon-mediated assited nanophotonic fabrication and their application".

In turn, I wish to thank Carra Feagaiga and the Nova Science Publisher editors for useful support during the preparation of this book.

ABOUT THE AUTHOR

Mario D'Acunto. M. Sci. degree in Physics from the University of Pisa in 1994, PhD degree in Materials Science at the Dept. of Mechanical and Nuclear Engineering, University of Pisa in 1999. Research Assistant at the Dept. of Physics, Dept. of Chemical Engineering and Materials Science, Dept. of Earth Science at the University of Pisa. Since 2009, he joined the Italian National Research Council (CNR) with a pioneering research activity connecting Machine Learning and Artificial Intelligence with Nanostructures. Currently, he is permanent researcher at the Institute of Structure of Matter (ISM-CNR), in Rome, and at the Institute of Information Science and Technologies, (ISTI-CNR), Pisa, Italy. His main interests, past and present, include theoretical and experimental skills in Surface Physics, Materials Science and Tribology, Image Processing and Analysis, Nonlinear dynamics, Microscopy techniques ranging from the molecular scale to optical range such as Scanning Probe Microscopy, Electron Microscopy, etc.

He is internationally recognized as a leading pioneer in the field of nanotribology, and his model on atomic wear has been named *D'Acunto model* by independent authors. He is the co-founder (with Ovidio Salvetti) since 2012 of the NanoICT laboratory, a *distributed-laboratory* with the main purpose to apply artificial intelligence and machine learning to nanostructures, in a special way on nanophotonic systems.

Chapter 1

INTRODUCTION: TAKING INSPIRATION FROM NATURE TO SOLVE COMPUTATION PROBLEMS

Nature-inspired Computation, and in a special way, bio-inspired computation, have attracted great interest in the last two decades, and, in particular, many optimization algorithms stimulated by real-world features have gained huge popularity. There are many reasons for such popularity and attention, and two main reasons are probably that such algorithms are flexible and versatile, and that they are very efficient in solving nonlinear design problems with real-world application. Nature-inspired computation has permeated into almost all areas of sciences, engineering and industries, from data mining to optimization, from computational intelligence to signal processing, from image analysis and vision systems to industrial applications. In fact, such algorithms due to their nature inspiration are one of the most active and popular research subjects with wide multidisciplinary connections.

The basic ideas underlying the nature-inspired computation can be backdated to the pioneering work of Church and Turing in the thirties of the last century. Indeed, a prevailing paradigm in classical computation theory, commonly recognized Church-Turing Thesis, affirms that no realizable computing device can be more powerful and efficient, aside from relative speedups, than a universal Turing machine (Church, 1932; Church, 1936, Turing, 1937; Calude and Păun, 2001, Ben Aman, 2005). As it is known for Turing machine is intended a hypothetical device that manipulates symbols on a strip of a physical recording tape according to a table of rules (Calude and

Păun, 2001). The Church-Turing Thesis is a precisely a thesis and not a theorem, nevertheless, many logicians and physicists challenged to define some insights from the Church-Turing Thesis into mathematical notion of probabilistic Turing machine adapted to simulate the logic of any computer algorithm. As a consequence, the Church-Turing Thesis has been used to approach formally the notion of intelligent being, that is stated with the following expression: *What is human computable is computable by a universal Turing machine*. This sentence equates information-processing capabilities of a human being with the *intellectual* capacities of a universal Turing machine. Moreover, this sentence implies also some questions on what types of computations are physically realizable and on the general problem on how translates in physical systems (electronic computers, for example) arithmetic operations, such as addition, subtraction, multiplication and division. Coherently with the Church-Turing Thesis, the notion of intelligence can be extended to the natural systems that can be traduced in terms of computational tasks and capability of Nature to operate as a *natural computer*.

In, this sense, nature-inspired computation is the computational version of the process of extracting ideas from nature to develop or improve computational systems, or using natural systems (like, DNA, atoms or molecules) to perform computation. Nature-inspired computing is a sub-branch of the most general natural computing, and can be defined as the field of research that, based or inspired by nature, allows the development of new computational tools, both hardware and software, The nature-inspired computation can be divided into two main branches (de Castro, 2007): *Computing inspired by nature* or *Computing with natural materials*.

In the first case, the basic idea is to develop computational tools, like algorithms, by taking inspiration from nature for the solution of complex problems. Through millions of years of trial-and-error using the mechanism of natural selection, nature has chosen specific solutions to problems such as survival and foraging for food in a hostile environment, involving the adaptation to totally different habitats.

In the latter case, computation is performed by using novel natural materials, where a novel computing paradigm comes out substituting or integrating the current silicon-based computers. Nature-inspired computation differs from natural computing, because does not consider a priority of inspiration from the *nature the simulation and emulation of nature by means of computing*. Nevertheless, both natural computing and nature-inspired computation represent multidisciplinary areas of investigation, involving computer scientists, physicists, chemists, engineers, biologists due to the necessity of integration of experimental and theoretical biology, physics, chemistry, empirical observation of nature with computational paradigms and algorithms.

de Castro proposed the scheme represented in figure 1.1 to illustrate the flowchart for natural computing, a correspondent scheme can be assumed for the nature-inspired computation.

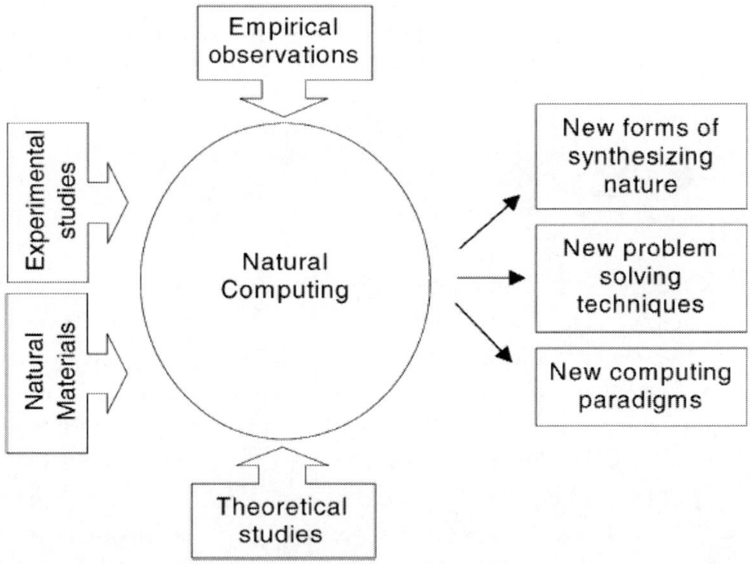

Figure 1.1. A schematic sketch representing the approaches used to develop natural computing. (Reproduced from (de Castro, 2007), with permission).

The basic motivation for inspiring computation from the Nature, it is that computation, be it mental, mechanic, molecular or silicon-based, is ultimately a physical process. To show this basic assumption, let us consider the following example *inspired* by the concept of entropy. In thermodynamics, the entropy S is a measure of the number of specific ways in which a thermodynamic system may be arranged, i.e., a sort of measure of disorder. According to the second law of thermodynamics the entropy of an isolated system never decreases and such systems spontaneously evolve towards thermodynamics equilibrium that corresponds to the configuration with maximum entropy. Systems not isolated, i.e., systems coupled to the environment, entropy may locally decrease, however, in irreversible processes, the entropy the system coupled to the environment (open system) increases.

The statistical definition of entropy was developed by Ludwig Boltzmann in the 70 decade of XIX century. Boltzmann showed that the interpretation of entropy in statistical mechanics is the measure of uncertainty about the microscopic nature of a system after its observable macroscopic properties, such as temperature, pressure and volume, have been taken into account. By a statistical point of view, for a given set of macroscopic variables, the entropy measures the degree to which the probability of the system is spread out over different possible microstates. The more such states available to the system with appreciable probability, the greater the entropy, i.e., entropy is a measure of the number of ways in which a system may be arranged. This definition is summarized by the expression

$$S = -k_B \cdot \sum_i p_i \cdot \ln p_i \tag{1.1}$$

where k_B is the Boltmann constant, equal to 1.38×10^{-23} J/K, (J is the Joule unity and K the Kelvin temperature), and p_i is the probability that the system is the i-th microstate. The entropy results to be a logarithmic measure of the number of the states with significant probability of being occupied. Von Neumann noticed that the two entropies are related by some constant factor. When the probability distribution of the system is changed so that the entropy is decreased by 1(unity, for example a bit), then the entropy is changed by a quantity $k_B \cdot \ln 2$ J/K and the system should dissipate $k_B T \cdot \ln 2$ joules of energy in the form of heat. Does the above analysis apply to computation? In 1961, Landauer has produced evidence for the affirmative answer. A computer to operate needs to be sure that distinct logical states are represented by distinct physical states. Each bit has two values, 0, 1, so it has one degree of freedom; it corresponds to one or more degress of freedom of physical states. A set of n bits possesses n degrees of freedom, corresponding to 2^n physical states. If, say, we reset n bits to all 0, then we have compressed 2^n logical states into a single state, this implies a loss of entropy. The irreversible loss information is equivalent to increase temperature in a physical system. As a consequence, operations in a computer cost energy. This cost is expressed by Landauer's principle (Landauer, 1961; Landauer, 1991): *Erasure of information is a dissipative process*. The quantification of such dissipation can be made with various simple examples.

An operation is *logically reversible* if it can be *undone* and if it can be run *backwards*, that is, if its inputs can always deduced from the outputs. Most logical gates are irreversible, a typical example is the NAND gate, which has two inputs bits and only one output bit. So, we cannot recover a unique input from the output bit because the result, say 1, can be obtained from three distinct inputs: (0,0), (0,1), (1,0). Assume, now, we operate the gate NAND with two Boolean variables, say, *a* and *b*, and suppose that the four initial states, (0,0), (0,1), (1,0), (1,1), have the same probability distribution, i.e., ¼. The initial entropy, which is calculated with Shannon's formula (here we use the capital letter *H* for the entropy, to be distinguished by the entropy as defined in thermodynamics)

$$H = -\sum_i p_i \cdot \log p_i \tag{1.2}$$

where p_i is the probability of the occurrence of event *i* and log is the logarithm in base 2, so resulting to be

$$H_{initial} = -4 \cdot \left(\frac{1}{4} \log \frac{1}{4} \right) = 2 \text{ bits} \tag{1.3}$$

That represents a system with only two possible states, 0 and 1, the outcome 0 appearing with probability ¼ and the outcome 1 appearing with probability ¾, consequently, the final entropy will be

$$H_{final} = -\left(\frac{3}{4} \log \frac{3}{4} + \frac{1}{4} \log \frac{1}{4} \right) = 2 - \frac{3}{4} \log 3 \text{ bits} \tag{1.4}$$

which means a loss of

$$H_{initial} - H_{final} = \frac{3}{4} \log 3 \text{ bits} \tag{1.5}$$

Assume, now, that we operate the gate $(a,b) \mapsto (a \vee b, a \vee b)$ and, again, suppose that the four initial states of the Boolean variables a, b have the same probability distribution, ¼. This gate has finally only three final states, namely (0,0), (1,0), (1,1), two of them with probability ¼ and one with probability ½. Consequently, the final entropy is

$$H_{final} = -\left(2 \cdot \frac{1}{4}\log\frac{1}{4} + \frac{1}{2}\log\frac{1}{2}\right) = \frac{3}{2}\,\text{bits.} \qquad (1.6)$$

In this case, the entropy loss due to the gate is ½ bits. Such examples show that the Landauer's principle can be enunciated in other words as: *information is inevitably physical*.

The key figure in nature-inspired algorithms is the *logic primitives*, on which the analysis of computational properties of structures can be built using various physical, chemical and biological phenomena (Hertz et al., 1991; Winfree et al., 1998; Tour, 2003; Aoki et al., 2004; Yanushkevich and Shmerko, 2008). Although the term logic primitive denotes a *technology-independent* computer unit, such unit becomes *technology-dependent* if the underlying natural phenomenon is specified (Yanushkevich and Shmerko, 2010). Natural phenomenon as well as the results of physical, chemical or biological processes can be *encoded* and *decoded* in terms of logic primitives. Encoding and decoding processes must be controlled for the resulting structure to contain the wanted properties. Hence, the natural properties are exploited to simplify the control functions of manufacturing. There are not analogies of such concepts in microelectronics. Instead of electrical signals representing streams of binary 1s and 0s, the natural processes, just an example of the many possible, the chemical concentrations of specific inducer molecules act as the input and output signals. These molecules interact with other molecules and bind specific molecular structures and such chemical process can be used as Boolean functions. The basic idea is to encode the particular features of chemical process in terms of logic primitives. A molecular primitive can be defined as a *switch* (two-terminal molecular device) and many-terminal molecular devices can be designed as logic gates by assembling the molecular primitives. Analogously, intermediate data structure is characterized by the properties such as (i) the ability to be encoded, (ii) recognition by topological properties, (iii) rules for assembling, and, (iv) ability to compose the universal set of logic operations (Crawley et al., 2005). Using the universal set of elementary Boolean functions, an arbitrary logic network can be designed.

The problem of computational completeness for nature-inspired systems requires a comment. Completeness, accordingly to Turing, is used to evaluate the computational properties of natural systems, thus addressing the highest level of abstraction (Bennett, 1973; Bennett and Landauer, 1985; Calude, 1988). In logic design of computing networks, we can formulate the completeness using the Post Theorem (Soare, 1987). In this case, the completeness is defined using the criteria of *minimal complete*, *redundant* and *decomposed* set of operations. To achieve the completeness of operation in the computation of an arbitrary logic function, some assembling rules for these primitives must be applied. For example, this type of completeness characterizes some types of DNA-based computation, where the rules of spatial configuration are specified and an arbitrary Boolean function is represented using the set of logic primitives.

In contrast to classical computing paradigms, many nature inspired structures can be implemented using techniques of templates. The templates carry out the information about computational properties. For example, fractals, that are characterized by multiscale self-affine structure, can be interpreted in terms of Boolean functions are useful as templates for tile self-assembly. In DNA computation, the tiles are DNA-based molecular structures moving randomly and the non-successive bonding of tiles performs incorrect computation, which can lead to error rate of nearly 8% (Amos, 2010). This feature is the base of the *randomly assembled computer*. In such type of computation, a network of randomly and sparsely interconnected nodes with binary behavior is assumed. The role of randomness in defining the rules of computation can be expressed as follows: give unreliable logic rules achieve the correct output values (Păun et al., 1998). This computation strategy presents still many unsolved questions. Von Neumann's approach declares that it is theoretically possible to achieve an acceptable level of fault-tolerance for the simplest imperfect logic cells using massive redundancy under certain constraints. So, since logic network models based on natural systems must be built taking into account the stochastic nature of device function process, then, the error models must be incorporated into the computational model in a sort of probabilistic logic network. This is the case of evolutionary and biocomputing algorithms, as well as self-assembly based computation (Doty, 2012).

Nature offers a myriad of examples. Only one, any sensory system that responds and adapts can naturally be viewed as an information processing device. Sensory system are characterized by fast response and slow adaptation to varying environmental cues. As sensory adaptive systems map environmental changes to changes of their internal degrees of freedom, they can be regarded as computational devices manipulating information. As described before, information is ultimately physical, and its manipulation subject to the entropic and energetic bounds of thermodynamics. Therefore, the fundamental costs of biological sensory adaptation can be clarified by tracking how the information the system has about its environmental is modified. These bounds are particularly relevant for small organisms, which unlike everyday computers operate at very low energies. Thus, one focus of bioinspired computation is to establish a general framework to the thermodynamics of information processing in sensory. Such general framework should help to quantify how during sensory adaptation information about the past is erased, while information about the present is gathered. *Amoeba* and *Escherichia coli* chemotaxis pathway are classical examples on how the animal cells receptors consume energy in the range of the information-theoretic minimum (Aono et al., 2007; D'Acunto et al., 2007). Bioinspired computation frameworks are also the basis for studies of nature-inspiring computation in solid state systems, as well as quantum systems and diffusion conditioned process (Naruse, 2014), only to cite a few.

1.1. Current Issues in Nature-Inspired Computation

Despite the wide popularity gained in the last two decades of nature-inspired Computation, there remain many challenging issues. Such challenging issues can be defined as: (i) gaps between theory and practice; (ii) classifications; (iii) parameters choice and (iv) large scale real-word applications.

i. Gaps between theory and practice: Nature-inspired algorithms work almost magically in practice, but it is not well understood why these algorithms work (Koziel and Yang, 2011). Except for a few cases such as genetic algorithms, simulated annealing, and swarm optimization, there are not many good results concerning the convergence analysis and stability of metaheuristic algorithms.
ii. Classifications: there are many ways to classify optimization algorithms. One possibility is to consider the number of agents, another one is based on the iteration procedure. In the first case, we have two possibilities: single agent or multiple agents. Genetic algorithms, particle swarm optimization are population-based algorithms, inspired genes or by swarming behavior of birds, such algorithms involve multiple agents interacting in a nonlinear manner. On the contrary, simulated annealing is a single agent algorithm. Another way of classifying algorithms is based on the core procedure

of algorithms. If an algorithms contains some randomness in the algorithm procedure, it is normally called stochastic, evolutionary, heuristic or metaheuristic. Here, heuristic is intended as *by trial and error*, while metaheuristic denotes a higher-level method by using certain selection mechanisms and information sharing (Fogel et al., 1966; Holland, 1975).

iii. Many nature-inspired algorithms have algorithms dependent parameters, and the appropriate setting of such parameters values will largely affect the performance of an algorithm. As a consequence, a challenging issue is deciding what values of parameters to use in an algorithm and how these parameters can be tuned so that they can maximize the performance on the algorithm of interest. There are two basic strategies. One is to run an algorithm with some trial values of key parameters, and the aim of the test runs is to get the best setting of these parameters. The other approach is to use a well-established algorithm to tune the parameters of another relatively new algorithm.

iv. Nature-inspired computation are very successful in solving many practical problems. However, the size, in term of variables, of these problems is relatively small. In the current literature, the algorithms have employed no more than hundred variables. On the contrary, linear programming solves problems with several millions of variables.

One example of nature-inspired operability for algorithms is the example of self-organization that is a ubiquitous process occurring in many systems, from physical and chemical to biological and artificial systems. Emergent phenomena such as Rayleigh-Bénard convection, Turing pattern formation and thunderstorms can all be seen as manifestation of self-organization (Turing, 1952; Cross and Hohenberg, 1993). Many aspects of self-organization can partly be understood using theories based on nonlinear dynamical systems, and far-from equilibrium multiple interacting agents. As suggested by Ashby, every isolated dynamic system, obeying to unchanged laws, will eventually develop some sort of organisms that are adapted to their environments (Ashby, 1962). For simple systems, going to equilibrium is trivial, on the contrary, for a complex system, if its size is to large that its equilibrium states are just a fraction of the vast number of possible states, and, if the system can evolve long enough, some self-organized structures may emerge. In addition, the changes occurring in the environment can stimulate the system to reorganize and re-adapt itself to such changes. If the system has sufficient perturbations or noise, often working at the edge of the chaos, some spontaneous formation of structures will emerge as the systems moves, far from equilibrium, selecting those states reducing uncertainty or entropy. The analogy with an optimization algorithm is immediate. An optimization algorithm can be viewed as a complex, dynamical system. If a convergence process can be considered as a self-organizing process, then there are strong similarities and links between self-organizing systems and optimization algorithms. And the features occurring in nature could be *translated* in algorithm to generate new and powerful computation.

The book provides an introductory tour of the most popular nature inspired computational strategies. The book is subdivided in two parts, anyone briefly describing the inspiration and motivation by natural processes and phenomena, main players, design principles, scope of each branch, current trends and open problems. In the first one, we focus the attention on the long tradition computing inspired by nature as Artificial and Spiking Neural Networks (chapter 2), Evolutionary and Genetic Algorithms (chapter 3), and Swarm Intelligence algorithms (chapter 4). In the second part, we present the emergent knowledge and technologies in Multiscale Nature processes (chapter 5), Quantum Computing and Quantum Cryptography(chapter 6), Encryption and Secure Communication system (chapter 7), Image processing and Vision systems (chapter 8), and finally on Nanophotonics Information (chapter 9).

REFERENCES

Amos M., 2010, Theoretical and Experimental DNA Computation, Springer, Berlin.

Aoki T., Homma N., Higuchi T., 2004, Evolutionary synthesis of arithmetic circuit structures, Artificial Intelligence in Logic Design, edited by Yanushkevich S.N., Kluwer, Dordrecht, 39-51.

Aono M., Hara M., Aihara K., 2007, Amoeba-based neurocomputing with chaotic dynamics, *Communications of ACM*, 50, 69-72.

Ashby W.R., 1962, Principles of the self-organization systems, in Principle of Self-Organization: Transactions of the University of Illinois Symposium, pp. 255-278, Pergamon Press, London, UK.

Ben-Amran A.M., 2005, The church-Turing Thesis and its Look-Alikes, *SIGACT News* 36(3), 113-116.

Bennett C.H., 1973, Logical reversibility of computation, *IBM J. Res. Develop.* 17, 525-532.

Bennett C.H., Landauer R., 1985, The fundamental physics limits of computation, *Scientific American*, July, 48-56.

Calude C., Theories of Computational Complexity, North-Holland, Amsterdam, 1988.

Calude C.S., Păun G., 2001, Computing with Cells and Atoms, Taylor & Francis, New York.

Church A., 1932, A set of Postulates for the Foundation of Logic, *Annals of Mathematics*, 33(2), 346-366.

Church A., 1936, An Unsolvable Problem of Elementary Number Theory, *American Journal of Mathematics*, 58(58), 345-363.

Crawley D., Nikolíc K., Forshaw M., 2005, 3D Nanoelectroncis Computer Architecture and Implementation, Institute of Physics Publishing, UK.

Cross M.C., Hohenberg P.C., 1993, Pattern Formation outside of equilibrium, *Reviews of Modern Physics*, 65(3), 851-1112.

D'Acunto M., Ciardelli G., Rechichi A., Montevecchi F.M., Giusti P., 2007, Nanotribological perspectives in Tissue Engineering, in Friction and Wear at Atomic Scale, Gnecco E. and Meyer E., eds., Springer, Berlin.

de Castro, L.N., 2007, Fundamentals of Natural Computing: an overview, *Physics of Life Reviews*, 4, 1-36.

Doty D., 2012 Theory of Algorithmic Self-assembly, *Communications of the ACM*, 55, 78-88.

Fogel L.J., Owens A.J., Walsh M.J., 1966, Artificial intelligence Through Simulated Evolution, J. Wiley & Sons, New York, NY.

Hertz J., Krogh A., Palmer R.G., 1991, Introduction to the Theory of Neural Computation, Addison-Wesley, Redwood City.

Holland J., 1975, Adaptation in Natural and Artificial Systems, University of Michigan Press, Ann Arbor, MI.

Koziel S., Yang X.S., 2011, Computational Optimization, Methods and Algorithms, Springer, Germany.

Landauer R., 1961, Irreversibility and heat generation in the computing process, *IBM J. Res. Develop.*, 5, 183-191.

Landauer R., 1991, Information is physical, *Physics Today*, 44, 23-29.

Naruse M., 2014, Nanophotonic Information Physics. Nanointelligence and Nanophotonic Computing, Springer, Germany.

Soare R.I., 1987, Recursively enumerable Sets and degrees, Springer-Verlag, Berlin.

Tour J.M., 2003, Molecular Electronics: Commercial Insights, Chemistry, Devices, Architecture and Programming, World Scientific, Hackensack, NJ.

Turing A.M., 1936, On Computable Numbers, with an Application to the Entscheidungsproblem, *Proceedings of the London Mathematical Society* 42(2), 230-65.

Turing A.M., 1952, The Chemical Basis of Morphogenesis, *Philosophical Transactions of the Royal Society of London*, 237(641), 37-72.

Winfree E., Liu F., Wenzler L.A., Seeman N.C., 1998, Design and self-assembly of two-dimensional DNA crystals, *Nature* 394, 539-544.

Yanushkevich S.N., Shmerko V.P., 2008, Introduction to Logic Design, Taylor &Francis/CRC Press, Boca Raton, FL.

Yanushkevich S.N., Shmerko V.P., 2010, Nature-Inspired Computing for Nanoelectronics, *Journal of Information, Control and Mangements systems*, 8(3), 265-283.

Chapter 2

ARTIFICIAL AND SPIKING NEURAL NETWORKS

The human brain can be described as a biological neural network that is as an interconnected web of neurons transmitting elaborate patterns of electrical signals. Neurons receive input signals and, based on such inputs, fire an output signal via on axon. The human brain works in an exceptional complexity way that, obviously, presents still many and many properties, behavior, and connection to be lighten. However, developing engaging animated systems with code does not require scientific accuracy on underlying processes, rather, we can simply to be inspired by the idea of brain function. In 1943, Warren S. McCulloch, a neuroscientist, and Walter Pitts, a logician, developed a first conceptual model of an artificial neural network (McCulloch and Pitts, 1943). In such model, they suggest the idea of a neuron, a single cell living in a network of cells that receives inputs, processes the inputs, and generates an output. Their work was not meant to accurately describe how the biological brain works. On the contrary, they focused the attention on how an artificial neural network (ANN) could be designed as a computational model based on the brain to solve certain kinds of problems. Their networks were based on simple neurons which were considered to be binary devices with fixed thresholds. The results of their model were simple logic functions such as *a or b* and *a and b*. In 1958, Rosenblatt stirred considerable interest in the field when designed and developed the so-called *Perceptron*, (Rosenblatt, 1958; Rosenblatt, 1962). The Perceptron had three layers with the middle layer known as the association layer. This system could learn to connect or associate a given input to a random output unit. Since the late 1979s and early 1980s the interest in the field of ANN based computing growth significantly in parallel to other techniques based on learning approach. In fact, the most common application of neural networks in computing today is to perform pattern recognition, with application ranging from optical character recognition to facial recognition. ANN is today an umbrella term for many techniques and algorithms together to fuzzy logic, neuro-computing, genetic computing, etc. defined generally as *soft computing*. On contrary to computational systems that are procedural (a program starts at the first line of code, executes it, and goes on the next, following instructions in a linear fashion), ANN does not follow a linear path, but information is processed in parallel throughout a network of nodes, the nodes being the neurons.

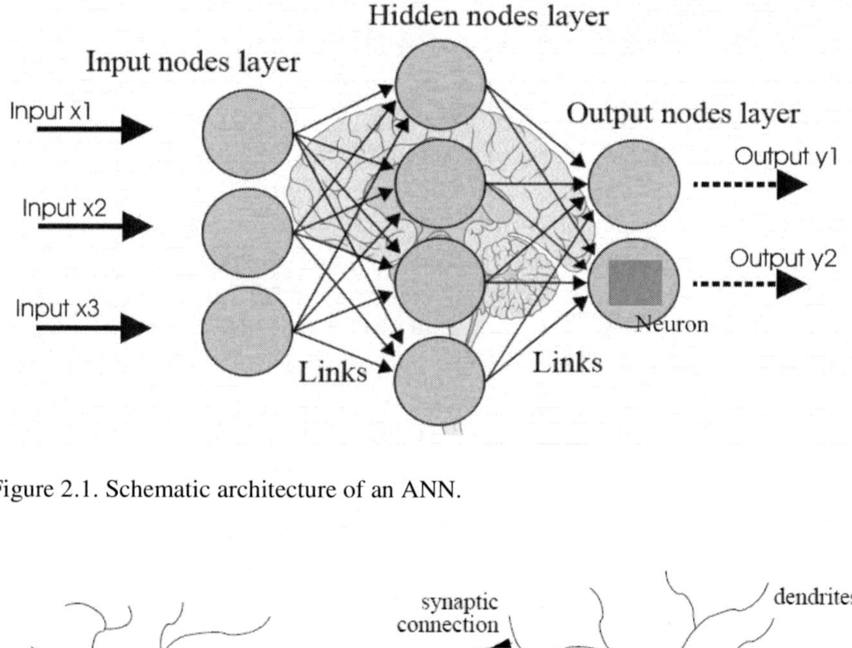

Figure 2.1. Schematic architecture of an ANN.

Figure 2.2. (Continued).

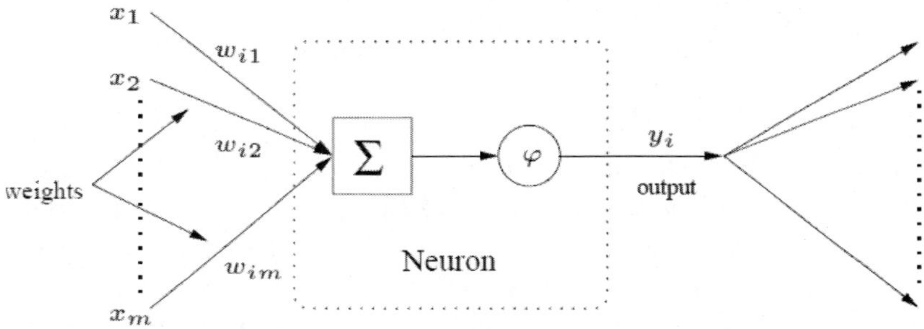

Figure 2.2. Above, elementary scheme of biological neurons. Below, internal structure of a node with its inputs (xi), weighted inputs (wi) and Sigmoid function.

In figure 2.1, it is represented a feed-forward ANN, characterized by the layout and behavior of their inner nodes, represented on figure 2.2. The nodes are arranged in input, output and middle layers with the last hidden from the outside. Each node in every layer is connected to every other node in the next layer guarantying the constant *forward flow* of information between layers. Nodes within the same layer are totally isolated from one another.

A large number of learning rules have been proposed, both for supervised learning (for teaching a network explicitly to do some tasks), and for unsupervised learning (self-learning features with external instructions). Supervised learning algorithms are for example gradient descent algorithms, such as error backpropagation, that fit the neural network behavior to some target function. Unsupervised learning in neural networks can be traced back to synaptic plasticity (Hebb, 1949) consisting in the ability of synapses to strengthen or weaken over time, in response to increases or decreases in their activity. Although, artificial neural networks have been proved to be very powerful in many domains, pattern recognition, control, bioinformatics, robotics, statistical tools, traditional neural networks suffer from intrinsic limitations, mainly for processing large amount of data or for fast adaptation to a changing environment. It has been evidenced as several characteristics, such as iterative learning algorithms or artificially designed neuron model and network architecture, are strongly restrictive compared with biological processing in natural neural networks (Paugam-Moisy and Bohte, 2011). In addition, new investigations in natural neuronal processing are stimulated and motivated by the evolution of thinking regarding the basic principles of brain processing. When the first neural networks were modeled, the prevailing belief was that intelligence is based on reasoning, and that logic is the foundation of reasoning. First application of neuron activity model designed by McCulloch and Pitts was addressed to show how thresholded binary neurons were skilled to build networks for computing Boolean functions (McCulloch and Pitts, 1943). Following the idea of Turing's work, they thought that in complex systems, intelligence could emerge from a very large network of neurons, combining huge numbers of elementary logic gates (Turing, 1950). Separately, neurobiological research has greatly progressed and the idea of Boolean decomposition of tasks has been abandoned for a long time for a long time. New knowledge on associative memory, learning, adaptation, and emotionality have replaced the basic notion of logic and reasoning as being fundamental to understanding how the brain processes information, while the concept of *time* emerged as a central feature in cognitive processing (Abeles, 1991). The advent of new brain imaging technologies, (electroencephalogram recording, functional magnetic resonance imaging, functional near infrared spectroscopy, etc.) has given the ability to record rapid changes in the internal activity of brain, and help elucidate the relation between brain activity and the perception of a given stimulus (Freeman, 1991). It is commonly recognized that cognitive process are most likely based on the activation of transient assemblies of neurons, although the underlying mechanisms are not yet understood well (Paugam-Moisy and Bohte, 2011). Real neurons spike, or better, neurons rely on pulses as an important part of information transmission from one neuron to another neuron (Maass and Bishop, 1999. In synthesis, a neuron can generate an action potential, the so-called *spike*, at the soma, the cell body of the neuron. This feature of real neurons became a central paradigm of a theory of spiking neural models. From an information processing, all spiking models share some common properties with their biological counterparts: (i) neurons process information coming from many inputs and produce single spiking output signals; (ii) their probability of firing (i.e., the generation of a spike) is increased by excitatory inputs and decreased by inhibitory inputs; (iii) Neurons dynamics is characterized by at least one state variable; when the internal variables of the model reach a certain state (in general, a threshold value), the model is supposed to generate one or more spikes. The basic assumption underlying the implementation of most of spiking neuron models is that it is the timing of spikes that carries the neural information rather than the specific shape of spikes (Olshausen, 1996; Gerstner and Kistler, 2002). The brief electric pulse travels along the neuron's axon with a duration of 1 or 2*ms*, figure 2.2 above. At the end of the axon, synapses connect one neuron to another, and the arrival of each individual spike, the synapses may release neurotransmitters along the synaptic cleft. These neurotransmitters are taken up by the neuron at the receiving end, and modify the state of that *postsynaptic* neuron, in particular the membrane potential, making the neuron more or less likely to fire for some duration of time (Purves et al., 2001). The transient impact a spike has on the neuron's membrane potential is commonly referred to as the postsynaptic potential, and it can potentially either inhibit the future firing, or excite the neuron, making it more likely to fire. A sequence of firing times can be described as a train of spiking pulse, $S(t)=\Sigma_i\delta(t-t_i)$, where i=1,2,… is the label of the spike and $\delta(.)$ is a Dirac function with $\delta(t)\neq 0$ for $t=0$ and $\int_{\Delta t}\delta(t)dt=1$, with Δt is a integration time interval enough large, figure 2.3.

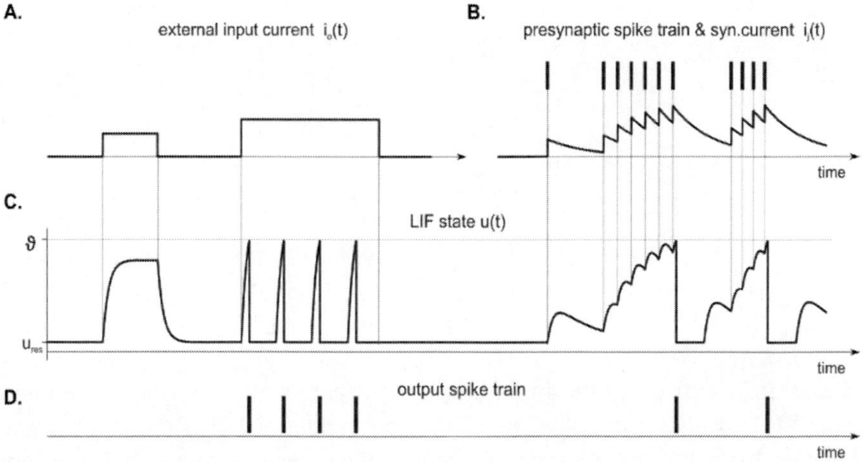

Figure 2.3. Example of the time evolution of the membrane potential $u(t)$ of a leaky-integrated-and-fire neuron (panel C) driven by an external input current $i_0(t)$ (panel A) or by a synaptic current $i_j(t)$ evoked by the sample presynaptic spike train (panel B). The currents $i_0(t)$ and $i_j(t)$ increase the membrane potential towards the firing threshold. Whenever the threshold is crossed the neuron emits a spike and the membrane voltage $u(t)$ is reset to a new value. The firing times of the neuron are represented as vertical bars in panel D. (Reproduced from (Ponulak and Kasinski, 2011), with permission).

Common spiking neuron models (Integrated-and-Fire; Leaky-Integrated-and-Fire, etc.) treat biological neurons as point dynamical systems, where the dynamics is described as follows (Ponulak and Kasinski, 2011):

$$C\frac{du(t)}{dt} = -\frac{u(t)}{R} + \left(i_0(t) + \sum w_j i_j(t)\right) \tag{2.1}$$

where $u(t)$ is the model state variable, that corresponds to the neural membrane potential, C is the membrane capacitance, R is the input resistance, $i_0(t)$ is the external current driving the neural state, $i_j(t)$ is the input current from the j-th synaptic input, and w_j represents the strength of the j-th synapse. In a model described by the Eq. (2.1), a neuron is supposed to fire a spike at time t_i, whenever the membrane potential u reaches a certain value v called a firing threshold. Immediately after a spike the neuron state is reset to a new value $u'<v$ and hold at that level for the time interval representing the neural absolute refractory period, figure 2.2. Arrival of a presynaptic spike at a synapse triggers an input signal $i(t)$ into the postsynaptic neuron. The input signal corresponds to the synaptic electric current flowing into the biological neuron and one largely employed its time dependence is (Ponulak and Kasinski, 2011):

$$i(t) = \int_0^{\infty} S_j(s-t)\exp(-s/\tau_s)ds \qquad (2.2)$$

where τ_s is the synaptic time constant and $S_j(t)$ denotes a presynaptic spike train. In figure 2.3, a typical response of the synapse model, as given by Eq. (2.2), to a sample input spike train is represented.

Neuroscience has made increasingly clear that in many situations, information is carried in the individual action potentials (Paugam-Moisy and Bohte, 2011). Rather than the form of the action potential, it is the number and the timing of spikes that play a significant role. This is particularly important for computation, because it has been recognized that the exact timing of spikes can be a means for coding information, as demonstrated in the electrosensory system of electric fish (Heiligenberg, 1991), in the auditory system of echo-locating bats (Kuwabara and Suga, 1993), and in the visual system of flies (Bialek et al., 1991). There is a long list of applications of artificial neural networks, as well as spiking neural networks, to a wide class of different problems. For a review of those methods we refer to Anthony and Bartlett (Anthony and Bartlett, 1999), and Ponulak and Kasinski (Ponulak and Kasinski, 2011).

2.1. Information Processing in Spiking Neurons

Each millisecond, thousands of spikes emitted by sensory neurons are processed by the brain, which decides what actions are the most appropriate for the sensed stimuli. In front of such brain activity, some issues arise: what processes enable such a fast information processing and how is information encoded in the neural signals? Or again, what is the temporal resolution of signals required to perform precise computations? Such issues concerning the neural representation of information are often referred to as a problem of neural code, strictly linked to rate coding and spiking code (Gerstner and Kistler, 2002). Many physiologists subscribe to the idea of a Poisson-like rate code to describe the way that neurons transmit information. However, Poisson rate codes seem hard to fit the impressively efficient rapid information transmission required for sensory processing in human vision, since only 100-150*ms* are sufficient for a human to respond selectively to complex visual stimuli, and in feedforwarded architecture of visual system this time is reduced to approximately 10*ms* (van Rullen et al., 2005; Girard et al., 2008). One possible answer to the realization of instantaneous rate code could be given by a pool of neurons firing spikes stochastically as a function of the stimulus: the so-called spike density code. However, maintaining such a set of neurons is expensive, as is the energetic code of firing so many spikes to encode a single variable. To address this problem several neural coding strategies based on spike timing have been proposed. In figure 2.4, some of such strategies are presented.

Time-to-first-spike is a model information, where the neural systems is encoded in the latency between the beginning of stimulus and the time of the first spike, figure 2.4A. Time-to-first-spike model enables ultra-fast information processing, as a decision on a stimulus can be commutated by the arrival of the first spike already within a few milliseconds. Such model has been considered for input discrimination in artificial tactile and olfactory sensors (Kim et al., 2010; Chen et al., 2011). Rank-order coding is another simple neural coding scheme, figure 2.4B, where information is encoded by the order of spikes in the activity of a neural population. Rank-order coding model assumes that each neuron emits only a single spike during a presentation of the image. This can be easily implemented in a feedforward network with inhibitory feedback connections. Based on such principles, rank-order coding scheme has been used to explain ultra-fast categorization observed in primate's visual system (Thorpe et al., 2001). Latency code is a model information where it is supposed to contain the exact timing of a set of spikes relative to each other, figure 2.4C. Since precisely timed patterns of spikes have been suggested to have a fundamental role in the nervous system in many functions controlling many forms of synaptic plasticity, as a consequence, changing the relative timing of presynaptic and postsynaptic spikes in a cortical neuron by a little as 10*ms* can determine whether a synapse is potentiated or depressed (Markram et al., 1997). Precisely timed sequences of spikes are typically observed in feedforward networks, since noise and inherent dynamics of recurrent networks can easily disrupt spike timing precision. In addition, as latency code is very efficient in terms of information capacity, some attempts to harvest precise spiking timing in recurrent networks have been made by exploring the idea of reservoir computation (Lestienne, 2001; Maass et al., 2002; Ponulak and Kasinski, 2010). Temporal coding mechanism for encoding and decoding spikes is represented in figure 2.5 (Paugam-Moisy and Bohte, 2011).

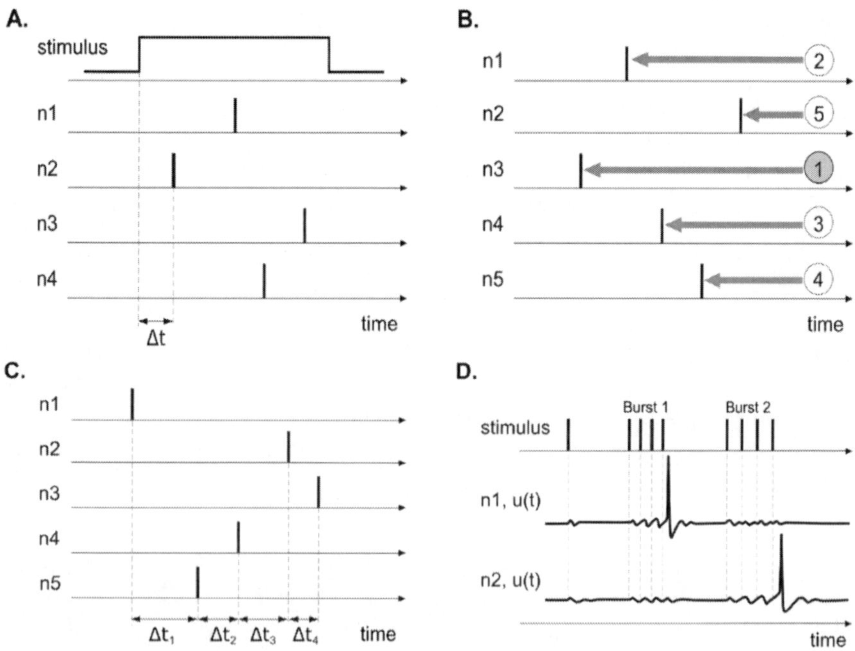

Figure 2.4. (Continued).

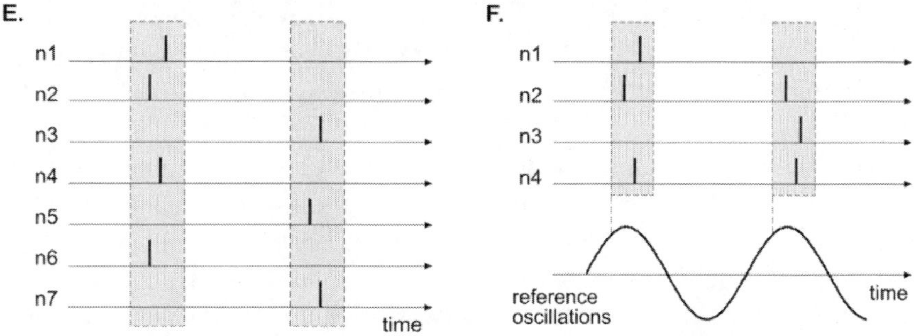

Figure 2.4. Spike-based information coding strategies: (A) time-to-first-spike; (B) rank-coding or spike-order coding, the number 1,..,5 in the circles indicate the order of spike arrival ; (C) latency coding based on the exact timing of spikes; (D) resonant burst coding; (E) coding by synchrony; (F) phase coding. *n#* represents the label of a neuron, Δt denotes the inter-spike latency, in turn, *u(t)* is the neuron model state variable. (Reproduced from (Ponulak and Kasinski, 2011), with permission).

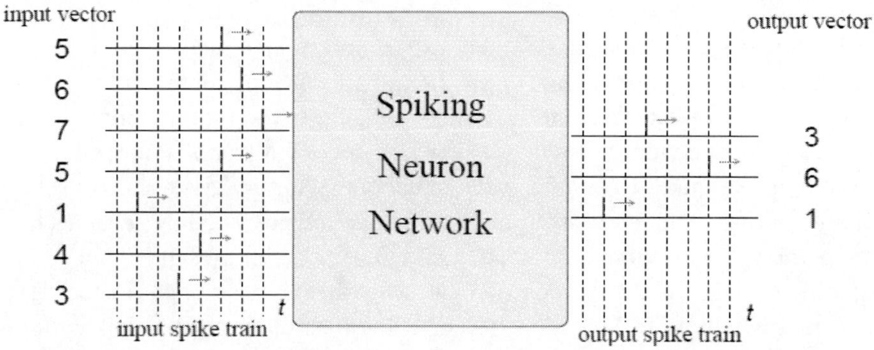

Figure 2.5. Schematic sketch of the temporal coding principle for encoding and decoding real vectors in spike trains. (Reproduced from (Paugam-Moisy and Bohte, 2011), with permission).

Other models of neural coding strategies represented in figure 2.4 refer to resonant burst model, coding by synchrony and phase coding. In resonant burst model the frequency of a burst of spikes determines which downstream neurons are activated, figure 2.4D (Izhikevich, 2002). Using the resonance phenomenon, a short burst can elicit strong post-synaptic response if the burst frequency is tuned to the eigen-frequencies of the membrane potential oscillations in the target neurons. The same burst would have a negligible effect on the postsynaptic membrane potential if the burst and eigen-frequencies are not tuned. This phenomenon could provide am effective mechanism for selective communication between neurons (Izhikevich, 2002). Coding by synchrony, figure 2.4E, is a model based on the assumption that neurons that encode different bits of information on the same object fire synchronously (Gray et al., 1989; Jefferys et al., 1996). This model is grounded on several experimental observations, for example, neurons in the visual cortex tend to synchronize their discharges with a precision in the millisecond range when activated with a single contour, whereas they act differently when activated by different contours moving in different directions (Gray et al. 1989). In the context of networks, neuronal synchronization is a mechanism improving information transmission through the network, as well as timing precision of spiking events (Diesmann et al., 1999). Figure 2.4F present the last neural coding strategies illustrated in this section, i.e., the phase coding. In phase coding model, times of emitted spikes are referred to the reference time point in a periodic signal. In this way neuronal spike trains can encode information in the phase of a pulse with respect to the background oscillations (Hopfield, 1995; Maass, 1996; Jensen and Lisman, 1996; Buzsaki, 2006).

It should be evidenced that the experimental and theoretical findings discussed in this section do not discard rate-based neural codes. To highlight the importance of rate base neural codes with precisely timing spikes let us consider the following considerations. From a combinatorial point of view, precisely timed spikes have a far greater encoding capacity given a small set of spiking neurons. The representational power of alternative coding schemes has been pointed out in figure 2.6, where a stimulus has been presented to a set of n spiking neurons and that each of them fires at most one spike in the next $T(ms)$ time window. If the code is to count the overall number of spikes fired by the set of neurons (population rate coding), the maximum amount of available information is $\log_2(n+1)$, since only $n+1$ different events can occur. In the case of a binary code, the output is an n-digits binary number, with obviously n as information coding capacity. A higher amount of information is transmitted with a timing code, provided that an efficient decoding mechanism is available for determining the precise times of each spike.

In practical cases, the available code size depends on the decoding precision, for example, for a $1ms$ precision, an amount of information of $n \times \log_2(T)$ can be transmitted in the T time window. In we consider the rank order coding model, since information is encoded in the order of the sequence of spike emissions, one among the $n!$ orders that can be obtained from n neurons, thus $\log_2(n!)$ bits can be transmitted, meaning that the order of magnitude of capacity is $n\log(n)$ (Paugam-Moisy and Bohte, 2011).

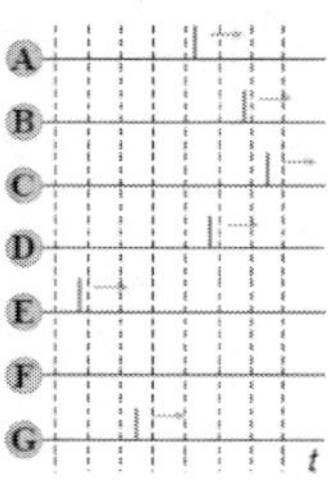

	count	latency	rank
A	1	5	3
B	1	6	5
C	1	7	6
D	1	5	4
E	1	1	1
F	0	–	–
G	1	3	2

Numeric examples:	count code	binary code	timing code	rank order
left (opposite) figure $n = 7, T = 7ms$	3	7	≈ 19	12.3
Thorpe et al. [164] $n = 10, T = 10ms$	3.6	10	≈ 33	21.8

Number of bits that can be transmitted by n neurons in a T time window.

Figure 2.6. Example of number of bits that can be transmitted the binary code 1111101 by n neurons for different time latency T and different coding schemes. (Reproduced from (Paugam-Moisy and Bohte, 2011), with permission).

2.2. Unsupervised and Supervised Learning

It is commonly thought that learning and memory in neural networks are based on the synaptic plasticity, i.e., the ability of synaptic connections to change their strength (Kwok and Yeung, 1997; Baudry, 1998). This ability is amplified by the co-existence of various forms of synaptic plasticity. Plasticity processes can differ on a time scale or in the conditions required for the induction (Lømo, 1966; Magleby and Zengel, 1976; Abbott and Nelson, 2000). Some forms of plasticity depend on the coincidence of pre- and postsynaptic activity and the concentration of specific chemicals (Citri and Malenka, 2008). However, without less of generality, we can focus the attention on models of learning for spiking neural networks that explore spike-timing based synaptic plasticity (Ponulak and Kasinski, 2011). Such models can be subdivided as unsupervised or supervised models.

Unsupervised learning is a process that takes place when the modification of synaptic strength, following a Hebbian process, is able to store information leading to the reorganization of connections within a neural network and under certain conditions may result in the emergence of new functions and formation of associative memories or formation of self-organizing maps (Hinton and Sejnowski, 1999). A Hebbian process is directly connected with the modality chose by the synapses to change their weights in order to store information. In such process, the change of the strength of the synaptic coupling, w_{ij}, can be expressed as $\Delta w_{ij} \propto v_i v_j$, where v_i represents the activity of the presynaptic neuron i and v_j the activity of the postsynaptic neuron j. The coupling is strengthened when both the neurons are simultaneously active and such two activities can be traditionally interpreted as neural firing rates. Recent neurophysiological findings have clarified that Hebbian plasticity is strongly influenced by the timing of individual spikes (Markram et al., 1997). Generally, presynaptic spikes preceding postsynaptic spikes have been observed to induce potentiation, while the reversed order of spikes induced synaptic depression. The dependence of synaptic plasticity on timing required a dynamical description of the change of the strength, as originally proposed by Hebb, this dynamical model has been first proposed by Gerstner and Kistler (Gerstner and Kistler, 2002)

$$\frac{d}{dt}w_{ij} = a_0 + a_1 S_j(t) + a_2 S_i(t) + a_3 S_j(t)\overline{S}_i(t) + a_4 \overline{S}_j(t) S_i(t) \tag{2.3}$$

where S_j and S_i are the pre- and postsynaptic spike trains, respectively, and the functions $\overline{S}_j$ and $\overline{S}_i$ are the low-pass filtered versions of S_j and S_i, respectively. $a_0,\ldots,a_4$, denote constant coefficients that control the rate of change in the synaptic efficacy. This phenomenon of synaptic plasticity dependence on spike timing is known as Spike-Timing-Dependent-Plasticity (STDP) (Ponulak and Kasinski, 2011). Another process, known as anti-STPD, has been observed. In this last process, some synapses can be weakened if the presynaptic input arrives shortly before the postsynaptic spike followed the post-synaptic one. STPD-like processes have assumed as important role in many applications of spiking neural networks in the context of unsupervised learning procedure.

The other wide class of artificial neural networks inspired learning methods is represented by supervised learning. Supervised learning was proposed as a successful concept of information processing already in the early years of the theory of neural computation (Rosenblatt, 1958; Widrow and Hoff, 1960). Essentially, such methods are based on the evidence that instruction-defined learning is also exploited by the brain. The most documented evidence for this type of learning in the central nervous system comes from studies on the cerebellum and the cerebellum cortex, also commonly referred as motor control and motor learning (Thach, 1996; Ito, 2000; Montgomery et al., 2002). Supervised learning is believed to be utilized by the neural motor centers to form internal representations of the body and the environment (Kawato and Gomi, 1992; Wolpert et al., 1998). Learning from instructions is supposed to control information representation in sensory networks (Gaze et al., 1970; Udin, 1985; Knudsen, 1991), and also contributes to the establishment of networks that support certain cognitive skills, such as pattern recognition or language acquisition.

Although there is a documented group of supervised learning models for rate-based neurons, spike-based coding scheme are still highly uncovered in this regard by the existing approaches. Only recently several concepts have been proposed to explain supervised learning in biologically realistic neuron models operating on the precise timing of particular action potentials (Kasinski and Ponulak, 2006). A Supervised Hebbian Learning (SHL) has been introduced to have a possible solution for the implementation of supervision in a biologically realistic manner (Ponulak and Kasinski, 2011). This model considers a spike-based Hebbian process, supervised by an additional *teaching* signal that should reinforce the postsynaptic neuron to fire at the target times and to remain silent in other times. Such teaching signal can transmitted to the neuron in a form of synaptic current or as intracellularly injected current, however, great advantages are obtained when the teaching signal modulating synaptic plasticity is supposed to have only a marginal direct effect on the postsynaptic somatic membrane potential (Legenstein et al., 2005).

Supervised learning methods have been developed for multi-layer feedforwarded or recurrent neural networks. In the case of artificial non-spiking neural networks with continuous activation functions backpropagation algorithm has been used to solve the problem of credit assignment in multi-layer networks. Analog implementation of error backpropagation in spiking networks, however, is difficult due to the complex discontinuous dynamics of spiking neurons. Bohte and coworkers were the first to propose an algorithm implementing a gradient descent-based error backpropagation for multi-layer spiking neural networks (Bohte et al., 2002). Successive modifications of their original algorithm were proposed with the objective to drop the limitation of first algorithm where each neuron was supposed to fire only once during a single simulation cycle (for a review of such methods, see Ponulak and Kasinki, 2011).

REFERENCES

Abbott L.F., Nelson S.B., 2000, Synaptic plasticity: taming the beast, *Nature Neuroscience,* 3, 1178-83.

Abeles M., 1991, Corticonics: Neural Circuits of the Cerebral Cortex, Cambridge Uniersiy Press, UK.

Anthony M., Bartlett P.L., 1999, Neural Network Learning: Theoretical Foundations, Camdridge University Press, UK.

Baudry M., 1998, Synaptic plasticity and learning and memory: 15 years of progress, *Neurobiology of Learning and Memory*, 70, 113-18.

Bialek W., Rieke F., de Ruyter R., van Steveninck R.R., Warland D., 1991, Reading a neural code, *Science*, 252, 1854-7.

Bohte S., Kok J., La Poutré H., 2002, Error-backpropagation in temporally encoded networks of spiking neurons by sparse temporal coding and multilayer RBF networks, *IEEE Trans. Neural Networks*, 13, 426-35.

Buzsaki G., 2006, Rhythms of the Brain, Oxford University Press, New York, NY.

Chen H.T., Ng K.T., Bermak A., Law M.K., Martinez D., 2011, Spike latency coding in a biologically inspired microelectronic nose, *IEEE Trans. of Biomedical Circuits Systems*, 5, 160-168.

Citri A., Malenka R.C., 2008, Synaptic plasticity: multiple forms, functions, and mechanism, *Neuropsychopharmacology*, 33, 18-41.

Diesmann M., Gewalting M.O., Aertsen A., 1999, Stable propagation of synchronous spiking in cortical neural networks, *Nature*, 402, 529-33.

Freeman W.J., 1991, The Physiology of Perception, *Scientific American*, 264, 78-85.

Gaze R., Keating M., Szekely G., Beazley L., 1970, Binocular interaction in the formation of specific intertectal neuronal connexions, *Proc. Royal Society B, Biol. Sciences*, 175, 107-47.

Gerstner W., Kistler W., 2002, Spiking Neuron Models. Single Neurons, Populations, Plasticity, Cambridge University Press, Cambridge, MA.

Girard P., Jouffrais C., Kirchner C.H., 2008, Ultra-rapid categorization in non-human primates, Animal Cognition, 11, 485-93.

Gray C.M., König P., Engel A.K., Singer W., 1989, Oscillatory responses in cat visual cortex exhibit intercolumnar synchronization which reflects global stimulus properties, *Nature*, 338, 334-337.

Hebb D.O., The Organization of Behavior, Wiley, New York, 1949.

Heiligenberg W., 1991, Neural Nets in Electric Fish, MIT Press, USA.

Hinton G., Sejnowski T.J., 1999, Unsupervised Learning. Foundations of Neural Computation, MIT Press, Cambridge, MA.

Hopfield J.J., 1995, Pattern recognition computation using action potential timing for stimulus representation, *Nature*, 376, 33-36.

Ito M., 2000, Mechanisms of motor learning in the cerebellum, *Brain Research*, 886, 237-245.

Izhikevich E.M., 2002, Resonance and selective communication via bursts in neurons having subthreshold oscillations, *Biosystems*, 67, 96-102.

Jefferys J.G., Traub R.D., Whittington M.A., 1996, Neuronal networks for induced *40 Hz* rhythms, *Trends Neuroscience*, 19, 202-08.

Jensen O., Lisman J.E., 1996, Hippocampal CA3 region predicts memory sequences: accounting for the phase precession of place cells, *Learning & Memory*, 3, 279-87.

Kasinski A., Ponulak F., 2006, Comparison of supervised learning methods for spike time coding in spiking neural networks, *International J. Applied Mathematics and Computer Science*, 16, 101-13.

Kawato M., Gomi H., 1992, A computational model of four regions of the cerebellum based on feedback-error-learning, *Biological Cybernetics*, 68, 95-103.

Kim E.K., Gerling G.J., Wellnitz S.A., Lumpkin E.A., 2010, Using force sensors and enural models to encode tactile stimuli as spike-based response, in Proceedings of the 2010 IEEE Haptic Interfaces for Virtual Environment and Teleoperator Systems, pp. 195-198, Boston, MA.

Knudsen E.I., 1991, Visual instruction of the neural map of auditory space in the developing optic tectum, *Science*, 5015, 85-87.

Kuwabara N., Suga N., 1993, Delay lines and amplitude selectivity are created in subthalamic auditory nuclei: the brachium of the inferior colliculus of the mustached bat, *J. of Neurophysiology*, 69, 1713-24.

Kwok T.Y., Yeung D.Y., 1997, Constructive algorithms for structure learning in feedforward neural networks for regression problems, *IEEE Trans. on Neural Networks*, 8, 630-45.

Legenstein R., Naeger C., Maass W., 2005, What can a neuron learn with spike-timing-dependent plasticity? *Neural Computation*, 17, 2337-82.

Lestienne R., 2001, Spike timing, synchronization and information processing on the sensory side of the central nervous system, *Progress in Neurobiology*, 65, 545-591.

Lømo T. (1966) Frequency potentiation of excitatory synaptic activity in the dentate area of the hippocampal formation, *Acta Physiologica Scandinavica*, 68(S277),128.

Maass W., 1996, Lower bounds for the computational power of networks of spiking neurons, *Neural Computation*, 19, 2124-48.

Maass W., Bishop C.M., 1999, Pulsed Neural Networks, MIT Press, USA.

Maass W., Natschlaeger T., Markram H., 2002, Real-time computing without stable states: A new framework for neural computation based on perturbations, *Neural Computation*, 14, 2531-60.

Magleby K.L., Zengel J.E., 1976, Long term changes in augmentation, potentiation, and depression of transmitter release as a function of repeated synaptic activity at the frog neuromuscular junction, *J. Physiology*, 257, 471-494.

Markram H., Luebke J., Frotscher M., Sakmann B., 1997, Regulation of synaptic efficacy by coincidence of postsynaptic APs and EPSPs, *Science*, 275, 213-15.

McCulloch W., Pitts W.H., 1943, A logical calculus of the ideas immanent in nervous activity, *Bulletin of mathematical Biophysics*, 5, 115-33.

Montgomery J., Carton G., Bodznick D., 2002, Error-driven motor learning in fish, *Biology Bulletin*, 203, 238-9.

Olshausen B.A., 1996, Emergence of simple-cell receptive field properties by learning a sparse code for natural images, *Nature*, 381, 607-09.

Paugam-Moisy H., Bohte S.M., 2011, Computing with Spiking Neuron Networks, in Handbook of Natural Computing, Rozenberg G., Baeck T., Kok J.N., Springer Verlag, Heidelberg.

Ponulak F., Kasinski A., 2010, Supervised learning in spiking neural networks with ReSuMe: sequence learning, classification and spike-shifting, *Neural Computation*, 22, 467-510.

Ponulak F., Kasinski A., 2011, Introduction to spiking neural networks: Information processing, learning and applications, *Acta Neurobiol. Exp.*, 71, 409-433.

Purves D., Augustine G.J., Fitzpatrick D., Katz L.C., LaMantia A.S., McNamara J.O., Williams S.M., 2001, Neuroscience, 2nd Edition, Sinauer Associates, Sunderland, MA.

Rosenblatt F., 1958, The Perceptron: A Probabilistic Model for Information Storage and Organization in the Brain, *Psychological Review*, 65(6), 386-408.

Rosenblatt F., 1962, Principles of Neurodynamics, Spartan Books, USA.

Thach W.T., 1996, On the specific role of the cerebellum in motor learning and cognition: Clues from PET activation and lesion studies in man, *Behavioral and Brain Sciences*, 19, 411-431.

Thorpe S.J, Delorme A., van Rullen R., 2001, Spike-based strategies for rapid processing, *Neural Networks*, 14, 715-26.

Turing A.M., 1950, Computing machinery and intelligence, *Mind*, 59, 433-460.

Udin S.B., 1985, The role of visual experience in the formation of binocular projections in frogs, *Cellular and Molecular Neurobiology*, 5, 85-102.

van Rullen R., Guyonneau R., Thorpe S.J., 2005, Spike times make sense, *Trends Neuroscience*, 28, 1-4.

Widrow B., Hoff M.E., 1960, Adaptive switching circuits, *IRE Wescon Convention Record*, 4, 96-104.

Wolpert D.M., Miall C.R., Kawato M., 1998, Internal models in the cerebellum, *Trends in Cognitive Sciences*, 2, 338-47.

Chapter 3

Genetic and Evolutionary Computation

Genetic and evolutionary computation can be considered as a sub-branch of artificial intelligence, which focuses on mimicking the high-level smart processes which characterize living beings, genetic and evolutionary computation with the purpose to provide computers with natural skills (adaptivity, self-improvement and learning) based on nature inspired algorithms.

The transposition into computers of the famous Darwin's theory consists of imitating the capability of a population of living organisms to adapt to its environment with selection and reproduction mechanisms. In the last forty years, terms as *evolutionary algorithms*, or *artificial Darwinism, genetic algorithms*, or *genetic programming* have become very popular (Davis, 1987; Goldberg, 1989; Back et al., 1997; Eiben and Smith, 2003). The common components of these techniques is the evolution of populations under the action of stochastic operators. The populations are generally represented as points in a search space. Evolution is normally organized into different generations and the engine of this evolution is based on *selection* and *genetic operators*. Selection is a *measurement* of the quality of an individual with respect to the problem to be solved. Genetic operators, usually recognized as *mutation* and *crossover* or *recombination*, produce individuals of a new generation. The efficiency of an evolutionary algorithm depends on the parameter settings with the general requirement that successive populations (generations) have to converge toward the global optimum of a performance function. Genetic algorithms have been used extensively to design new multiscale materials for finding the energy global minimum of crystalline solids (Lonie and Zurek, 2011) and clusters of adatoms in surface physics (Sierka, 2010).

Evolutionary techniques are generally zero-order stochastic optimization methods, where the only information which is required is the value of the function to be optimized at the sample points (Koza, 1992; Schwefel, 1995; Zitzler et al., 2000; Hamda et al., 2002). One advantage is that such methods are particularly useful to treat irregular, complex, or badly conditioned functions. However, one main disadvantage is that the computation time can be long. As a consequence, evolutionary techniques are usually recommended when other more classical and rapid method fail, in addition, classical optimization methods can be successfully hybridized with evolutionary techniques.

Despite the attractive simplicity of an evolutionary process, figure 3.1, the development of an efficient evolutionary algorithm is a difficult task, since an evolutionary stochastic process is very sensitive to parameter and algorithm setting. This implies that the building of an efficient evolutionary algorithm is based on a good, if not excellent, knowledge of the problem to be solved, as well as on a good understanding of the underlying evolution mechanisms.

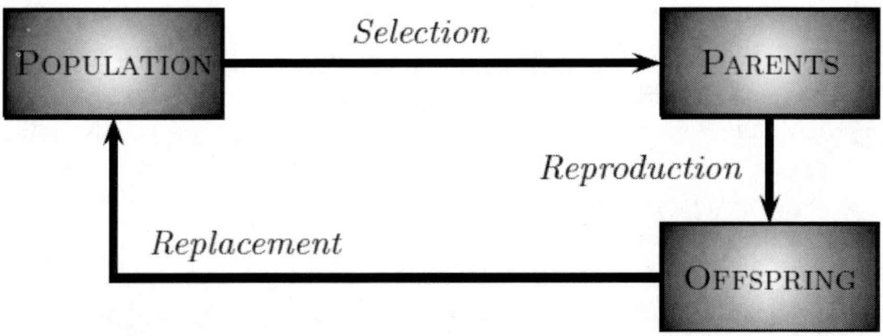

Figure 3.1. Example of a flow chart of an evolutionary algorithm.

A primary advantage of evolutionary computation is that it is conceptually simple. The procedure may be written as difference equation (Abraham et al., 2006):

$$x[t+1] = s(v(x[t])) \tag{3.1}$$

where $x[t]$ is the population at time t under a representation x, v is a random variation operator, and s is the selection operator. In addition, evolutionary algorithm performance is representation independent, and evolution algorithms can also be combined with more traditional optimization techniques. This combination may be as simple as the use of a gradient minimization used after primary search with an evolutionary algorithm or it may involve simultaneous application of other algorithms. Since traditional methods of optimization are not robust to dynamic changes requiring, in many cases, a complete restart in order to provide a solution, evolutionary algorithms, on the contrary, can be used to adapt solutions to changing circumstance. But, the greatest advantage of evolutionary algorithms comes from the ability to address problems for which there are no human experts. Although human expertise should be used when it is available, it often proves less than adequate for automating problem-solving routines.

A common strategy in evolutionary algorithms can be represented as follows. Let us start with the concept of individuals and environment, *individuals* represent solutions or points of a search space, also called *environment.* On such environment, a maximum of a fitness function or *evaluation function* is searched. Individuals are usually represented as a code (real, binary, of fixed or variables size, simple or complex), they can be considered as *genotypes* (chromosomes or genomes). While the corresponding solutions, that are vectors of the search space, the environment, are the *phenotypes*. A common target to be achieved in evolutionary algorithms, is that an evolutionary algorithm must evolve its population in a way that makes individuals more and more *adapted* to the environment. The maximum adaptation corresponds to the maximized fitness function.

A common approach is to start with a population of individuals, with each individual corresponding to a potential solution to the considered problem. The operation of initialization is used to fix some random initial conditions. Selection function decides which individuals of the current population are going to reproduce. Such function is normally associated to the *quality* of individual, where quality is defined by the *fitness function.* The simplest selection function is the so-called proportional selection, implemented with a biased random shot, where the probability of selecting an individual is directly proportional to its fitness function value (Cagnoni et al., 2008):

$$P(i) = \frac{fitness(i)}{\left(\sum_{k=1}^{popsize} fitness(k)\right)} \tag{3.2}$$

Other selection rules and schemes include concepts such as scaling, i.e., the selection linearly scales the fitness function at each generation in order to get a maximal fitness that is C times the average fitness of the current population, and C measures the selective pressure, usually fixed between 1.2 and 2 (Goldberg, 1989). Another alternative selection scheme is the so-called *ranking* that allocates to each individual a probability that is proportional to its rank in a sorted list according to fitness. Again, another selection choice is the tournament, where individuals are randomly selected in the populations independently to their fitness values and chooses the best. The selective pressure is linked to the size and efficiency of the tournament.

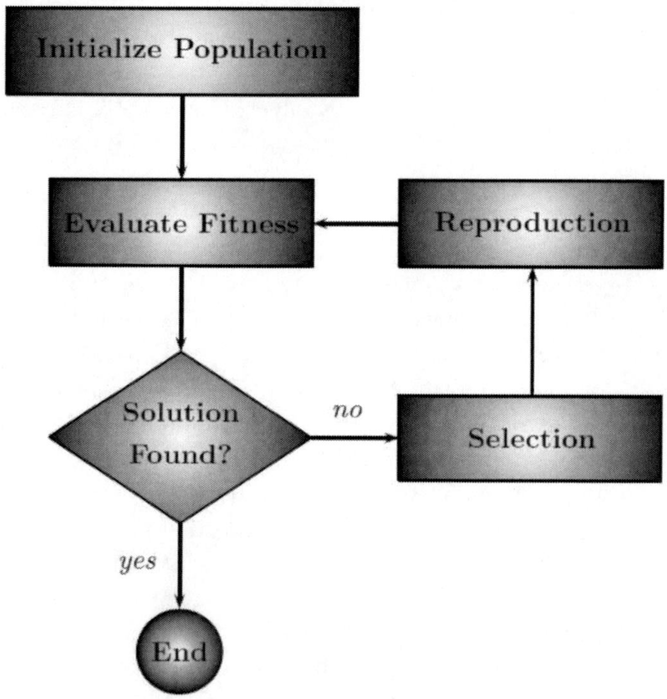

Figure 3.2. Flow chart of basic genetic algorithm iteration.

Reproduction operator generates offspring, generally, a number of parents equal to the desired number of offspring, i.e., 2 parents produce 2 children, but also other less-conventional schemes can be programmed (2 parents for 1 child, and, generalizing, n parents for p children, with $n>p$, or $n<p$). Reproduction operator includes two main variation operators such as

crossover, or recombination, that recombines genes of parents, and mutation, that slightly perturbs the genome. Both such operations are quantified by correspondent probabilities factors. Crossover and mutation tend to concentrate the population near good (or best) individuals. On the contrary, mutation limits the attraction of the best individuals in order to let the population explore other areas of the search space. To show how the crossover operates, we have to use the binary encoding representation of genes. In binary string encoding representation of a genetic algorithm, a phenotype (parameters) can be converted to genotypes. Knowing the ranges of each problem variable, this can be represented using a suitable binary string. The genotype (chromosome) is than represented as for example

Chromosome A:	1101101111010011011O
Chromosome B:	11011110101010001111O.

The crossover operator selects genes from parent chromosomes and creates a new offsprings. The simplest way to do this is to choose randomly some crossover point and everything before this point is copied from the first parent and then everything after a crossover point is copied from the second parent. For example, (| denotes the crossover point):

Chromosome A:	**11111 | 00100110110**
Chromosome B:	10011 | 11000011110
Offspring A:	**11111** | 11000011110
Offspring B:	10011 | **00100110110**

where crossover bits are randomly copied from the first or from the second parent. After crossover, mutation can take place. Mutation changes randomly the new offsprings. For binary encoding mutation is performed by changing a few randomly chosen bits from 1 to 0 or from 0 to 1. Mutation depends on the encoding as well as the crossover, for example, mutation could exchange two genes:

Chromosome A:	110**1**111000011110
Chromosome B:	1101100**0**100110110
Offspring A:	110**0**111000011110
Offspring B:	1101101**1**00110110

Evaluation operator computes the quality of new individuals. This operator is the only one that normally uses the function to be optimized. The basic requirement of estimations made using the evaluation operator is the definition of a probability or at least a rank for each solution.

Replacement operator controls the composition of generation $n+1$. This operator is strictly connected to the Elitism that is often recommended for optimization tasks in order to keep the best individuals from a population into the next one. Usual strategies involve the direct transmission of a given percentage of the best individual in the next population. There are two main evolution strategies for elitism, (i,o) or $(i+o)$ producing o offsprings of a population of i individuals. The strategy (i,o) controls elitism via the difference i-o, i.e., the i-o best individuals are kept and completed by o offsprings. The strategy $(i+o)$ selects the i best individuals for the next generation from an intermediate population of size $i+o$.

In turn, the stopping operator stops the evolution program at the right moment. A usual strategy is to stop evolution after a fixed number of generations, or when stagnation occurs. Since a good control of the stopping criterion strongly influences the efficiency of the algorithm, a good practice is to define one *a priori* set of evolution parameters, such as population size, crossover and mutation probabilities, selective pressure, replacement percentage, etc. For a review on the wide number of application of evolutionary computation, we refer to Banzhaf (Banzhaf, 2013).

Although the evolutionary computation roots date from the late 1950s and the early 1960s, only from the 1990s onwards the field of evolutionary and genetic computation suffered a major growth. The main current trends in the field include theoretical investigations, applications to dynamic, multi-modal, multi-objective and constrained optimization. Also, investigations unto evolutionary robotics, evolutionary hardware and evolutionary electronics would know a large impact in such emergent technologies, as well as biological applications and bioinformatics, applications in data mining, games, arts and music. Implementation of genetic programming will continue to benefit in coming years from new approaches that include results from developmental biology and epigenetics. The use of bioinspiration, based on the deep understanding of natural evolution, has led to some very substantial progress in the implementation of artificial systems that show human-level problem-solving abilities. Open problems and main challenges include the design of high-performance evolutionary algorithms, the incorporation of domain knowledge into the algorithms, the development of on-line evolutionary systems in which adaptation and evolution occur simultaneously, the identification of the main classes of problems to which evolutionary algorithms are the most suitable approaches. Achieving artificial intelligence in computing machines is still far in the future, however, in restricted steps in that direction have been taken. As suggested by Banzhaf, a major component of any future system that could truly lay claim to the property of intelligence will be bioinspired to evolutionary intelligence and genetic programming paradigms.

3.1. EVOLUTIONARY PROGRAMMING

The basic Evolutionary programming (EP) method operates according to the following steps: (i) choose an initial population; (ii) new offspring's are created by mutation. In such scheme, the number of solutions in a population is highly relevant to the speed of optimization. Any offspring solution is assessed by computing its fitness. Generally, s stochastic tournament is sufficient to determine n different solutions, considering that EP method typically does not use any crossover as a genetic operator.

It should be noted that, when comparing EP to genetic algorithms, one can identify some significant differences. While genetic algorithms are implemented by having arrays of bits representing chromosome, in EP techniques there are no such restrictions for the representation, since the representation follows from the problem. In fact, EP typically uses an adaptive mutation operator in which the severity of mutations is often reduced as the global optimum is approached while genetic algorithms use a pre-fixed mutation operator. The scheme to adapt the mutation step size widely employed is the meta-evolutionary technique, where the variance of the mutation distribution is subject to mutation by a fixed variance mutation operator that evolves along with the solution (Fogel et al., 1966; Fogel, 1999). Similar approach is used in evolution strategies algorithm (Koza, 1992). Evolution strategies merely concentrate on translating the fundamental mechanisms of biological evolution for technical optimization problem. The parameters to be optimized are often represented by a vector of real numbers, while another vector of real numbers defines the strategy parameters which controls the mutation of the objective parameters. Both object and strategic parameters form the data-structure for a single individual, so, for example, a population P of i individuals could be described as $P=(c_1,c_2,\ldots, c_{i-1}, c_i)$ where the nth chromosome c_n is defined as $c_n=(op, sp)$, where $op=(o_1,o_2,\ldots,o_i)$, is the object parameters and sp=$(s_1,s_2,\ldots,s_i)$ is the strategy parameters (). Differently than for EPs, evolution strategies employ crossover and mutation operators. The mutation operator in evolution strategy is defined as component wise addition of normal distributed random numbers. Both the objective parameters and the strategy parameters of the chromosome are changed by mutation. A mutant's object-parameters vector can be expressed as $op(mut)=op+N(sp)$, where $N(x)$ is the Gaussian distribution of mean-value 0 and standard deviation x. The strategy parameters mutation step size is done by adapting the standard deviation sp, for example, $sp(mut)=(sp\cdot\alpha)$, where $\alpha=(\alpha_1, \alpha_2, \ldots \alpha_i)$ is a random value vector and $\cdot$ denotes scalar product. For two chromosomes, $c_1=(op(c_1), sp(c_1))$ and $c_2=(op(c_2), sp(c_2))$ the crossover operator is defined using conditional probability $C(c_1,c_2)=((op(c_1),i|op(c_2),i);(sp(c_1),i|\ sp(c_2),i))$, and i a randomly assigned value so that 50% selection probability for $op(c_{1,2})$ and $sp(c_{1,2})$.

3.2. Genetic Programming

Genetic programming (GP) corresponds to a representation of variable-length structures as trees, figure 3.3. Initially designed to handle LISP program, the richness and versatility of the variable-size tree representation are reason of the large impact of GP (cagnoni et al., 2008). Indeed, many optimization, command or control problems can be formulated as a program induction problem. Recently, GP has been shown to achieve human competitive results in computer vision (Trujillo and Olague, 2006).

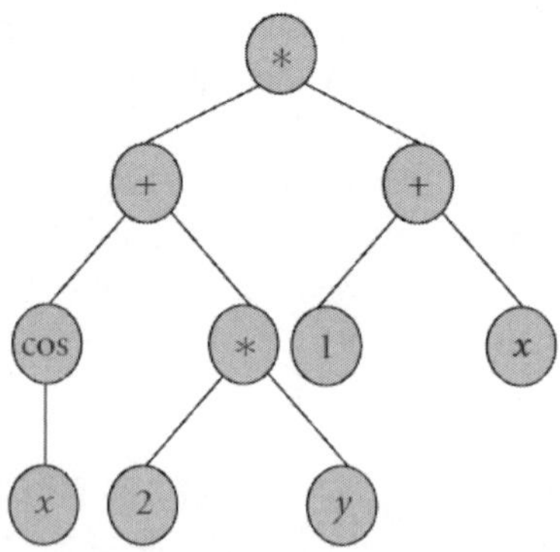

Figure 3.3. Example of a tree representation of the function (cos(x)+2*y)*(1+x). (Reproduced from (Cagnoni et al., 2008), with permission).

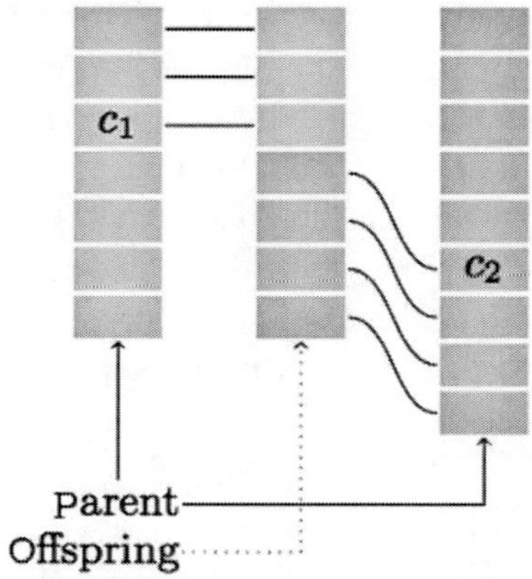

Figure 3.4. Exchanging blocks of codes in tree-based.

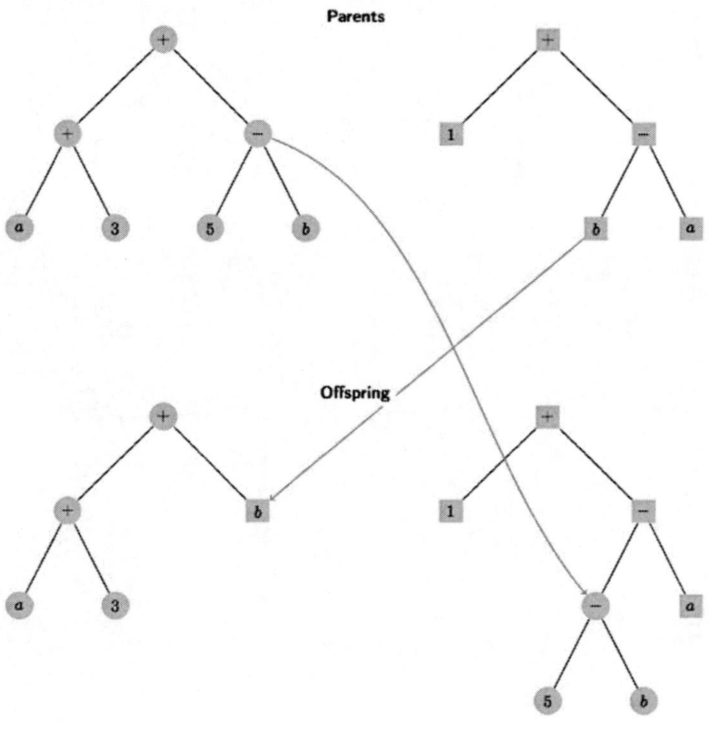

Figure 3.5. Exchanging subtrees in tree-based representation of programs.

A GP algorithm explores a search space of recursive programs made of elements of a function set, of a variable set, and of a terminal set (i.e., data and constants). Individuals of the population are programs that, when executed, produce the solution to the problem to be found, figure 3.4.

Crossover operators operate as subtree exchanges, figure 3.5. Mutations are more complex, and several mutations have to be used, producing different types of perturbations on the genome structure, as suppression or addition of a node, modification of the content of a node. Mutations operate both on the constants or discrete variables.

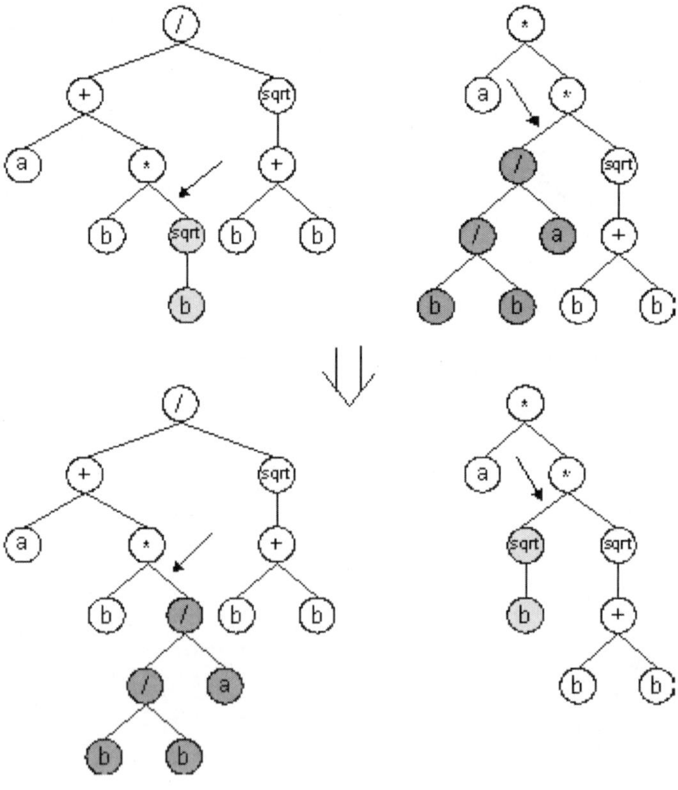

Figure 3.6. Tree representation of a crossover operator.

A parse tree is a structure able to check the interpretation of a computer program. Functions are written a nodes, their arguments as leaves. A subtree is a part of a tree that is under an inner node of this three. When the tree is cut out from its parent, the inner node can become a root node and the subtree is then a valid tree of its own. The creation of an offspring from the crossover operation is carried out by deleting the crossover fragment of the first parent and then inserting the crossover fragment of the second parent. A sample crossover operation is shown in figure 3.6. In GP the crossover operation is accomplished by taking randomly selected subtrees in the individual and exchanging them.

Mutations are found in two versions. The simplest type is to replace a function or a terminal by a function or a terminal, respectively. In the second type, an entire subtree can replace another subtree. Both the types are illustrated in figure 3.7.

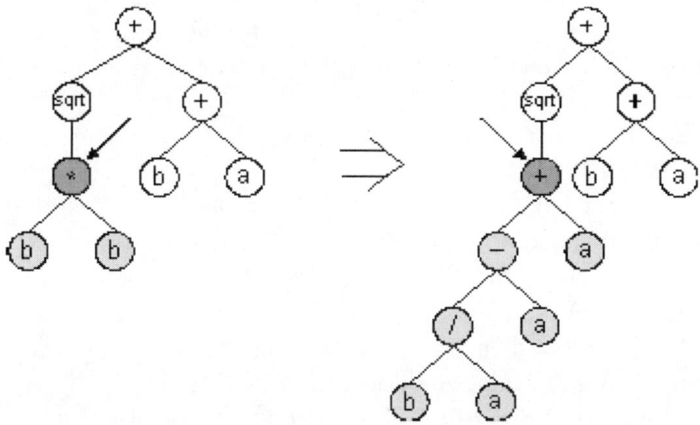

Figure 3.7. Tree representation of a mutation operator.

In GP programming, the set of functions and terminals that will be used in a specific problem has to be chosen carefully. A solution may be very complex to be found or not to be found at all, if the set of functions is not powerfully enough. As in any evolutionary computation programming, the generation of first population of individuals plays a leading role for successful implementation of GP strategy. However, other factors influence the best performance of the algorithm, such as size of the population, percentage of individuals that participate in the crossover/mutation, etc. One specific advantage of GP is that no analytical knowledge is needed, but restrictions on how the structure of solutions should be formulated. In addition, GP programs scale with the problem size. Many variants of GP algorithm can be found in literature, as Linear Genetic Programming or gene Expression Programming, just to name a couple, for a review of such variants, please refer to (Abraham et al., 2006).

REFERENCES

Abraham A., Nedjah N., de Macedo Mourelle L., 2006, Evolutionary Computation: from Genetic Algorithms to Genetic Programming, *Studies in Computational Intelligence*, 13, 1-20.

Back T., Fogel D.B., Michalewicz Z., 1997, Handbook of Evolutionary Computation, Oxford University Press, UK.

Banzhaf W., 2013, Evolutionary Computation and Genetic Programming, in Engineered Biomimicry, Elsevier, North-Holland.

Cagnoni S., Lutton E., Olague G., 2008, Genetic and Evolutionary Computation for Image Processing and Analysis, Hindawi, Eurasip Book Series on signal processing and Communications.

Davis L., 1987, Genetic Algorithms and Simulated Annealing, Pittman, London, UK.

Eiben A.E., Smith J.E., 2003, Introduction to Evolutionary Computing, Springer, New York, NY.

Fogel D.B., 1999, Evolutionary Computation: Toward a New Philosophy of machine Intelligence, 2nd ed. IEEE Press, Piscataway, NJ.

Fogel L.J., Owens A.J., Walsh M.J., 1966, Artificial intelligence Through Simulated Evolution, J. Wiley & Sons, New York, NY.

Goldberg D.E., 1989, Genetic algorithms in Search, Optimization, and Machine Learning, Addison-Wesley, Reading, MA.

Hamda H., Jouve F., Lutton E., Schoenauer M., Sebag M., 2002, Compact unstructured representations for evolutionary design, *Applied Intelligence*, 16(2), 139-155.

Koza J.R., 1992, Genetic Programming, MIT Press, Cambridge, MA.

Lonie D.C., Zurek E., 2011, XtalOPT: An open-source evolutionary algorithm for crystal structure prediction, *Computer Physics Communication*, 182, 372-87.

Schwefel H.P., 1995, Numerical Optimization of Computer Models, 2nd edition, J. Wiley & Sons, New York, NY.

Sierka M., 2010, Synergy between theory and experiment in structure resolution of low-dimensional oxides, *Progress in Surface Science*, 85, 398-434.

Trujillo L., Olague G., 2006, Synthesis of interest point detectors through genetic programming, *Proceedings of the 8th Annual Conference on Genetic and Evolutionary Computation*, pp. 887-894, Seattle, W.

Zitzler E., Deb K., Thiele L., 2000, Comparison of multiobjective evolutionary algorithms: empirical results, *Evolutionary Computation*, 8(2), 173-195.

Chapter 4

MACHINE LEARNING AND SWARM INTELLIGENCE

One important series of natural phenomena depending on social behavior stimulated many computational strategies and algorithms. Many animal species show interesting social interactions, like knowledge sharing or behavioral imitation, with varying degrees of complexity. A common feature of social animals is that they gain a survival advantage by joining in groups and interacting with each other. For instance schools of fishes have an advantage in escaping predators, as each individual fish can be a kind of lookout for the whole group. Herding animals are advantaged in finding food when they adopt cooperative behavior, since if one animal finds a source of food, the others will watch and follow. Probably, insect colonies are the most famous example, of collective organization. Insects, such as ants, bees, wasps and termites, live in self-organized colonies, and any individual is specialized in a set of tasks, according to its morphology, age or change connecting individual behavior with collective performance. Therefore, these organisms perform various activities simultaneously inside the colony, displaying collective swarm intelligence.

The interesting aspect of this kind of collective processes is that they point out *self-organization* and *emergent* characteristics. Such two characteristics are also desired properties for a computational model. Indeed, the possibility of a system, whose single parts are quite simple to program, but whose overall behavior is complex and adaptable, is very appealing. The field of research focused on developing such systems and applying them to solve a wide range of problems is often referred to with the term *Swarm Intelligence* (Dorigo and Stützle, 2004; Garnier et al., 2007).

Since the '90 decade of the last century, several algorithms inspired to collective behavior have been proposed (Dorigo, 1992; Dorigo et al., 1996; Dorigo and Gambardella, 1997; Dorigo et al., 1999). The application areas of these algorithms regard well studied optimization problems like NP-hard problems (Traveling Salesman problem, Quadratic Assignment Problem, Graph problems), network routing, clustering, data mining, job scheduling, robotic and sensors networks control. Particle Swarm Optimization (PSO) and Ant Colonies Optimization (ACO) are currently the most popular algorithms in the swarm intelligence domain.

4.1. Swarm-inspired Algorithms

Swarm intelligence algorithms have been an interesting alternative for providing satisfactory solutions in real-world discrete and combinatorial problems. Since such problems are usually challenging and require computationally intensive algorithms, many of swarm intelligence algorithms have been used in the continue version. However, to apply them to a discrete problem requires adaptation, hybridization, or modification the original algorithms to manage those sort of problems. The methods used to achieve this objective are the most diverse, because this seems to be a remarkably opportunity, either developing new methodological approaches or applying to specific discrete/combinatorial problems. Future work aims to a more extensive research on different discretization methods and encoding schemes, focusing on expanding the range of possibilities on using continuous algorithms to discrete problems. This will generate in the future more alternatives to combine the desired continuous algorithm with combinatorial and binary problems. Here, we detail about some widely employed swarm-inspired algorithms.

4.1.1. Particle Swarm Optimization (PSO)

PSO is a population-based search algorithm and is initialized with a population of random solutions, called particles. Unlike in the evolutionary computation techniques, each particle in PSO is also associated with a velocity. The basic scheme provides that particles fly through the hyperdimensional search space of the problem with velocities which are dynamically adjusted according to their historical behaviors and with the aim to emulate the success of other individuals. Therefore, the particles swarm has the tendency to organize itself flying towards the better and better search area over the course of search process. PSO was first introduced to simulate birds seeking food (Dorigo and Blum, 2005). In such application to birds, the following scenario is assumed: a group of birds are randomly searching food in an area. There is only one piece of food in the area being searched. Initially, the birds do not know where the food is. However, they know how far the food is and the peers' positions. The question is: given the ignorance of where the food and knowing the positions of the rest of the swarm what's the best strategy to find the food? The best strategy could be to follow the bird which is nearest to the food. PSO is an example of metaheuristic algorithm (Blum and Roli, 2003; Yang, 2010b; Yang and Karamanoglu, 2013). PSO learns from the scenario and uses it to solve the optimization problems. PSO is initialized with group of random particles xi and then searches for optima by updating each generation. At each generation, each particle is updated by two best choices. The first one is the best previous location (i.e., the position giving the best fitness value) a particle has achieved so far and denoted by the value pi. At each iteration, the p value vector of the particle with the best fitness in the neighborhood, designed l and g for example, and the p vector of the current particle are combined to adjust the velocity along each dimension. Therefore, that velocity is used to compute a new position for the particle. The adjustment to the velocity conditioned by the individual's previous best position, p, is considered as the cognition component, and the portion influenced by the best in the neighborhood is considered as the social component (Kennedy, 1992; Kennedy, 1997; Krause et al., 2013). The mathematical expressions that translate the PSO as described are (Kennedy and Eberhart, 1997; Shi and Eberhart, 1998)

$$v_i^{t+1} = \omega v_i^t + \chi_1 \vartheta_1 (p_{il} - x_{il}) + \chi_2 \vartheta_2 (p_{ig} - x_{ig}) \tag{4.1a}$$

$$x_i^{t+1} = x_i^t + v_i^t \tag{4.1b}$$

where ω is an inertia function and takes the values between 0 and 1, χ_1 and χ_2 are two random numbers generated within the range [0,1], θ_1 and θ_2 are two learning factors which control the influence of the cognitive and social components, respectively. In many applications, it is useful to consider the particles' velocity clamped into the range $[v_{min}, v_{max}]$ (often v_{min} is 0) which serves as a constraint to control the global exploration ability of particle swarm and the likelihood of particles leaving the search space is reduced. A basic scheme of PSO is represented in figure 4.1

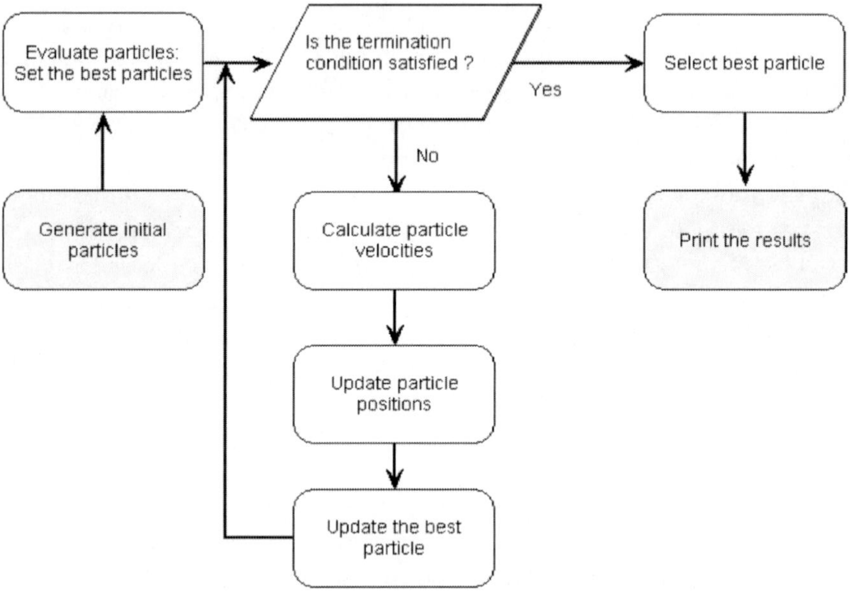

Figure 4.1. A basic scheme of PSO. (Reproduced from (Grosan et al., 2006), with permission).

PSOs have a long series of applications in various fields. A detailed description subdivided following the topics of applications cane found in (Krause et al., 2013).

4.1.2. Ant Algorithms

Ant algorithms translates in computational tools the foraging behavior of social ants. Ants essentially use pheromone as a chemical messenger, and the pheromone concentration can be considered as the indicator of quality solutions to a problem of interest.

As the solution is often linked with the pheromone concentrations, the search algorithms often produce routes and paths marked by the higher pheromone concentrations, therefore, ants based algorithms are particularly suitable for discrete optimization problems. In addition, the movements of ants is controlled by pheromone, which will evaporate over time, as a consequence, ant algorithms will lead to premature convergence to the local (often wrong) solutions. Therefore, ant algorithms work very well when time-dependent pheromone concentration is well accounted. The ant algorithms have two important issues that must be taken into due consideration: the probability of choosing a route and the evaporation rate of pheromone. For a network routing problem, the probability of ants at a particular node *i* to choose the route from node *i* to node *j* is given by (Dorigo and Stütle, 2004, Yang and Karamanoglu, 2013)

$$p_{ij} = \frac{\phi_{ij}^{\alpha} d_{ij}^{\beta}}{\sum_{i,j=1}^{n} \phi_{ij}^{\alpha} d_{ij}^{\beta}} \tag{4.1}$$

where ϕ_{ij} is the pheromone concentration of the route between *i* and *j*, d_{ij} is the desirability of the same route, $\alpha>0$, and $\beta>0$ are the influence parameters (their typical values are $\alpha\approx\beta\approx2$). A priori knowledge about the route is often required, and a relation as $d_{ij} \propto 1/s_{ij}$ must be bounded, where s_{ij} is the distance which implies that shorter routes will be selected due to their shorter traveling time, and thus the pheromone concentrations on these routes are higher. If the traveling time is shorter, less amount of pheromone has been evaporated during this period.

4.1.3. Bee Algorithms

Bee algorithms are inspired by the foraging behavior of honeybees in nature. Such algorithms use partially pheromone concentrations, rather, they focus the characteristics on waggle dance, polarization, and nectar maximization used to simulate the allocation of the forager bees along flower patches and thus different search regions in the search space (Nakrani and Tovey, 2004; Karaboga, 2005; Pham et al., 2005; Yang, 2005). In the honeybee-based algorithms, forager bees are allocated to different food sources to maximize the total nectar intake (for a review lecture, see Yang 2010a; Parpinelli and Lopes 2011). Yang developed a virtual bee algorithm where pheromone concentrations can be linked with objective functions directly (Yang, 2005). Karaboga developed a first artificial bee colony optimization algorithm (Karaboga, 2005). In such algorithm, the bees in a colony are divided into three groups: employed bees (forager bees), onlooker bees (observer bees), and scouts. Unlike the honeybee algorithm, which has only two groups of bees (forager bees and observer bees), the bees in such algorithm are more specialized (Karaboga, 2005, Afshar et al., 2007).

Like to the ants-based algorithms, bee algorithms are also very flexible in dealing with discrete optimization problems. In principle, they can solve both continuous optimization and discrete optimization problems, for example, combinatorial optimization such as routing and optimal paths has been successfully solved by ant and bee algorithms.

4.1.4. Firefly Algorithms

Firefly algorithms are based on the flashing patterns and behavior of fireflies. They were first developed by Yang (Yang, 2008; Yang, 2009). The rules governing such algorithms can be synthesized as follows (Krause et al., 2013): (i) Fireflies are unisexual; (ii) The attractiveness between fireflies is proportional to the brightness; (iii) The brightness of a firefly is determined by the landscape of the objective function.

Those three rules state that one firefly will be attracted to other fireflies regardless their sex. Since the attractiveness is proportional to the brightness, the attractiveness decreases as the distance between two fireflies increases. For any two flashing fireflies, the less brighter one will move toward the more brighter one, and, if there is no brighter one than a firefly, it will move randomly.

By an algebraic point of view, the rules above described can be quantified as follows. The movement of a firefly i is attracted to another, more attractive (brighter) firefly j is determined by (Yang and Karamanoglu, 2013)

$$x_i^{t+1} = x_i^t + \beta_0 e^{-\gamma r_{ij}^2}\left(x_j^t - x_i^t\right) + \alpha \varepsilon_i^t \tag{4.2}$$

where β_0 is the attractiveness at a distance r=0, and the second term is due to the attraction. The third term is randomization with α being the randomization parameter, and ε is a vector of random numbers drawn from a Gaussian distribution. It is interesting to note that if β_0 =0, the Eq.(4.2) describes a simple random walk. Therefore, the randomization ε can easily be extended to other distributions such as Lévy flights (Chechkin et al., 2008). The Lévy flights essentially provides a random walk whose random step length is drawn from a Lévy distribution which has an infinite variance with an infinite mean. The steps essentially form a random walk process with a power-law step-length distribution with a heavy tail, and new solutions should be generated by Lévy walk around the best solution obtained so far. This will often speed up the local search (Pavlyukevich, 2007). Firefly algorithms have attracted much attention, and their efficiency when applied over a wide range of test problems has been demonstrated (Sayadi et al., 2010; Apostolopoulos and Vlachos, 2011; Yang, 2011b).

4.1.5. Cuckoo Search

Cuckoo search algorithms are the latest nature-inspired metaheuristic algorithms developed by Yang and Deb (Yang and Deb, 2009). Such algorithms are based on the brood parasitism of some cuckoo species. Cuckoos are birds area characterized other than beautiful sound, by the fact that such species lay their eggs in communal nets, though they may remove others eggs to increase the hatching probability of their own eggs. Many cuckoo species anbage the obligate brood parasitism by laying their eggs in the nests of other host birds (commonly other species). The rules describing such behaviors are synthesized as follows (Burnwal and Deb, 2013): (i) Each cuckoo lays one egg at a time and dumps it in a randomly chosen nest. (ii) The best nests with high-quality eggs will be carried over to the next generation. (iii) The number of available host nests is fixed. The egg laid by a cuckoo is discovered by the host bird with a probability $p \in [0,1]$. In the case $p=1$ corresponding to the certainty that the egg is of another species, the host bird can either get rid the egg or simply abandon the nest and build a completely new nest.

The implementation can be developed based on the simply representation of the three rules: each egg in a nest represents a solution, and each cuckoo can lay only one egg (thus representing a solution). The goal is to use the new and potentially better solutions to replace a not-so-god solution in the nests. This representation can be easily extended to a more complicated case where each nest has multiple eggs representing a set of solutions. A basic algorithm using the cuckoo search approach employs a balanced combination of a local random walk and the global explorative random walk, controlled by a switching parameter p. The local random walk can be written as (Yang and Deb, 2009)

$$x_i^{t+1} = x_i^t + \alpha n \otimes H(p - \varepsilon) \otimes \left(x_j^t - x_k^t\right) \quad (4.3)$$

where x_j and x_i are two different solutions selected randomly by random permutation, $H(u)$ is a Heaviside function, ε is a random number drawn from a uniform distribution, and n is a step size. The global random walk can be carried out by using Lévy flights

$$x_i^{t+1} = x_i^t + \alpha L(n, \lambda) \quad (4.4)$$

whereα>0 si the step-size-scaling factor, which should be related to the scales of the problem of interests, and $L(n, \lambda)$ is a Lévy distribution, and a choice can be (Pavlyukevich, 2007)

$$L(n, \lambda) = \frac{\lambda \Gamma(\lambda) \sin(\pi\lambda / 2)}{\pi} \cdot \frac{1}{n^{1+\lambda}} \quad (4.5)$$

Eq. (4.5) is a stochastic equation for a random walk, whose next step-location depends on the current location (the first term in 4.5) and the transition probability (the second term). In many cuckoo search algorithms, a substantial fraction of the new solutions should be generated by the far field randomization and whose locations should be far enough from the current best solution ensuring that the systems does not get trapped in a local minimum or maximum (Yang and Deb, 2010; Gandomi et al., 2013).

4.1.6. Bat Algorithms

Bat-inspired algorithms were firstly developed by Yang (Yang, 2010c; Yang, 2011a). They take inspiration by the echolocation behavior of microbats. Echolocation is a type of sonar, able to detect prey, avoid obstacles, and locate their roosting crevices in the dark. Microbats emit a very loud sound pulse and listen to the echoes that bounce back from the surrounding objects. Depending on the species, their pulse varies in property and can be correlated with their hunting strategies. Some bat species use short, frequency-modulated signals to sweep through about an octave, while others more often use constant-frequency signals for echolocation. In addition, their signal bandwidth varies depending on the species and is often increased by using more harmonics. The translation of bat echolocation characteristics in algorithms is based on three idealized rules: (i) All bats use echolocation to sense distance, and it is assumed that they know the difference between food/prey and background barriers in some magical way. (ii) A bat roams randomly with a velocity v_i at position x_i with a fixed frequency range $[f_{min}, f_{max}]$, varying its emission rate $\rho \in [0,1]$ and loudness L_0 to search for pray, depending on the proximity of their target. (iii) Although the loudness can vary in many ways, it is assumed that the loudness varies from a large positive value of L_0 to a minimum constant value L_{min}. The algebraic system deriving from such rules is described as follows (Yang, 2011a):

$$
\begin{aligned}
&f_i = f_{\min} + \eta\left(f_{\max} - f_{\min}\right); \qquad && v_i^{t+1} = v_i^t + f_i\left(x_i^t - x^*\right); \\
&x_i^{t+1} = x_i^t + v_i^t && \\
&A_i^{t+1} = \alpha A_i^t && \rho_i^t = \rho_i^0\left[1 - \exp(-\beta t)\right]
\end{aligned}
\tag{4.6}
$$

where η is a random number drawn from a uniform distribution and x^* is the current bets solution found so far during iterations, α is a constant and denotes a sort of cooling factor as in simulated annealing, and β also is a constant and stabilizes the rate of emission to a fixed value. Bat algorithms, as well as other swarm algorithms, have been introduced too recently, and their application is still limited. Anyway, their use to solve many optimization problems in a wide range of applications is easily predictable.

4.1.7. Flower Pollination Algorithm

Flower pollination algorithm was recently developed by Yang (Yang, 2012) taking inspiration by the flow pollination process of flowering plants. The term pollination cover a series of complex processes and the rules stimulating the algorithm can be synthesized as (Yang, 2012): *(i) Biotic and cross-pollination can be considered as a process of global pollination process, and pollen-carrying pollinators move in a way that obeys Lévy flights; (ii) For local pollination, abiotic and self-pollination are used; (iii) Pollinators such as insects can develop flower constancy, which is equivalent to a reproduction probability that is proportional to the similarity of two flowers involved; (iv)*

The interaction or switching of local pollination and global pollination can be controlled by a switch probability p∈[0,1], with a slight bias toward local pollination.

The algebraic translation of such rules can be made as follows. First, global pollination must be distinguished by local pollination. In principle, flower pollination can occur at all scales, both local and global. In reality, adjacent flowers or flowers in the not-so-far-away neighborhood are more likely to be pollinated by local flower pollen than those far away. Under such scheme, rule (i) can be represented mathematically as

$$x_i^{t+1} = x_i^t + L(\lambda)(x_i^t - g^*) \tag{4.7}$$

where x_i is the pollen i or and g^* is the current bets solution found among all solutions at the current generation (iteration). $L(\lambda)$ is the Lévy flight distribution, similar to Eq.(4.5) and corresponds to the strength of the pollination when the insect may move over a long distance with various distance steps. For local pollination, the rules (ii) and (iii) are represented by

$$x_i^{t+1} = x_i^t + \varepsilon(x_i^t - x_k^t) \tag{4.8}$$

where x_j and x_k are pollen from different flowers of the same plant species. If they come from the same species or selected from the same population, Eq. (4.8) describes a random walk if we draw ε from a uniform distribution with values falling in the range [0,1]. Rule (iv) essentially regards the reasonable values of a switch probability p between common global pollination and intensive local pollination.

4.2. Swarm Intelligence, Data Mining and Knowledge Discovery

Data mining is the application of specific algorithms for extracting patterns from data. Many goals of knowledge discovery are achieved following some data mining methods. Such methods regard (i) *Clustering*, i.e., the identification of a finite set of categories or clusters to describe the data; (ii) *Summation*, i.e., the derivation of summary for association of rules and the rule of multivariate visualization techniques; (iii) *Regression*, corresponding to learn a function which maps a data item to a real-valued prediction variable and the discovery of functional relationships between variables; (iv) *Classification*, corresponding to learn a function that classifies a data item into one of several predefined classes. Other methods involve *Dependency modeling*, i.e., finding a model which describes significant dependencies between variables, *Deviation Detection* that should discovery the most significant changes in data from previously identified values, and *Cascading classifiers*, a term denoting a class of methods used to solve pattern recognition problems combining improvement of classification accuracy and the reduction of the complexity.

Sousa et al. have proposed the use of PSO as a tool for data mining (Sousa et al., 2003; Sousa et al., 2004). In their approach, three different Particles Swarm Data Mining Algorithms were implemented and tested against a Genetic Algorithm and a Tree Induction Algorithm. From the obtained results, PSO proved to be a suitable candidate for classification tasks. Thus, a second approach was dedicated to improving one of the Particle Swarm optimizer variants in terms of attribute type support and temporal complexity. The data sources used for experimental testing are considered as a *de facto* standard for rule discovery algorithms reliability ranking, indicating that PSO algorithms are competitive, not only with other evolutionary techniques, but also with industry standard algorithms (Shelokar et al., 2004; Grosan et al., 2006).

Oliveira et al. proposed of using PSO algorithm inside cascading classifiers methods for finding thresholds in order to improving the error-reject trade-off yielded by class-related reject thresholds (Oliveira et al., 2005). It has been proved the PSO is very effective in solving real valued global optimization problems. In addition, the authors have applied the PSO algorithm to optimize the thresholds of a cascading classifier system devoted to recognize handwritten digits in order to show the benefits of such an algorithm. In a cascading classifier the inputs rejected by the first stage and handled by the next ones using costlier features or classifiers.

Chen et al. proposed a combination of evolutionary procedure with PSO to design hierarchical fuzzy systems Takagi-Sugeno Fuzzy Systems (TS-FS) (Chen et al., 2006). A TS-FS model is described by fuzzy IF-THEN rules which represents local input-output relations of a nonlinear systems. The overall fuzzy model of a TS-FS system is achieved by fuzzy blending of the linear system models. The hierarchical structure is evolved using Probabilistic Incremental Program Evolution with specific instructions. The fine tuning of the IF-THEN parameters encoded in the structure is accomplished using PSO. When compared to the hierarchical TS-FS, the proposed hybrid approach exhibits competing results with high accuracy and smaller size of the hierarchical architecture.

Cluster analysis has become an important technique in exploratory data analysis, pattern recognition, machine learning and neural computing. In the field of clustering, K-means algorithm is the most popularly used algorithm to find a partition that minimizes mean square error measure. Although K-means is an extensively useful clustering algorithm, it suffers from several limitations. The objective function of the K-means is not convex and hence it may contain local minima. The PSO clustering algorithm performs a globalized search in the entire solution space. In many applications, PSO, K-means and PSO clustering algorithm have been applied showing that the hybrid PSO algorithm can generate more compact clustering results than the K-means algorithm.

Ye and Chen introduced an evolutionary PSO learning-based method to optimally cluster *N* data points into *K* clusters (Ye and Chen, 2005). Such method automatically detects the cluster centers of geometrical structure data sets. The special alternative metric introduced by the PSO method is considered to improve the traditional K-means clustering algorithm to deal with various structure data sets (Ahmadyfard and Modares, 2008).

Swarming agents in networks of physically distributed processing nodes may be used for data acquisition, data fusion, and control applications. In such applications, it is generally used an architecture for active surveillance systems where simple mobile agents collectively process real time data from heterogeneous sources (Rana et al., 2011).

Kuo et al. proposed an ant K-means clustering method (Kuo et al., 2005). Ant K-means algorithm modifies the K-means locating the objects in a cluster with the probability, which is updated by the pheromone, while the rule of updating pheromone is according to total within cluster variance (Tsai and Kao, 2011).

Shelokar et al. developed an ant colony optimization metaheuristic as a rule based machine learning method (Shelokar et al., 2004). The learning algorithm addresses the problem of knowledge acquisition in terms of rules from example cases by developing and maintaining the knowledge base through the use of (i) simple mechanism *a priori* known, (ii) pheromone trail information matrix, and (iii) use of available heuristic information. Therefore, the performance of ant colony classifier is compared with the well-known decision tree algorithm in term of the predictive accuracy on test cases and simplicity of rules discovered.

The application of swarm intelligence to data mining in medicine is impressive (Krasnogor et al., 2007). Just to cite a couple of examples, Bursa and Lhotska presented a clustering application based on ant colony for automatic recognition of patterns in biological signals (Bursa and Lhotska, 2007). The data used in that work are Electrocardiograms and Electroencephalograms. Mangat proposed a combination of PSO with ant colony optimization to improve the rule extraction methods to mine patient data over medical database to detect common risk factor for a wide range of diseases (Mangat, 2010).

REFERENCES

Afshar A., Haddad O.B., Marino M.A., Adams, B.J., 2007, Honey-bee mating optimization (HBMO) algorithms for optimal reservoir operation, J. *Franklin Inst.*, 344, 452-462.

Ahmadyfard A., Modares H., 2008, Combining PSO and K-means to enhance data clustering, *Proceedings of Telecommunications International Symposium*, pp. 688-691.

Blum C., Roli A., 2003, Metaheuristics in combinatorial optimization: overview and conceptual comparison, *ACM Computing Surveys*, 35, 268-308.

Burnwal S., Deb S., 2013, Scheduling optimization of flexible manufacturing system using cuckoo search-based approach, *Int. J. Advanced Manufacturing Technology*, 64(5-8), 951-959.

Bursa M., Lhotska L., 2007, Modified ant colony clustering method in long-term electrocardiogram processing, *Proceedings of the 29th Annual International Conference of the IEEE EMBS*, pp. 3249-3252.

Chechkin A., Metzler R., Klafter J., Gonchar V., 2008, Introduction to the Theory of Lévy Flights, In: Anomalous Transport: Foundations and Applications, Klages R., Radons G., Sokolov I.M., eds, Wiley-VCH, Weinheim.

Dorigo M., 1992, Optimization, learning and Natural Algorithms, PhD thesis, Politecnico di Milano, Italy.

Dorigo M., Maniezzo V., Colorni A., 1996, Ant system: optimization by a colony of cooperating agents, *IEEE Transactions on Systems, Man and Cybernetics, Part B*, 26, 29-41.

Dorigo M., Gambardella L.M., 1997, Ant colony system: A cooperative learning approach to the traveling salesman problem, *IEEE Transactions on Evolutionary Computation*, 1(1), 53-66.

Dorigo M., Di Caro G., Gamardella L.M., 1999, Ant algorithms for discrete optimization, *Artificial Life*, 5(2), 137-142.

Dorigo M., Stützle T., 2004, Ant Colony Optimization, MIT Press, Cambridge, MA.

Dorigo M., Blum C., 2005, Ant colony optimization theory: A survey, *Theoretical Computer Science*, 344(2-3), 243-278.

Gandomi A.H., Yang X.S., Alavi A.H., 2013, Cuckoo search algorithm: a metaheuristic approach to solve structural optimization problems, *Engineers with Computers* 29(1), 17-35.

Garnier S., Gautrais J., Theraulaz G., 2007, The biological principles of swarm intelligence, *Swarm Intelligence*, 1(1), 3-31.

Grosan C., Abraham A., Chis M., 2006, Swarm Intelligence in Data Mining, *Studies in Computational Intelligence*, 34, 1-20.

Karaboga D., 2005, An Idea Based on Honey Bee Swarm for Numerical Optimization, *Technical Report TR06*, Erciyes University, Turkey.

Kennedy J., 1992, Thinking is social: Experiments with the adaptive culture model, *Journal of Conflict Resolution*, 42, 56-76.

Kennedy J., 1997, The Particle Swarm: Social Adaptation of knowledge, In: *Proceedings of IEEE Service Center,* pp. 303-308, Piscataway, NJ.

Krasnogor N., Nicosia G., Pavone M., Pelta D., 2007, *Nature Inspired Cooperative Strategies for Optimization,* Springer, Berlin.

Krause J., Cordeiro J., Parpinelli R.S., Lopes H.S., 2013, A survey of Swarm Algorithms Applied to Discrete Optimization Problems, Swarm Intelligence and Bio-Inspired Computation, Elsevier, North-Holland.

Mangat V. 2010, Swarm Intelligence Based technique for Rule Mining in Medical Domain, *International Journal of Computer Applications*, 4(1), 19-24.

Nakrani S., Tovey C., 2004, On honey bees and dynamic server allocation in internet hosting centers, *Adaptive Behavior*, 12(3-4), 223-240.

Parpinelli R.S., Lopes H.S., 2011, New inspirations in swarm intelligence: a survey, *Int. J. Bio-Inspired Computation*, 3, 1-16.

Pavlyukevich I., 2007, Lévy flights, non-local search and simulated annealing, *J. Computational Physics*, 226, 1830-1844.

Pham D.T., Ghanbarzadeh A., Koc E., Otri S., Rahim S., Zaidi M., 2005, The Bees Algorithm, *Technical Note, Manufacturing Engineering Center*, Cardiff University, UK.

Rana S., Jasola S., Kumar R., 2011, A review on particle swarm optimization algorithms and their applications to data clustering, *Artificial Intelligence Review*, 35(3), 211-222.

Sayadi M.K., Ramezanian R., Ghaffari-Nasab N., 2010, A discrete firefly metaheuristic with local search for makespan minimization in permutation flow shop scheduling problems, *Int. J. Industrial Engineering Computations*, 1, 1-10.

Shelokar P.S., Jayaraman V.K., Kulkarni B.D., 2004, An ant colony classifier system: Application to some process engineering problems, *Computers & Chemical Engineering*, 28(9), 1577-1584.

Shi, Y., Eberhart R.C., 1998, A modified particle swarm optimizer, In: Proceedings of the IEEE Congress on Evolutionary Computation, pp. 69-73, Piscataway, NJ.

Tsai C.Y., Kao I.W., 2011, Particle swarm optimization with selective particle regeneration for data clustering, *Expert Systems with Applications*, 38(6), 6565-6576.

Yang X.S., 2005, Engineering optimization via nature-inspired virtual bee algorithms, *Artificial Intelligence and Knowledge Engineering Applications: A Bioinspired Approach, Lecture Notes in Computer Science*, 3562, 317-323, Springer, Berlin.

Yang X.S. 2008, Nature-Inspired Metaheuristic Algorithms, first ed. Luviner Press. UK:

Yang X.S., 2009, Firefly algorithms for multi modal optimization, *Fifty Symposium on Stochastic Algorithms, Foundation and Applications, Lecture Notes on Computer Science*, Watanabe O., Zeugmann T., eds, 5792, 169-178, Springer, Berlin.

Yang X.S., 2010a, Nature-Inspired Metaheuristic Algorithms, 2nd ed. Luviner Press, UK.

Yang X.S., 2010b, Engineering Optimization: An Introduction with Metaheuristic Applications, J. Wiley & Sons, NJ.

Yang X.S., 2010c, A new metaheuristic bat-inspired algorithm, *Nature Inspired Cooperative Strategies for Optimization, studies in computational Intelligence*, 284, 65-74, Springer, Berlin.

Yang X.S. 2011a, Bat algorithm for multi-objective optimization, *Int. J. Bio-Inspired Computation*, 3(5), 267-274.

Yang X.S., 2011b, Chaos-enhanced firefly algorithm with automatic parameter tuning, *Int. J. Swarm Intelligence Research*, 2(4), 1-11.

Yang, X.S., 2012, Flower pollination algorithm for global optimization, *Proceedings of the 11th International Conference on Unconventional* *computation and Natural computation, lecture notes in Computer Science*, 7445, pp.240-249, Springer, Berlin.

Yang X.S., Deb S., 2009, Cuckoo search via Lévy flights, *Proceedings of the World Congress on Nature & Biologically Inspired computing, IEEE publications*, pp.210-214, USA.

Yang X.S., Deb S., 2010, Engineering optimization by cuckoo search, *Int. J. Math. Modelling and Numerical Optimization* 1(4), 330-343.

Yang X.S., Karamanoglu M., 2013, Swarm intelligence and Bio-Inspired Computation: an Overview, Swarm Intelligence and Bio-Inspired computation, Elsevier, North-Holland.

Ye F., Chen C.Y., 2005, Alternative KPSO-Clustering Algorithm, *Tamkang Journal of Science and Engineering*, 8(2), 165-174.

Chapter 5

NANOSTRUCTURES INSPIRING COMPUTATION

Nanoscience and nanotechnology are the study and application of objects with dimensions of 1-200 nanometers (*nm*). One nanometer is a billionth of a meter ($10^{-9}m$). To give an idea a sheet of newspaper is about one hundred thousand nanometers thick. Nanoscience and nanotechnology involve the ability to see and to control atoms and molecules on nanoscale down to individual objects. The possibility to study the matter on such nanoscale has been made thank to the advent of scanning probe microscopies (Scanning Tunneling Microscopy and Atomic Force Microscopy) in the 1980s (Binnig et al., 1982; Binnig et al., 1986). Although nanoscience and nanotechnology are relatively new, nanoscale materials were used for centuries. Gold nanoparticles were used in the so-called *Lycurgo cup*, manufactured by Roman artists in the IV Century B.C. (Freestone et al., 2007), and alternate-sized gold and silver particles created colors in the stained glass windows of medieval churches hundreds of years ago (Jin et al., 2001). The artists back then just didn't know that the process they used to create these beautiful works of art actually led to changes in the composition of the materials they were working with. Today's scientists and engineers are finding a wide variety of ways to deliberately make materials at the nanoscale to take advantage of their enhanced properties such as higher strength, lighter weight, increased control of light spectrum, and greater chemical reactivity than their larger-scale counterparts.

There are two general ways to produce nanomaterials. The first way is to start with a bulk material and then break it into smaller pieces using physical, mechanical, chemical or other form of energy. This way is defined *top-down* procedure (Whitesides and Grzybowski, 2002; Walt, 2003). The second way consists to synthetize the material from atomic or molecular species via chemical reactions, allowing for the precursor particles to grow in size. This procedure is known as *bottom-up* (Lieber, 2002; Hecht, 2003; Zhang, 2003). In a bottom-up scheme, methods to produce nanoparticles from atoms are chemical processes based on transformations in solution such as sol-gel processing, chemical vapor deposition, plasma or flame spraying synthesis, laser pyrolysis, atomic or molecular condensation. In addition, nanoparticles of a wide range of materials (including both a variety of organic and biological compounds, but also inorganic oxides, metals and semiconductors) can be processed using chemical *self-assembly* techniques (Walt, 2003). These techniques exploit selective attachment of molecules to specific surfaces, biomolecular recognition and self-ordering principles (one basic example is the preferential docking of DNA strands with complimentary base pairs) as well as well-developed chemistry for attaching molecules onto clusters and substrates (for example, thiol (-SH) end groups to gold atoms, here S denotes the sulfur atom and H the hydrogen atom) and other techniques like reverse micelle, sono- and photo-chemical synthesis to realize 1-D, 2-D and 3-D self-assembled nanostructures (Huck, 2005; D'Acunto and Pingue, 2009). The molecular building blocks grow as parts of a dendritic structure that join tighter in a perfect short- or long-scale order without an effective driving force. The nanostructured growing with self-assembly procedure is the core of bottom-up procedure and the growing structures can maintain their basic chemical and physical properties on larger scales than nanoscale, for example, in bulk, and inexpensively. The self-assembly characteristic of natural systems on nanoscale can be considered as an example of *natural intelligence* and *nature learning*. Self-assembly is particularly useful because it allows the aggregation of structures too small to be manipulated individually into the ordered arrays of patterns that often give function to the materials. The development of hierarchically ordered structures is the basic manifestation of nature learning operating on structures in which self-assembly has been at work at different scales, each bridging a different property. A phenomenon as simple as crystal formation is a process of self-assembly. A useful known example is the self-assembly of atoms and molecules into stable crystalline CdSe quantum dots (cadmium-selenium nanoparticles having diameters of tens of nm), and the subsequent self-assembly of the nanoparticles into three-dimensional photonic crystals (Zrenner, 2000).

Nanomaterials can be classified according to their size, or functions. Another property useful for classification is the structure. As the dimensions of structures become smaller, their ratio of surface-to-volume increases. Molecules are essentially a surface being the smallest nanostructure. The ability to make materials with high ratios of surface-to-volume by building them from nanostructures is an important opportunity for surface science and technology. The confinement of the system properties to a surface is crucial in nanotechnology. Surfaces and interfaces are intrinsically nanoscale structures that are key in determining the properties and behavior of many systems of large interest due their possible employment in information communications technologies (Tour, 2003; Crawley et al., 2005). A surface determines many properties for materials, such as wettability, adhesion, friction, susceptibility to corrosion, fracture resistance, optical, biocompatibility, and many others (Stepanow et al., 2008). Self-assembly has already made a large contribution to surface science through the introduction of self-assembled monolayers (alkanethiolates chains on gold or silvers film), which allow significant control and tenability of the surface properties.

Why should computation have anything to do with nanoscience, beyond the obvious role of developing software-modeling tools? It is commonly recognized that while the computing revolution was about the systematic manipulation of information, nanoscience is about the systematic manipulation of matter (Chen et al., 2003). However, many of the traditional forms of manual control are simply not possible at small scales. Automating the growth of molecular structures it is impossible with hands, and the machine they operate. We must learn to program molecules to manipulate themselves. This learning can be reversed, the programming of the molecules can generate new algorithms. DNA is the basic example. DNA is the molecule of choice in many labs, not only for its biological properties but for its information-bearing properties. It is easy to synthesize and its physical properties are well understood. Computation with DNA will be described in section 5.1.

Self-assembly plays an important role to create nanoscale circuits in molecular electronics, where the random variation in the connection between components are used in the sense of probabilistic logic network. In section 5.2 will be presented the state of the art on how to produce reliable circuits in spite of the random variation of connections. Finally, in section 5.3 logic primitives associated to quantum dots arrays will be discussed and section 5.4 will be dedicated to the computation models based on the property of self-similarity that characterizes fractal structures.

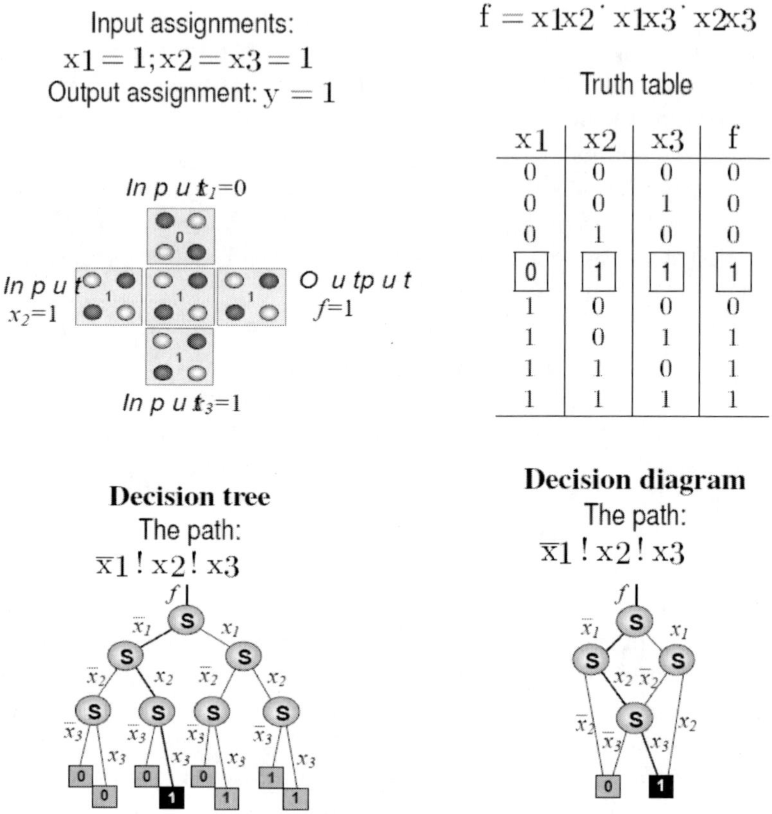

Figure 5.1. Example of a Boolean majority function $f{=}M(x_1,x_2,x_3){=}x_1x_2 \vee x_1x_3 \vee x_2x_3$ and the related data structure. (Reproduced from (Yanushkevich and Shmerko, 2010), with permission).

A common description of such topics could be based on molecular information processing based on two nature-inspired functions: self-assembly and conformational dynamics, both working in combination (Crawley et al., 2005). Starting by the pioneering paper of Wang (Wang, 1961), molecular assembling is usually formulated as a topological problem. The source data to be specified in any problem are: (i) a finite set of unit size square elements, where top and bottom sides of each element is encoded by symbols over a finite alphabet; (ii) a region where these elements must be located; (iii) the rules for local assembling of such elements, (iv) the rules for global assembling. The problem can be synthetized saying that it to put the elements into specified regions, given the desired function. A computational step consists of one element bonding to others according to given rules that match input labels of one element to the output labels of order one or two adjacent elements. Since assembling a small number of elements can be controlled, this strategy can be transferred to large-size problems thank to self-assembling rules so that, guided by the self-replicating natural phenomenon, the successive bonding of element performs a computation, for example, the evaluation of a Boolean function given its inputs. The computation of any Boolean function requires the definition of libraries of logic primitives built using the requirements to computing Boolean functions, see figure 5.1 and table 5.1.

Figure 5.1 reports the example of Boolean majority function of three variable. Another similar example could be the AND function, by assigning the input x_3=0, the AND function is implemented using the majority function f=$M(x_1,x_2,0)=x_1x_2 \vee x_1 \cdot 0 \vee x_2 \cdot 0=\underline{x_1x_2}$ (Yanushkevich and Shmerko, 2010). Table 5.1 report all the logic primitive function and correspondent algebraic form.

Table 5.1. Tabulated form of a Boolean function y for the given assignments of variables x_1 and x_2 (with the row of the truth table), the logic primitive, and the correspondent algebraic form. (Reproduced from (Yanushkevich and Shmerko, 2010), with permission)

Tabulated form (x_1 x_2 y)	Logic primitive	Algebraic form
0 0 0	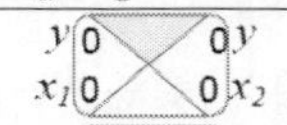	$y = x1 \cdot x2$ for $x1 = x2 = 0$
0 0 1		$y = \overline{x1}\overline{x2}$ for $x1 = x2 = 0$
0 1 0	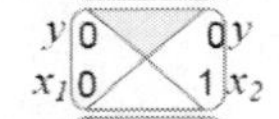	$y = x1 \cdot \overline{x2}$ for $x1 = 0; x2 = 1$
0 1 1		$y = \overline{x1}x2$ for $x1 = 0; x2 = 1$
1 0 0		$y = \overline{x1} \cdot x2$ for $x1 = 1; x2 = 0$
1 0 1		$y = x1\overline{x2}$ for $x1 = 1; x2 = 0$
1 1 0		$y = \overline{x1} \cdot \overline{x2}$ for $x1 = 1; x2 = 1$
1 1 1		$y = x1x2$ for $x1 = x2 = 1$

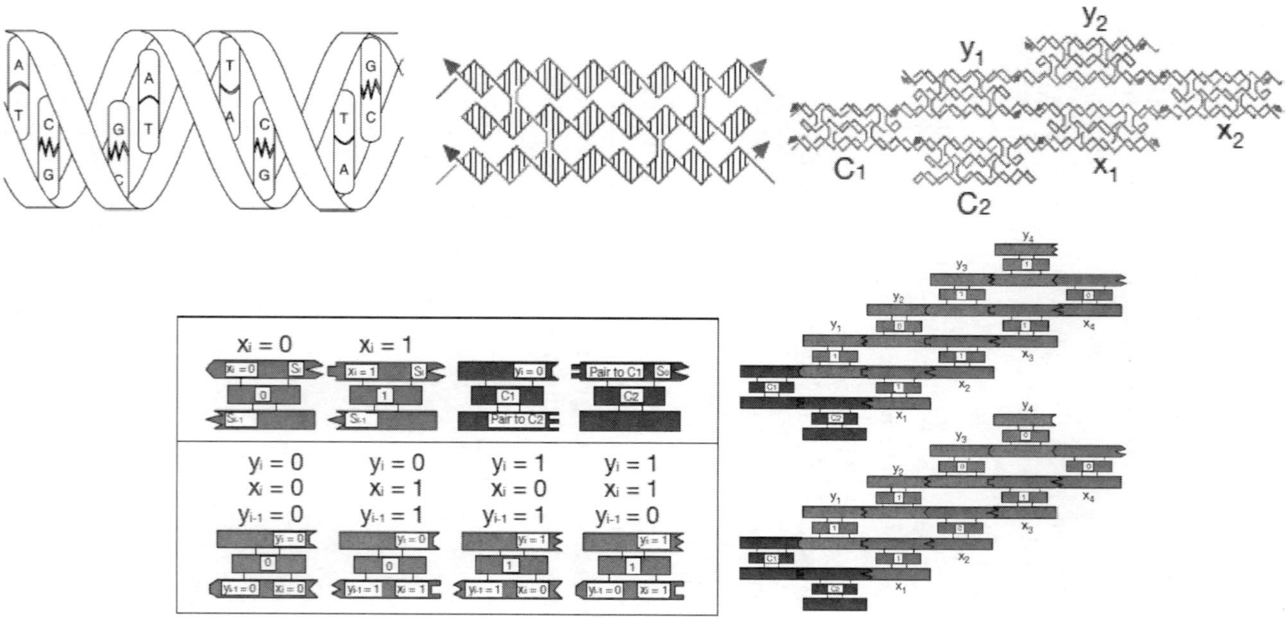

Figure 5.2. Calculation of cumulative XOR by self-assembly of DNA tiles. From the top, on left, the double helix of DNA. Adenine (A) is complimentary to Thymine (T), and Cytosine (C) is complimentary to Guanine (G). Middle, an individual triple-crossover tile forming three double helical domains; arrowheads indicate 3′ ends. On the right, after calculation, at the end of the assembly, the reporter strand running through the x diagonal array, around the corner, and then back up the y diagonal array is ligated, thereby associating the calculated output with the input. Bottom images, from left, the three helical domains are drawn as rectangles, flanked by sticky ends shown as geometrical shapes. The value of each tile is in the central rectangle. In the image, two x tiles, four y tiles and the initialization corner tiles, C1 and C2, are represented. On the right, the image reports two performed calculations. The values of each tile are the same as on the left. The sticky ends are the same. The tiles are shown assembled to perform the cumulative XOR calculation. The operations are designed to proceed from lower left to upper right, this is because the x_i and C1 and C2 tiles have longer sticky ends than y_i tiles. (Reproduced with modification from (Mao et al., 2000), with permission).

Any arbitrary Boolean function can be computed using this collection of logic primitives and the rules of assembling. A logic primitive operatively corresponds to a particular configuration of two switches given the assignments of the input and output variables. Logic primitives can be converted into various data structures and interpreted using switches, tabulated forms, decision trees or diagrams. As a consequence computing using the logic primitives can be associated with the paths in decision trees and diagrams. The path in a decision tree (from the root node to the terminal node) for a Boolean function corresponds to the logic primitive.

5.1. Nanoscale Self-Assembling Computation: The Case of DNA

One definition of self-assembled algorithm is that such algorithm describes the self-assembly of a structure whose total number of components (and their sizes) is much greater than the number of different types of components (Adleman, 1994; Dotty, 2012). Since a component type is reused many times, it has no way of knowing where it is going to end up in the structure, so only local information is available to guide its attachment. DNA tile assembly has the potential to reuse a small number of tile types to create large structures (Mao et al., 2000; Rothemund, 2006; de Castro, 2008). In figure 5.2, the basic features of the DNA tile model are schematically presented.

An example of laboratory example of cumulative XOR calculations with denaturing gels is reported in figure 5.3.

Since Adleman's molecular computer encoded the solution to a Hamiltonian path problem in DNA (Adleman, 1994), several developments and applications of DNA computation have been recently reported (Benenson, 2012; Miyamoto, 2013). It has been estimated that DNA computation can operate at over 1000 teraflops as well as store a single bit of information in one cubic nanometer, with speed and storage capacities greatly exceeding silicon computation devices. Analogously to DNA, ribonucleic acid (RNA) and microRNA logic gates have been used a wide series of biological applications ranging from cellular targeted delivery (Hemphill and Deiters, 2013), to pH sensing in *Caenorhabditis elegans* (Surana et al., 2011). Inside animal cells DNA logic gates are employed for the computation of endogenous biological inputs independent of protein components and gene expression systems (Rinaudo et al., 2007) or detect microRNA in vivo (Xie et al., 2011).

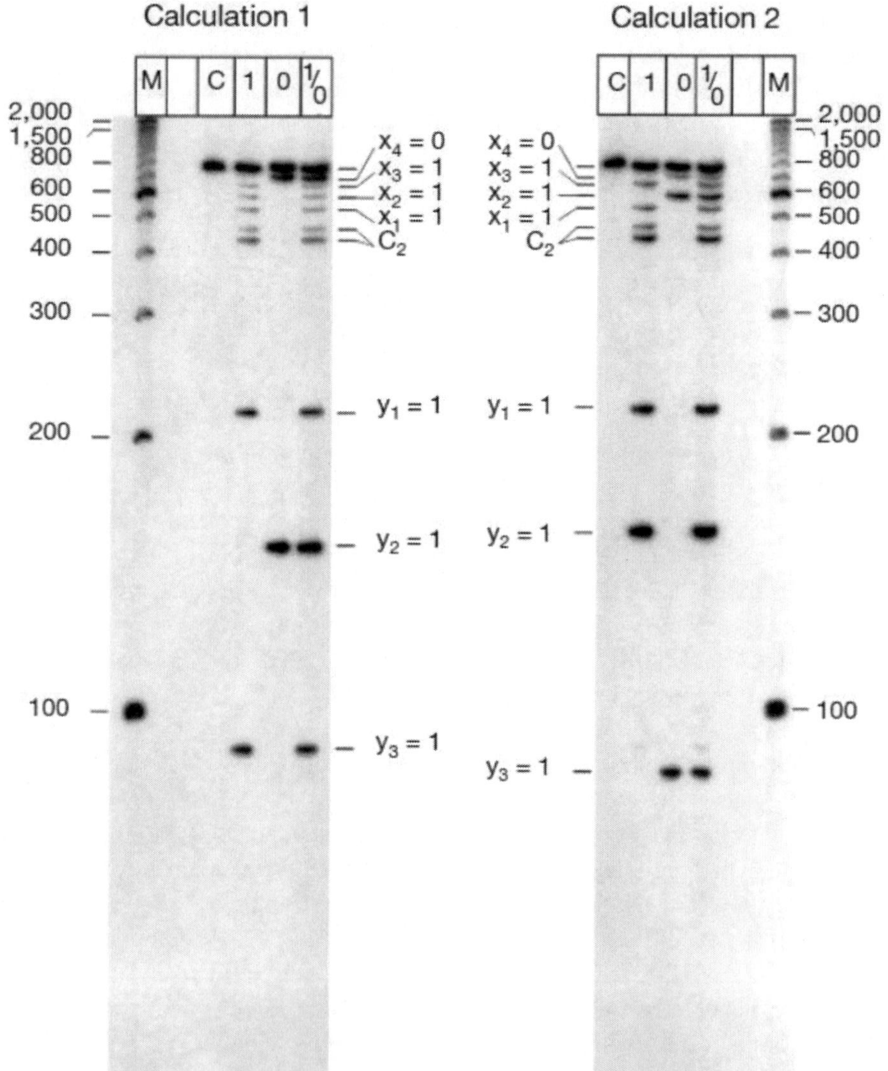

Figure 5.3. Cumulative XOR calculations expressed though two 6% denaturing gels. For detailed description see (Mao et al., 2000). (Reproduced with permission).

5.2. Self-assembled Molecular Circuits

Compared to micro-electronics, nano-electronics is still in its childhood, more or less as micro-electronics was just before the advent of transistor in the 1940s. The passage from the micro-electronics towards the nano-electronics cannot be thought with a top-down approach. Lithography that is the principal technique to create electronic micro-components, can create microscale circuits with many components, high yield and low cost unit, but this combination of capabilities is not yet possible for molecular-scale devices. On the contrary, a bottom-up approach could create a large number of molecular devices designed by self-assembling molecules. In principle, self-assembly can produce complex nanoscale structures as demonstrated by biological processes and can create a wide range of structures at many length scales. However, the current physical and chemical self-assembly technology at the nanoscale is limited to creating simple, regular or random structures. For nanoscale circuits, the basic challenge is to design components simple enough to fabricate complex circuits by self-assembly. One possibility is to use arrays of parallel micron-long nanowires. Two of these arrays, placed orthogonally with molecules between the crossed wires, can be configured to provide electronic memory and logic circuits (Hogg et al., 2006). However, although such configuration increases the area of the circuit, the advantage is minimal when applied to a large number of components. An alternative approach could be represented by addressing wires to demultiplexer circuits. Unfortunately, demultiplexers require a complex pattern of connections, which can't be fabricated at the nanoscale by current technology. The solution could be represented by fabricating demultiplexers at the nanoscale using random self-assembly (Rachlin and Savage, 2008). The idea is to consider a regular self-assembly process to create an array of many parallel nanowires (deHon et al., 2005; Hogg et al., 2006). Ordinary micron-scale lithography makes the small number of micron-scale address wires. Connections between these sets of wires are formed with two-way AND logic elements at their cross points, figure 5.4. These connections can be formed by a feasible random physical process allowing control over the density of connections but not their precise location, thereby precluding the complex connection pattern of a standard demultiplexer. Since such connections are fabricated by self-assembly methods, this involve many defects and uncertainty in the circuits.

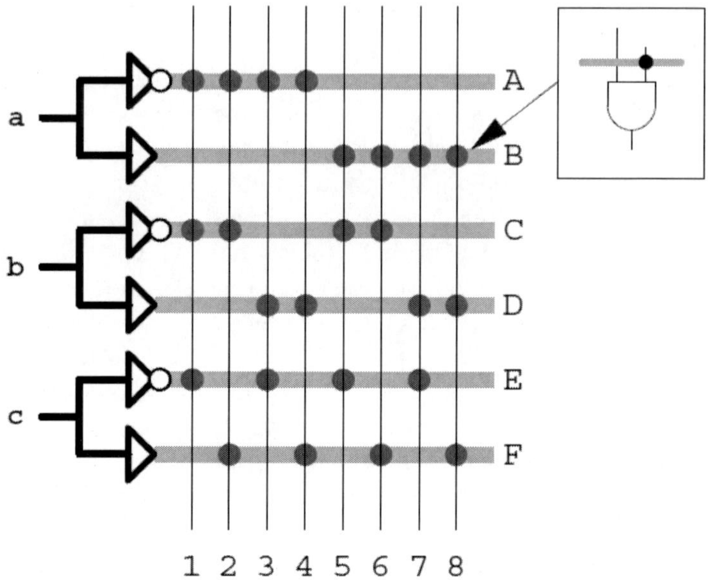

Figure 5.4. Schematic sketch of a demultiplexer circuit with 8 data wires (1, . . ., 8) and 6 addressing wires. The binary pattern of connections shown in the picture has valid addresses consisting of alternating 0's and 1's, which can be provided externally by 3 wires (a, b, c), each connected to two addressing wires, one of which is via an inverter circuit. Inset: Logic element corresponding to a connection. (Reproduced from (Hogg et al., 2006), with permission).

By an experimental point of view, the demultiplexer represented in figure 5.4 gives some advantages. It is much easier to establish random interconnections between data wires and addressing wires than accurately defined interconnections. The random connections can be done chemically using a chemical process which has a specific change of happening (~50%). One example of such a process is using a randomly-deposited, colloidal-sized dot (diameters of nanometers) to either make electrical contact or not between a nanowire and a microscopic address wire. The se dots consist of conductive particles. To use a random assembly process, we simply introduce enough connections over the whole extent of the data wires so each data wire has probability p to connect to each of the addressing wires, where p can be selected with any value between 0 and 1. A probability p=1/2 of a connection means the contact area, A, between a data and address wire has probability ½ to have no nanoparticles. In a grid geometry, this area could hold $\alpha = A/d^2$ particles, where d is the diameter of the particle (say 5nm). If ρ is the probability a grid point to be occupied by a nanoparticle, we have that $(1-\rho)^{\alpha}=1/2$, giving $\rho=0.017$. Thus the contact area will have, on average, $\rho\alpha=0.69$ particles. This value is larger than ½ because we have an equal probability to have either no particles in the contact area or at least one particle.

One critical point of a scheme of demultiplexer report in figure 5.4 is the definition of threshold conditions for random connectivity (Chen et al., 2003; deHon et al., 2005). Let us consider *N* data wires and *M* addressing wires, we generate a connectivity matrix in which each element is independently selected to be 1 with a specified probability *p*. Following the example suggested by Hogg et al., (Hogg et al., 2006), consider the matrix

$$\begin{pmatrix} 0 & 1 & 1 & 0 \\ 1 & 1 & 0 & 1 \\ 0 & 0 & 1 & 1 \end{pmatrix}$$

The two 1's in the first row indicate the first addressing wire connects to the 2nd and 3rd data wires. Thus, comparing the first and second columns, we note that turning on the connections for the second data wire also turns on those for the first. Similarly, the last columns address also activates the first. As a consequence, this set of connections only allows uniquely addressing two of the four data wires, namely the first and third. In general, we can consider each column of the connection matrix as a specified set of connections. If the number of addressing wires, *M*, increases, the chance two addresses conflict in this way decreases. Thus we can expect that sufficiently large *M* will give unique addresses with high probability. In addition, increasing the number of data wires, *N*, makes it more likely that at least two of them will conflict, in this case, the system will not be fully addressable. However, many authors declare that the research on self-assembled molecular nanocircuits focused on such problem will be able to find a suitable solution in less time that it might be thought.

5.3. Quantum Dots Networks and Logic Computation

Quantum dots networks are also commonly known as quantum cellular automata, they represent nanostructures considered as one of the emerging technologies useful for future computers (Lent et al., 1993; Chopard and Droz, 1998; Delgado, 2007). A quantum dots is a nanocrystal made of a semiconductor materials where excitons are confined in all the three spatial dimensions, so that the electronic properties are intermediate between those of bulk semiconductors and of discrete molecules. One basic property of quantum dots is that the band gap, which determines the frequency range of emitted light, is inversely related to its size since, due the spatial confinements of excitons, the electronic characteristics of a quantum dot are strongly related to its size and shape. The other advantage of quantum dots is that the excitation and emission of quantum dots can be highly tunable. In addition, the size of a quantum dot may be set when it is made, so that its conductive properties may be carefully controlled. But the property of quantum dots motivating this section, is that quantum dots assemblies consisting of arrays, or networks of quantum dots of many different size forming gradient multilayer-layer nanofilms, can be made exhibiting a range of desirable emission properties (Brus, 1984; Murray et al., 2000). Quantum dots can be considered as qubits for quantum computation and this topic is described in the next chapter. Here, we focus the attention on quantum dots arrays as logic primitives (Yanushkevich and Shmerko, 2010).

In the traditional silicon-based technology, information is represented by voltages and currents, and a wire crossing requires a bridge out the plane. On the contrary an advantage of quantum dots is the ability to cross wires on a plane. Given the physical properties of quantum dots, each logic primitive is represented by four quantum dots in a square array (Tougaw and Lent, 1994; Lent and Tougaw, 1997; Shukla and Bahar, 2004; macucci, 2006, Yanushkevich and Shmerko, 2008). Electrons should be able to tunnel between the dots, but are unable to leave this square array. Moreover, electrons are forced to reside in diagonally opposite dots of the square due to electrostatic repulsion. The two ground-state polarizations are energetically equivalent, and can be interpreted as logic 0s and 1s. In quantum dots cells, different wires carrying different binary values can cross each other at the same level without any interference or crosstalk. Unlike silicon-based technology, where metal layers are used to implement connections without performing any functions, the multi-layers of quantum dots networks can be used as active components. In locally connected structures, the range of interaction and the connection complexity of each basic geometry (cell) of quantum dots are independent on the number of cells. Therefore, these structure are scalable and massively parallel.

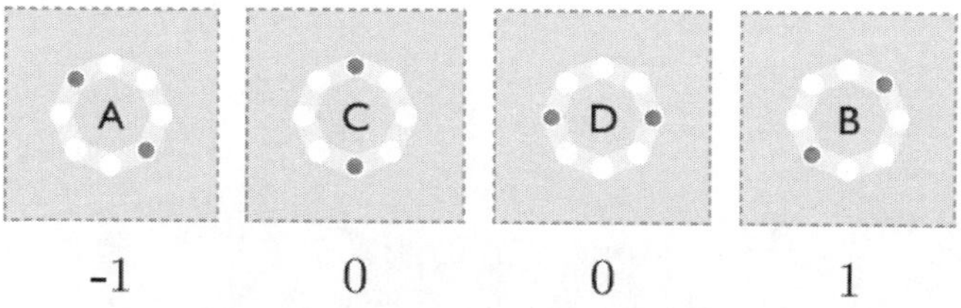

Figure 5.5. Example of a ternary quantum-dot cell with the four distinct electron arrangements, i.e., the four possible states marked A, B, C, and D, that correspond to the maximal inter-electron separation. (Adapted from (Pečăr et al., 2008), with permission).

Here, we give an example of hyper-controlled-not (hyper-CNOT) gate implemented by manipulating four quantum dot-cavity system (Ren and Deng, 2014). Quantum dot –cavity system is composed by a single charged quantum dot confined in a double-sided optical resonant microcavity. The resonant microcavity is composed by two distributed partially reflective Bragg reflectors with low loss for on-resonance transmission, moreover, the double sided cavity is made two-mode so that can support both polarization modes. In such system, the quantum dot is located at the center of a double-sided cavity. When an excess electron is injected into quantum dot, the singly charged quantum dot shows the optical resonance of a negatively charged exciton consisting of two electrons bound to one hole. As a consequence, the negatively charged exciton, accordingly to Pauli's exclusion principle, shows spin-dependent transitions interacting with circularly polarized lights and the input-output relation of such double-sided quantum dot-cavity system can be calculated from the Heisenberg equations of motion for the cavity field operator and the negatively charged exciton dipole operator (Walls and Milburn, 1994). The principle of the spatial-CNOT gate constructed on the quantum-dot-cavity system as proposed by Ren and Deng is based on the reflection and the transmission rules of circularly polarized lights interacting with the quantum dot- cavity system (Ren and Deng, 2014). Another promising candidate for the implementation of a future multi-valued processing platform is the ternary quantum dot cellular automata. The principal functionally complete set of a binary logic system comprises binary conjunction, disjunction and negation and the corresponding binary quantum dots system. Ternary logic represents a generalization of binary logic so one cannot simply use the binary functionally complete set. The extension of a binary quantum dot system to a ternary quantum dot has been proposed, figure 5.5 (Pecăr et al., 2008).

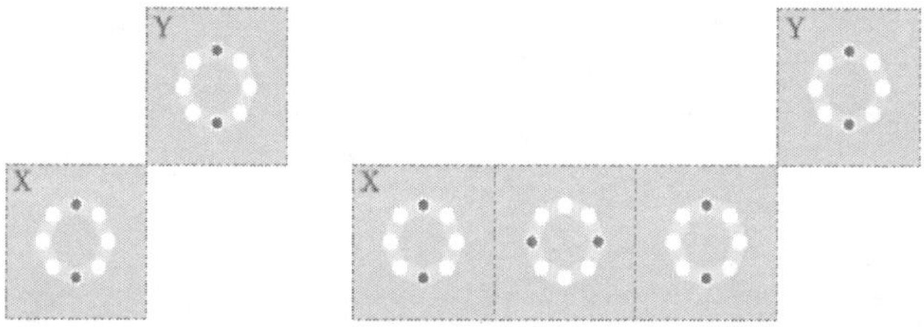

x	X	Y	y
-1	A	B	1
0	C	C	0
0	D	D	0
1	B	A	-1

Figure 5.6. The core of a ternary inverter (left) and the extension of the input section (middle). The behavior matches the truth table of ternary negation, right. (Reproduced from (Pecăr et al., 2008), with permission).

In a ternary quantum dot cell, eight quantum dots are arranged in a circular pattern with two mobile electrons. The electrons can only reside at quantum dots or tunnel between adjacent quantum dots, but cannot tunnel outside the cell. The Coulomb interaction between the electrons causes them to localize in quantum dots that ensure their maximal separation which corresponds to the energetic minimal state. In figure 5.5, the four arrangements, which correspond to the ground states (energetic minimal states), are marked as A, B, C and D. The four state can be interpreted as logic values. By arbitrary definition, A is interpreted as logic value -1, B as logic value 1 and C and D as 0. The reliability of the behavior of quantum dot cells as in figure device depends foremost on the reliability of the switching process, consisting in the transition of a cell's state that corresponds to one logic value to a state that corresponds to another and vice versa. This is achieved by means of the adiabatic switching concept, where a cyclic signal, namely adiabatic clock, is used to control the cell's switching dynamic. Recent results on the ternary switching configuration showed that the correct behavior of logic states requires a synchronized data transfer to be scalable in more complex architectures (Pecăr and Lebar Bajec, 2011). In order to construct more complex structures, an inverter core must be defined so that if a logical value x corresponds to the state input cell X and logical value y to the state of output cell Y it can be seen that the quantum dot cell must act as a ternary inverter, figure 5.6. Moreover, complex structures can be built connecting the inverter core to other primitives. This is achieved by means of wires, figure 5.6.

Similar geometries can be developed for converting, for example, parallel data lines into data stream. This conversion allows different pieces of data to be reduced to a time-dependent series of values on a single wire. In quantum dots arrays this can be made introducing clocking zones consecutive 90-degree phases.

5.4. Fractals for Computation Models

Fractal geometry is the geometry of nature and its core concept is the self-similarity (Mandelbrot, 1983). Self-similarity can be defined as an invariance with respect to scaling. Due to some characteristics of self-similarity (regularity and periodicity of structures), self-similarity can be strongly juxtaposed to self-assembly. As a natural consequence scale invariance, fractal based computation can be implemented using certain physical and chemical phenomena, such as crystal morphology and patterning. In crystal morphology, physical parameters, such as concentration, temperature, pressure and the order of assembly affect crystal growth and morphology. Since these parameters can be controlled, then the crystal growth can be described in terms of logic function computation. Analogously to crystal growth, fractals also describe the assembly of DNA helices and microtubules, as well as others phenomena and morphologies as broccoli, threes and lightning bolts.

Logic primitives can be used for the interpretation of the self-assembly process I terms of Boolean function computation. In terms of logic primitives, each type of fractal can be characterized by (i) self-assembly dynamics, (ii) class of the implemented Boolean functions, and (iii) computing performance (Butler et al., 2001; Rothemund et al., 2004). The basic idea underlying this connection is the relationship between the tabulated form of a Boolean function distributed in the fractal structure and the properties of this function, such as symmetry and polynomial terms. One example of conversion of fractal structure into logic primitive is to use a predefined pattern, see previous section. In this section, we limit to consider a Sierpinski triangle as pattern (Rothemund et al., 2004). The Sierpinski triangle is a type of fractal structure, with attractive fixed set with the overall shape of an equilateral triangle, subdivided recursively into smaller equilateral triangles, figure 5.7. The Sierpinski triangle for a Boolean function $f(x_1,x_2,\ldots,x_n)$ is a triangle formed by

Exclusive OR (XOR) addition of 0s and 1s starting from the bottom row, which is the truth vector of f. Let a Boolean function f of three variables x_1,x_2,x_3, be given by a truth table, or truth vector, F=$[00101011]^T$, figure 5.7. This function can be represented by a decision tree whose terminal nodes represent the truth vector. The Sierpinski triangle is then constructed from the truth vector, and it results in the coefficient vectors of the polynomial forms of this function.

Truth table

x1	x2	x3	f
0	1	0	0
0	1	1	0
1	0	0	1
1	0	1	0
1	1	0	1
1	1	0	0
1	1	0	1
1	1	0	1

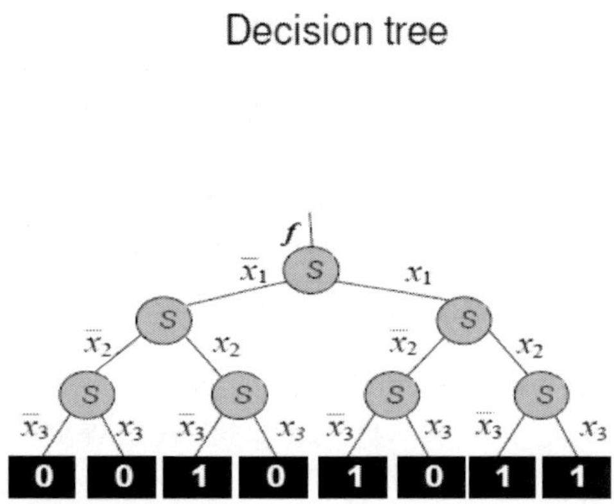

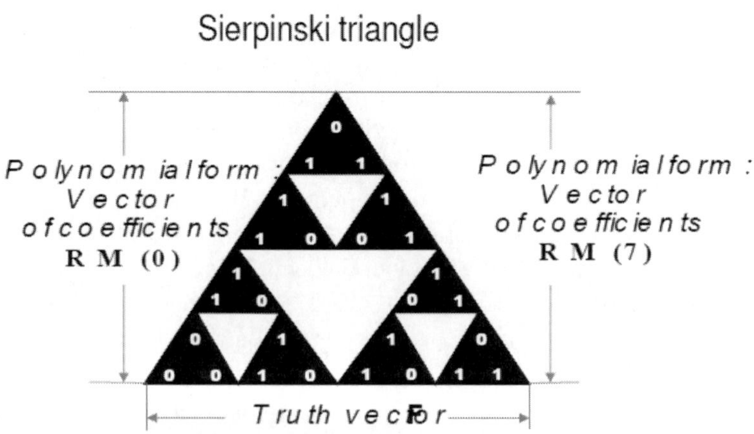

Figure 5.7. Relationship between Boolean function $f(x_1,x_2,x_3)$ and its truth vector F=$[00101011]^T$, decision tree, and Sierpinski triangle. (Reproduced from (Yanushkevich and Shmerko, 2010), with permission).

Another type of triangle-like fractal structure is the transeunt triangle (Yanushkevich and Shmerko, 2010). They have found application for the description of crystal-like process because of perfect relations to logic function description. Transeunt triangles represent data structures for symmetric Boolean functions. A Boolean function f of n variables x_1, $x_2,\ldots,x_n$ is totally symmetric if and only if it is unchanged by any permutation of variables. A totally symmetric function is completely specified by a carrier vector F with a_i coefficients, with $0 \leq i \leq n$, such that Boolean function f is a_i for all assignments to x_1, $x_2,\ldots,x_n$. For example, a Boolean function $f=\overline{x}_1\overline{x}_2\overline{x}_3 \vee x_1x_2x_3$ is totally symmetric, and the correspondent carrier vector is F=[1 0 0 1]. Manipulation of transeunt triangles can be accomplished using *forward* and *inverse* procedures. The forward procedure is defined as the converting of a symmetric Boolean function given in tabulated form into a polynomial form using a suitable vector of coefficients. On the contrary, an inverse procedure can be specified as the computation of a symmetric Boolean function given in polynomial form and represented by vector of coefficients. The final result of such computation are the values of polynomial expressions.

REFERENCES

Adleman L.M., 1994, Molecular computation of solutions to combinatorial problems, *Science*, 266, 1021-24.

Benenson Y., 2012, Biomolecular computing systems: principles, progress and potential, *Nature Reviews Genetics* 13, 455-68.

Binnig G., Rohrer H., Gerber C., Weibel E., 1982, Surface Studies by Scanning Tunneling Microscopy, *Physical Review Letters*, 49(1), 57-60.

Binnig G., Quate C.F., Gerber C., 1986, Atomic Force Microscope, *Physical Review Letters*, 56, 930-34.

Brus L.E., 1984, Electron-electron and electron-hole interactions in small semiconductor crystallites: the size dependence of the lowest excited electronic state, *J. Chem. Phys.*, 80, 4403-4409.

Butler J.T., Dueck G.W., Yanushkevich, Shmerko V.P., 2001, On the number of generators of transeunt triangles, *Discrete Applied Mathematics*, 108, 309-16.

Chen Y., Jung G.Y., Ohlberg D.A.A., Li X., Stewart D. R., Jeppesen J. O., Nielsen K.A., Stoddart J.F., Williams R. S., 2003, Nanoscale molecular-switch crossbar circuits, *Nanotechnology*, 14, 462-468.

Chopard B., Droz M., 1998, Cellular Automata Modeling of Physical Systems, Cambridge University Press, UK.

D'Acunto M., Pingue P., 2009, Novel Polymers and Nanopatterning, in *Nanotechnological applications of novel polymers,* Mohsen Adeli Eds, Transworld Research Network, India.

deHon A., Copen Goldstein S., Kuekes P.J., Lincoln P., 2005, Nonphotolithographic nanoscale memory density prospects, *IEEE Transactions on Nanotechnology*, 4, 215-228.

Delgado C.A.P., 2007, Quantum Cellular Automata: Theory and Applications, PhD thesis, University of Waterloo, Waterlo, Ontario, Canada, http://www.iqc.ca/publications/theses/caperez_phd.pdf .

Dotty D., 2012, Theory of Algorithmic Self-Assembly, *Communications of the ACM*, 55(12),78-88.

Freestone I., Meeks N., Sax M., Higgitt C., 2007, The Lycurgus Cup- A Roman Nanotechnology, *Gold Bulletin*, 40(4), 270-277.

Hecht S., 2003, Welding, organizing, and planting organic molecules on substrate surface-promising approaches towards nanoarchitectonics from the bottom up, *Angew. Chem. Int. Ed Engl.* 42, 24-26.

Hemphill J., Deiters A., 2013, DNA Computation in mammalian Cells: MicroRNA Logic Operations, *J. Am. Chem. Soc.*, 135, 10152-10518.

Hogg T., Chen Y., Kuekes P.L., 2006, Assembling nanoscale circuits with randomized connections, *IEE Transactions on Nanotechnology*, 5, 110-122.

Huck W.T.S., 2005, Nanoscale Assembly. Chemical Techniques, Springer, Berlin.

Jin R., Cao Y., Mirkin C.A., Kelly K.L., Schatz G.C., Zheng J.G., 2001, Photoinduced conversion of silver nanospheres to nanoprisms, *Science,* 294, 1901-03.

Lent C.S., Tougaw P.D., Porod W., Bernstein G.H., 1993, Quantum cellular automata, *Nanotechnology*, 4, 49-57.

Lent C.S., Tougaw P.D., 1997, A device architecture for computing with quantum dots, *Proc. IEEE*, 85, 541-47.

Lieber C.M., 2003, Nanoscale science and technology: building a big future from small things, MRS Bulletin, 28, 486-491.

Macucci M., 2006, Quantum Cellular Automata: Theory, Exoerimental and Prospects, Imperial College Press, London.

Mandelbrot B.B., 1983, The Fractal Geometry of Nature, H. Holt and Company edition.

Mao C., le Bean T.H., Relf J.H., Seeman N.C., 2000, Logical computation using algorithmic self-assembly of DNA triple-crossover molecules, *Nature* 407, 493-96.

Miyamoto T., Razavi S., Derose R., Inoue T., 2013, Synthesizing Biomolecule-based Boolean Logic Gates, *ACS Synthetic Biology* 2(2), 72-82.

Murray C.B., Kagan C.R., Bawendi M.G., 2000, Synthesis and characterization of monodisperse nanocrystals and close-packed nanocrystal assemblies, *Ann. Rev. Mater. Sci.*, 30, 545-610.

Pečăr P., Ramšak A., Zimic N., Mraz M., Lebar Bajec I., 2008, Adiabatic pipelining: a key to ternary computing with quantum dots, *Nanotechnology*, 19, 495401(1-12).

Pečăr P., Lebar Bajec I., 2011, The Key Elements of Logic Design in Ternary Quantum-Dot Cellular Automata, Unconventional Computation (UC) 2011, Lecture Notes on Computer Science, 6714, pp. 177-188, Springer, Berlin

Rachlin E., Savage J.E., 2008, Nanowire addressing with randomized-contact decoders, *Theoretical Computer Science*, 408, 241-61.

Ren B.C., Deng F.G., 2014, Hyper-parallel photonic quantum computation with coupled quantum dots, *Scientific Reports*, 4, 4623(1-7).

Rinaudo K., Bleris L., Maddamsetti R., Subramanian S., Weiss R., Benenson Y., 2007, A universal RNAi-based logic evaluator that operates in mammalian cells, *Nature Biotechnology*, 25, 795-801.

Rothemund P.W.K., Paradakis N., Winfree E., 2004, Algorithmic Self-Assembly of DNA Sierpinski Triangles, *Plos Biology*, 2(12), e424.

Rothemund P.W.K., 2006, Folding DNA to create nanoscale shapes and patterns, *Nature* 440, 297-302.

Shukla S.P., Bahar R.I., 2004, Nano, Quantum and Molecular Computing, Kluwer, Dordrecht.

Surana S., Bhat J.M., Koushika S.P., Krishanan Y., 2011, An autonomous DNA nanomachine maps spatiotemporal pH changes in a multicellular living organism, *Nature Communications*, 2, 340-44.

Stepanow S., Lin N., Barth J.V., 2008, Modular assembly of low dimensional coordination architectures on metal surfaces, *J. Physics: Cond. Matter*, 20, 184002-17.

Tougaw P.D., Lent C., 1994, Logical devices implemented using quantum cellular automata, *J. Appl. Phys.*, 75, 1818-25.

Walls D.F., Milburn G.J., 1994, Quantum Optics, Springer-Verlag, Berlin.

Walt D.R., 2002, Nanomaterials: Top-to-bottom functional design, *Nature Materials*, 1, 17-18.

Wang H., 1961, Proving Theorems by pattern Recognition, *Bell System Technical J.*, 40, 1-37.

Whitesides G.M., Grzybowski B., 2002, Self-assembly at all scales, *Science*, 295, 2418-2421.

Xie Z., Wroblewska L., Prochazka L., Weiss R., Beneson Y., 2011, Multi-input RNAi-based logic circuit for identification of specific cancer cells, *Science*, 333, 1307-11.

Yanushkevich S.N., Shmerko V.P., 2008, Introduction to Logic Design, Taylor & Francis, CRC Press, Boca Raton, FL.

Yanushkevich S.N., Shmerko V.P., 2010, Nature-Inspired Computing for Nanoelectronics, *J. of Information, Control and Managements Systems*, 8(3), 265-283.

Zhang S., 2003, Building from the bottom up, *Materials Today*, 6, 20-27.

Zrenner A., 2000, A close look on single quantum dots, *J. Chem. Phys.*, 112, 7790-7798.

Chapter 6

QUANTUM COMPUTING

In a classical digital computer, information is stored as bits, each of which represents a zero or a one, and n-long vectors are manipulated to model functional evaluation and to implement algorithms. The stability of the stored information and the reliability of such manipulations is based on classical physics and it is assumed that one can examine storage devices to determine the information of their contents without affecting the effective values of such contents. On the contrary, if information is stored using quantum physics the context is radically different. For example, at the quantum level a storage bit could represent both zero and one simultaneously, and measurements and manipulations of those quantum bits must be carried out using different processes that can be modeled as matrix operations. As a consequence, the physical context in which information is represented becomes an important aspect of the theory.

The study of the role of quantum mechanics in the theory of computation has begun in the early 1980s with the publications of Paul Benioff, who considered a quantum mechanical model of computers and the computation process (Benioff, 1982A; Benioff, 1982B). Hence, similar questions were presented shortly thereafter by Richard Feynman by asking what kind of computer should be used to simulate physics. His answering led him to the belief that with a suitable class of quantum machines one could, at least in principle, imitate any quantum system. Nevertheless, quantum computing was definitively recognized as a new frontier of computation only in 1994, when Peter Shor published a factoring algorithm for a quantum computer that finds the prime factors of a composite integer N more efficiently than is possible with the known algorithms for a classical computer (Shor, 1994).

To begin to describe quantum algorithms, we need an understanding of the physical phenomena that motivate quantum mechanics. Quantum mechanics is a general term used to refer to the mathematical framework that describes quantum physics. Quantum physics is the theoretical and experimental framework that explains and describes the behavior of objects with atomic dimensions. A quantum computer is a system that uses quantum-mechanical phenomena to perform computation and operations on data. Before to detail the basic properties of a quantum computer and the fundamental characteristics of quantum computation we have to define the properties of quantum mechanics.

6.1. Basic Properties of Quantum Mechanics

The mathematical structure of quantum mechanics is quite sophisticated. Thus, the basic ideas of quantum mechanics can be described looking at the behavior of atomic scale systems as measured in experiments. The controversial results if such experiments are analyzed with classical mechanics framework led to the necessity to introduce quantum mechanics in the 1920s decade. One basic experiment is the two-slit experiment for electrons (Sakurai, 1985). In such experiment, a source produces a mono-energetic stream of electrons which move in a uni-dimensional direction. An absorbing screen, perpendicular to the electron stream, has two narrow slits through which the electrons can pass on their way to counters on a second screen set beyond the first screen. When only one of the slits is open, the counters record a pattern of impacts that resembles a truncated normal distribution, that is the distribution waited for a stream of electrons impinging on one slit. On the contrary, if both slits are open and sufficiently close one each another, than the distributions of impact show interference and the pattern of observed counts with two slits open is not the sum of the patterns of counts obtained by opening each slit separately. A further development in the two-slit experiment is the impinging of electron in separated time, in this case, the wave-like behavior of interference suggest that each electron is somehow interfering with itself, which is in strong contrast with the idea that each electron must have gone through exactly one of the slits. Since the patterns are more confused, we can gain only a probabilistic knowledge which slit each electron traverses. Another fundamental experiment that opened the doors to quantum concepts, is the Stern-Gerlach experiment (Sakurai, 1985). Thank to such experiment, it has been found that the electrons, as well as other elementary particles, have an intrinsic angular momentum, called *spin*, which can be experimentally detected by beaming a stream of electrons through an appropriate inhomogeneous magnetic field. The original experiment of Stern and Gerlach was performed on silver atoms that have a single valence electron, so that the physical properties conditioned by the spin, essentially depending by the spin of the single electrons. But the most important consequence of the Stern-Gerlach experiment was the possibility to observe some effect directly connected to the existence of a quantized spin for the electronic beam. For example, instead of observing a continuum of deflections, the electronic beam is deflected in a finite number of ways. In particular, it was observed that certain particles have spin ½, which means that the interfering electronic beam splits into exactly two subbeams. Implications from this phenomenon are strongly important for quantum computing as will be shown later. If an electronic beam is moving along the x-axis, and if the magnetic field is arranged to have a large inhomogeneous component in a direction perpendicular to the x-axis, say, for example, in the z-direction, then one subbeam diverges (up) in the positive z-axis direction and the other diverges (down) in the negative z-axis direction. In addition, it is impossible to predict whether a single electron will go up or down, the two subbeams have equal intensity, and to the two subbeams can be associated two values: a z-spin up or being in a state $(z,+)$ and the particles in the second subbeam as having z-spin down or as being in a state $(z,-)$. If a subsequent measurement is made on the beam $(z,+)$, for example, using the same apparatus, then only one beam emerges, i.e., the $(z,+)$ beam itself, as would be expected intuitively. In this case, in the second experiment, the behavior of the particles in the $(z,+)$ subbeam can be predicted, they will emerge in state $(z,+)$. Analogous behavior is observed in other directions, so that if a subsequent Stern-Gerlach experiment with the inhomogeneity in the y direction, a so-called *y-oriented* Stern-Gerlach experiment, is performed on the $(z,+)$ subbeam, for example, two new subbeams are observed, denoted by $(y,+)$ and $(y,-)$ in the obvious notation. Again, the two new subbeams will have equal intensity although in which y-direction an individual electron goes cannot be predicted. Nevertheless, if a second z-oriented Stern-Gerlach measurement is made on the $(y,+)$ (say) subbeam which was selected from the $(z,+)$ subbeam, then both a $(z,+)$ subbeam and a $(z,-)$ subbeam are detected in equal intensity. This implies that the measurement of the y-spin orientation has erased the effect of the first z-spin measurement on the surviving electron. This phenomenon is completely counterintuitive and has not a classical physics counterpart. Moreover, the analogy with the wave phenomena can be easily found. The analogy is as follows: supposed to send a beam of light through three polarized filters and (say) the polarization directions of the first and third filters are at right angles, and (say) the polarization of the middle filter is at 45 ° angle to each of the other two. If the middle filter is removed from the experiment, no light is observed passing through the third filter, as is to be expected. But, if the middle filter is in place, light polarized in the direction of the third filter is observed. Moreover, after the second filter the selective effects of the first filter on the polarization seem to be vanished. From the experiments of the two-slits system, Stern-Gerlach apparatus, and light polarization, we reach to several conclusions. Electrons show wave-like behavior and light exhibits particle-like behavior. Another conclusion is on the probabilistic behavior of matter at microscale, the outcome of a future measurement of a system cannot always be predicted with certainty, but one is able to predict future behavior only with a prescribed probability. As in the Stern-Gerlach z-spin experiment, one can predict with certainty that an electron in the $(z,+)$ state will go up in a subsequent z-oriented experiment but can only predict the behavior of the electron in a subsequent y-oriented experiment with a certain probability. A series of conclusions regard somehow the limit of the experiment performance, or better, the necessity to distinguish between the evolution of the system under investigation and the measurement of the same system. As in the Stern-Gerlach experiment, sending a spin ½ particle through the device is an example of the former, measuring which trajectory the particle took is an example of the latter. In addition there is a limit to the accuracy of simultaneous measurements of certain physical properties such as position and momentum. This lack of knowledge is denoted as the Heisenberg uncertainty principle. In turn, any theory describing the behavior of matter at the atomic scale cannot ignore the effect an observation has on the physical system.

Acceptance of such conclusions and of subsequent models does not come easily, and the debate over various aspects of the quantum theory is still open. Here, we suggest some readings to the interested reader, (Hirvensalo, 2000; Pittenger, 2000; Nielsen and Chuang, 2010), and drop the debate going to describe briefly, the basic formalism need to discuss the quantum computing challenges.

In quantum mechanics, the possible states of a system are represented by unit vectors, called state vectors. Formally, these reside in a complex separable Hilbert space, generally called associated Hilbert space of the system, that is well defined up to a complex number of norm 1 (the phase factor). In other words, the possible states are points in the projective space of a Hilbert space, usually called the complex projective space. The exact nature of the Hilbert space is dependent by the system and the observable needs to describe the physics of the system. Any observable is represented by a maximally Hermitian linear operator acting on the state space, and any eigenstate of the observable corresponds to an eigenvector of the operator, while the associated eigenvalue corresponds to the value of the observable in that eigenstate.

The standard notation used to represent a vector in a vector space is $|\mathbf{x}\rangle$, where **x** is a label for the vector. The notation $|\cdot\rangle$, referred to as *ket*, identifies **x** as a column vector. Any *ket* $|\mathbf{x}\rangle$ has a dual *bra* $\langle\mathbf{x}|$, which is the conjugate transpose of $|\mathbf{x}\rangle$. Since the state of a quantum system can be described by a unit-length vector in a Hilbert space, the state space of a quantum system (the quantum state space) can be described in terms of vector and matrices or using a standard notation involving *bra* and *ket* states, i.e., the *bracket* or *Dirac notation* (Dirac, 1982; de Castro, 2007). The terminology *bracket notation* is so defined because the *inner product* of two states is represented by a *bracket*, $\langle\mathbf{x}'|\mathbf{x}\rangle$, which consists of a left part $\langle\mathbf{x}'|$, the *bra*, and a right part $|\mathbf{x}\rangle$, the *ket*. The inner product between the two vectors results in a complex number, while the notation $|\mathbf{x}'\rangle\langle\mathbf{x}|$ represents the outer product of vectors $|\mathbf{x}'\rangle$ and $|\mathbf{x}\rangle$, and results in a matrix.

Any state of a quantum system can be written as a linear combination of a number of basis states, the so-called *superposition of basis states*:

$$\mathbf{c}_1|\mathbf{x}_1\rangle + \mathbf{c}_2|\mathbf{x}_2\rangle + \ldots + \mathbf{c}_n|\mathbf{x}_n\rangle \tag{6.1}$$

where $\mathbf{c}_i$, i=1,…,n, are complex numbers called *amplitudes*, with the property $\sum_i |\mathbf{c}_i|^2 = 1$. Each value $|\mathbf{c}_i|^2$ corresponds to the probability that the system can be found at state $\mathbf{x}_i$. Analogously, $|\mathbf{x}\rangle$ and $|\mathbf{x}'\rangle$ can be combined to give a tensor product that is a form of putting together vector spaces to form larger vector spaces allowing the combination of quantum states. As a consequence, the state space of a composite system is the tensor product of the state spaces of the component physical systems. For example, two classical bits can be combined is a further composite system as 00, 01, 10 or 11. The value of any combination can be written as the product of the individual bits, i.e., $|\mathbf{x}\rangle \otimes |\mathbf{x}'\rangle$ (also abbreviated as $|\mathbf{x}\rangle|\mathbf{x}'\rangle$ or $|\mathbf{xx}'\rangle$). There are some quantum composite systems that cannot be written as a tensor product of states of its component systems, this property is known as *entanglement*. For example, assuming that the first system is an arbitrary state $|\mathbf{x}\rangle_A$ and the second system in another arbitrary state $|\mathbf{x}'\rangle_B$, if the state of the composite system cannot be written as the tensor product $|\mathbf{x}\rangle_A \otimes |\mathbf{x}'\rangle_B$, then the states are said to be entangled. The general state of a composite system has the form

$$\sum_{\mathbf{x},\mathbf{x}'} \mathbf{c}_{\mathbf{xx}'} |\mathbf{x}\rangle_A |\mathbf{x}'\rangle_B \tag{6.2}$$

From the Eq. (6.2), we can have a representation of two-qubits states, as the Bell states, for example (Sakurai, 1985):

$$\beta_{00} = \frac{1}{\sqrt{2}}\left(|00\rangle_{AB} + |11\rangle_{AB}\right);\ \beta_{01} = \frac{1}{\sqrt{2}}\left(|01\rangle_{AB} + |10\rangle_{AB}\right);$$

$$\beta_{10} = \frac{1}{\sqrt{2}}\left(|00\rangle_{AB} - |11\rangle_{AB}\right);\ \beta_{11} = \frac{1}{\sqrt{2}}\left(|01\rangle_{AB} - |10\rangle_{AB}\right) \tag{6.3}$$

Another important aspect of quantum computation is the time evolution of qubits. In quantum mechanics the evolution of a quantum system corresponds to how it changes over time. Because the modeling of quantum mechanics must (i) model interference phenomena, (ii) model nondeterministic predictions, and (iii) allow for evolution of a quantum system as distinct from its measurement, we must distinguish between closed and open system. If the quantum system is closed, its evolution can be described by a unitary transformation operator **U** that relates the state $|\mathbf{x}_2\rangle$ of the system at time t_2 to the state $|\mathbf{x}_1\rangle$ at time t_1 by the unitary transformation

$$|\mathbf{x}_2\rangle = \mathbf{U}|\mathbf{x}_1\rangle \tag{6.4}$$

and the effect of the unitary transformation **U** on a state is described by the corresponding rotation of the correspondent vector in the appropriate Hilbert space. Examples, of unitary transformation are the Pauli matrices, that are a set of three 2×2 complex matrices which are Hermitian and unitary

$$\sigma_0 = \mathbf{I} = \begin{bmatrix} 1 & 0 \\ 0 & 1 \end{bmatrix}; \ \sigma_1 = \mathbf{X} = \begin{bmatrix} 0 & 1 \\ 1 & 0 \end{bmatrix}; \ \sigma_2 = \mathbf{Y} = \begin{bmatrix} 0 & i \\ -i & 0 \end{bmatrix};$$
$$\sigma_3 = \mathbf{Z} = \begin{bmatrix} 1 & 0 \\ 0 & -1 \end{bmatrix} \tag{6.5}$$

In *classical* world, the information is physically stored as bits (an entity that assumes value 0 *or* 1) in standard computers, and the devices realizing a bit can be a combination of transistors and other integrated circuit elements with a distribution of charge determining the state of the bit. On the contrary, when information is stored at atomic scales, quantum effects take place and the scenario changes completely. In this case, the qubit can assume both value 0 *and* 1, simultaneously. Analogously, measurements and manipulations affect the contents of a qubit and can be modeled as matrix operations. Quantum information is described by a state in a two-level system with two basic states conventionally labeled as $|0\rangle$ and $|1\rangle$. Such states form an orthogonal basis for a two-dimensional complex vector space resulting as *computational basis states*. Such states possess all the mathematical properties of Hilbert space vector, so, it is possible to form linear combinations of the basis states, *superposition*, which correspond to a *pure* qubit state:

$$|\mathbf{x}\rangle = \mathbf{c}_1|0\rangle + \mathbf{c}_2|1\rangle \tag{6.6}$$

where $\mathbf{c}_1$ and $\mathbf{c}_2$ are complex numbers, with the property $\sum_{i=1,2}|\mathbf{c}_i|^2 = 1$. The superposition of basis states implies that an infinite amount of information can potentially be encoded in a single qubit by appropriately defining the amplitudes $\mathbf{c}_1$ and $\mathbf{c}_2$. If in standard computing, n bits can be used to represent 2^n states, so that a string of 2 bits allows the states 00, 01, 10, 11, instead, a n-qubit system carries out n computational basis states denoted as

$$|\mathbf{x}'\rangle = \sum_{\mathbf{x}=00...0}^{11...1} \mathbf{c}_{\mathbf{x}} |\mathbf{x}\rangle \tag{6.7}$$

where, as usual, $\mathbf{c}_{\mathbf{x}}$ are complex numbers and $\sum_{\mathbf{x}} |\mathbf{c}_{\mathbf{x}}|^2 = 1$. Therefore, *n* qubits can represent any complex unit vector in a Hilbert space of dimension 2^n, having one dimension for each classical state. An ordered system of *n* qubits is known as *quantum register* (de Castro 2007). Analogously to classical computation, the elementary operations can be used to manipulate bits in standard computers producing logic functions and operations. For example, a logic gate is an electronic device used to perform a simple logic function and to construct larger logic systems. Common gates are the NOT, which operates on a single bit, and the AND and OR gates that operate on two or more inputs. Some classical gates, such as the OR and XOR gates, have the property that the operations they perform on the inputs are not invertible. For quantum gates the situation changes. Quantum gates, i.e., the analogous of logic gates in standard computers, are the basic units of quantum algorithms and quantum computers. The simplest example of a quantum gate acting on a single bit is the quantum NOT gate. While the classical NOT gate maps 1→0 and 0→1, the quantum NOT gate maps the state $|0\rangle \rightarrow |1\rangle$ and $|1\rangle \rightarrow |0\rangle$. This operation can be represented by matrix notation (**A**) as follows:

$$\begin{aligned} \mathrm{NOT}|0\rangle = \mathbf{A}|0\rangle = \begin{bmatrix} 0 & 1 \\ 1 & 0 \end{bmatrix}\begin{bmatrix} 1 \\ 0 \end{bmatrix} = \begin{bmatrix} 0 \\ 1 \end{bmatrix} = |1\rangle \\ \mathrm{NOT}|1\rangle = \mathbf{A}|1\rangle = \begin{bmatrix} 0 & 1 \\ 1 & 0 \end{bmatrix}\begin{bmatrix} 0 \\ 1 \end{bmatrix} = \begin{bmatrix} 1 \\ 0 \end{bmatrix} = |0\rangle \cdot \end{aligned} \tag{6.8}$$

Hence, any unitary matrix transformation may be used as quantum gate, this implies that, in contrast to standard gates, quantum gates are invertible. The Pauli matrices, relations (6.6), correspond to well-known quantum gates. Consequently, matrix **I** can represent the identity gate and the matrix **A** is the NOT gate, as represented in Eqs. (6.8). Transformations can be built from unitary matrices, as an example, another transformation that is commonly used in quantum computation is the *Hadamard* gate, **H**,

$$\mathbf{H} = \frac{1}{\sqrt{2}}\begin{bmatrix} 1 & 1 \\ 1 & -1 \end{bmatrix} \quad (6.9).$$

When applied to n bits, the Hadamard gate generates a superposition of all 2^n possible states:

$$\mathbf{H}|0\rangle = \frac{1}{\sqrt{2}}\begin{bmatrix} 1 & 1 \\ 1 & -1 \end{bmatrix}\begin{bmatrix} 1 \\ 0 \end{bmatrix} = \frac{1}{\sqrt{2}}\begin{bmatrix} 1 \\ 1 \end{bmatrix} = \frac{1}{\sqrt{2}}(|0\rangle + |1\rangle)$$
$$\mathbf{H}|1\rangle = \frac{1}{\sqrt{2}}\begin{bmatrix} 1 & 1 \\ 1 & -1 \end{bmatrix}\begin{bmatrix} 0 \\ 1 \end{bmatrix} = \frac{1}{\sqrt{2}}\begin{bmatrix} 1 \\ -1 \end{bmatrix} = \frac{1}{\sqrt{2}}(|0\rangle - |1\rangle). \quad (6.10)$$

Quantum circuits can be built combining quantum state transformations and the notation is similar to that of many layouts of classical circuits. The information flows from left to right, the horizontal lines represent wires and vertical lines connecting two or more qubits represent coupling terms, figure 6.2(a), and the squared boxes with special symbols correspond to gates, figure 6.2(b).

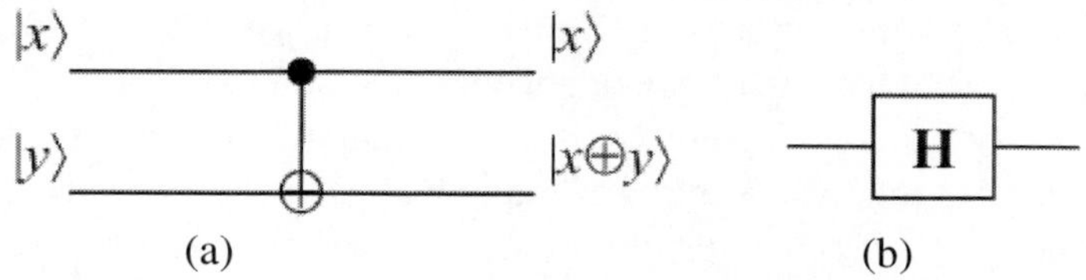

Figure 6.2. Examples of quantum circuits and gates. (a) Controlled-NOT gate. (b) Hadamard gate symbol. (Reprinted from (de Castro, 2007), with permission)

6.2. Quantum Cryptography

Quantum systems can be used to achieve cryptographic tasks, such as secret and secure communications. As usual in cryptographic scenarios, Alice and Bob are widely separated and wish to communicate. They are connected by an ordinary bidirectional open channel and uni-directional quantum channel, directed from Alice to Bob and vice versa, figure 6.3.

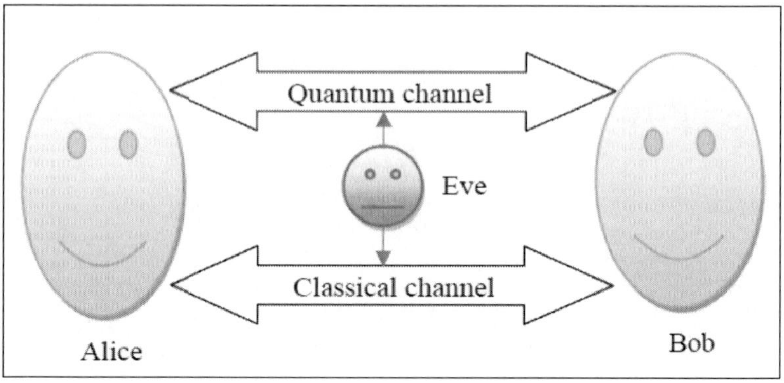

Figure 6.3. Example of a Quantum Key Distribution (QKD) model. Alice and Bob are two users who are connected through quantum and classical communication channel, wishing to communicate securely. Eve is the conventional name given to the adversary in cryptology. (Reproduced from (Lopes and Sarwade, 2014), with permission).

In quantum cryptography (QC) the quantum properties described in the introduction can used to produce a secure communication between Alice and Bob. These properties seem to be a set of negative rules stating things that cannot be done. For examples (Lütkenhaus N., 1999): (i) One cannot take a measurement without perturbing the system; (ii) One cannot determine simultaneously the position and the momentum of a particle with arbitrarily high accuracy. (iii) One cannot simultaneously measure the polarization of a photon in the vertical-horizontal basis and simultaneously in the diagonal basis. (iv) One cannot draw pictures of individual quantum processes. (v) One cannot duplicate an unknown quantum state. QC transforms such axioms in a secure communication provided the communication is quantum, that is, quantum systems carry the information, for example, individual photons. When this is the case, axiom (i), stats that Eve cannot get any information about the communication without introducing perturbations that would reveal her presence. How this could happen, image that Alice codes information in individual photons, which she sends to Bob. If Bob receives the photons unperturbed, then, according to the basic axiom (i), the photons were not measured. No measurement implies that Eve did not get any information about the photons because following the quantum characteristics of the system, acquiring information implies carrying out measurements. Consequently, after exchanging the photons, Alice and Bob can check whether someone was listening. It is enough to compare a randomly chosen subset of their data using a public channel, if Bob receives this subset unperturbed, then he can sure that eavesdropping is not working. In order to ensure that axiom (i) applies, Alice encodes her information in non-orthogonal states (see section 6.1). Alice and Bob could discover any eavesdropper, but only after they have exchanged their message, it would of course be much better to ensure their privacy in advance and not afterwards. To achieve this, Alice and Bob could not use the quantum channel to transmit information, but only to transmit a random sequence of bits, that represents the key. If the key is unperturbed, then quantum physics guarantees that no one has gotten any information about this key by eavesdropping the quantum communication channel, i.e., performing a measurement. In this case, Alice and Bob can safely use this key to encode messages. But, if unfortunately, the key turns out to be perturbed, then, Alice and Bob simply disregards it. Since the key does not contain any information, they have not lost any.

Since its invention in 1984 by Bennett and Brassard (Bennet and Brassard, 1984), quantum key distribution (QKD) has led to a change of paradigm with respect to the existing classical cryptographic schemes. While the latter ones establish their security on mathematical assumptions, the security of QKD relies on the fact that the devices of the legitimate parties, Alice and Bob, and the eavesdropper, Eve, are governed by quantum physics. Security proofs of QKD schemes exploit well-established quantum features such as the non-cloning theorem, or the non-shareability (monogamy) of entanglement. The common schemes in all these protocols is the following: Alice and Bob first establish some correlations by performing some measurements on a quantum state, or, similarly, Alice sends some quantum states that are later measured by Bob. Hence, exploiting the quantum formalism, Alice and Bob bound Eve's information and draw up a secret key by a public communication. A correlation is a conditional probability distribution $P(a,b|x,y)$, where a and b are Alice and Bob's output data, respectively, and x and y are their choices of inputs. For instance, x and y could be their choice of measurements settings and *a and b* are the obtained results. But the basic assumption in any protocol is that Alice and Bob know how the correlation $P(a,b|x,y)$ has been established. Therefore, all security proofs of QKD are based not only on [illegible]lidity of the quantum formalism, but also on the assumption that Alice [illegible]fectly know how their correlation is established. This perfect [illegible] the legitimate partners know the dimensions of the [illegible]uantum systems. Just in case Alice and Bob do [illegible] *a priori*, they have exploit a well- [illegible]om some observed correlation,

$P(a,b|x,y)$, without having to care about the practical details needed for the correlation distribution. This last condition makes the QKD device independent. In fact, an immediate necessary condition for some correlation to be secure under this device independent requirement, is that $P(a,b|x,y)$ should not allow a description in terms of local classical variables (Acin et al., 2006): $P(a,b|x,y) \neq \sum_{\gamma} p_{\gamma} P(a|x,\gamma) P(b|y,\gamma)$. If not, the adversary Eve may hold a copy of the γ's. This necessary condition implies that the correlation $P(a|x,\gamma)$ must violate a Bell inequality (Bell, 1964; Sakurai, 1985). As a result, any security proof of QKD in this more general device-independent scenario exploits the properties related to the quantum non-locality (Ekert, 1991).

As mentioned, the first protocol for QC was proposed in 1984 by C.H. Bennett and G. Bressard, hence the name BB84 as this protocol is known (Bennet and Brassard, 1984). The protocol was originally presented using the language of spin ½, but clearly it works for any two-level quantum system. The protocol uses four quantum states that constitute two bases, for example, the states up $|\uparrow\rangle$, down $|\downarrow\rangle$, left $|\leftarrow\rangle$, and right $|\rightarrow\rangle$. The bases are maximally conjugate in the sense that any pair of vectors, one from each basis, has the same overlap, e.g., $|\langle\uparrow|\leftarrow\rangle|^2=1/2$. Such states are the *qubits* and, conventionally, one attributes the binary value 0 to states $|\uparrow\rangle$ and $|\rightarrow\rangle$, and the value 1 to the other two states. In the first step, Alice sends individual spins to Bob in states chosen at random among the four states as represented in figure 6.4, where the spin states $|\uparrow\rangle, |\downarrow\rangle, |\leftarrow\rangle$, and $|\rightarrow\rangle$ are identified as the polarization states *horizontal, vertical*, +45° and -45°, respectively. The individual spins could be sent all at once or one after the other, the only restrictions being that Alice and Bob be able to establish a one-to-one correspondence between the transmitted and the received spins. Hence, Bob measures the incoming spins in one of two bases, chosen at random, using a random-number generator, independent from that of Alice. At this point, whenever they use the same basis, they get perfectly correlated results. On the contrary, whenever they use different bases, they get uncorrelated results. Hence, on average, Bob obtains a string of bits with a 25% error rate. This error rate is so high that standard error correction schemes would fail. But the BB84 protocol, Alice and Bob know which bits are perfectly correlated, i.e., the ones for which Alice and Bob used the same basis and which ones are completely uncorrelated, i.e., all the other ones. If, for each bit, Bob announces publicly in which basis he measured the corresponding qubit, then Alice can reveals only whether or not the state in which she encoded that qubit is compatible with the basis announced by Bob. If the state is compatible, they keep the bit; if not, they disregard it, so that in this way, about 50% of the bit string is discarded. This shorter key obtained after basis reconciliation is called the *sifted key* (Marand and Townsend, 2008).

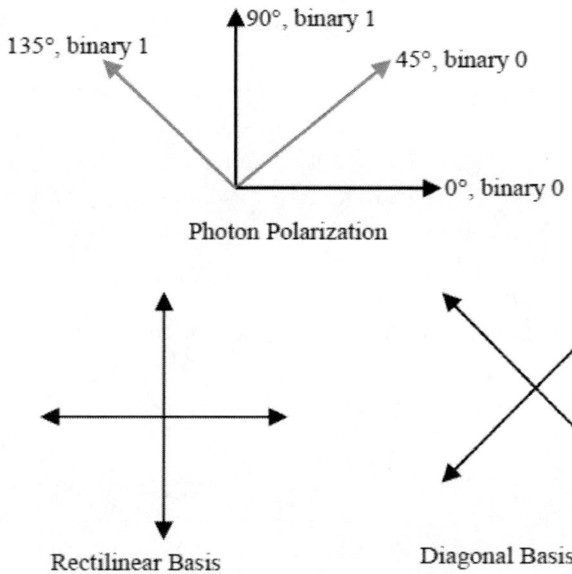

Figure 6.4. BB84 protocol: Alice generates a sequence of random numbers and encodes them using basis as shown in figure. Alice chooses this basis randomly and transmits the polarized photons to Bob. Hence, Bob measures the polarization of each received bit by choosing a random basis per bit. According to theory of probability, Alice and Bob are expected to choose same basis for more than 50% of cases on average.

In the BB84 protocol is interesting to note that: (i) Alice and Bob use a public channel, the only requirement is that this channel is authentic rather than confidential. Indeed, Eve can listen to all the communication on the public channel, but she cannot modify it. (ii) Neither Alice nor Bob can decide which key results from the protocol, because it is the conjunction of both of their random choices that produces the key. If Eve intercepts a qubit propagating from Alice to Bob, and Bob does not receives an expected qubit, he simply tells Alice to disregard it. Hence Eve only lowers the bit rate (theoretically down to zero), but she does not gain any useful information. To do a real eavesdropping, Eve must send a qubit to Bob and send this qubit in its original state, keeping a copy for herself.

BB84 have used quantum properties in such an efficient manner, that it has become the base for quantum cryptography. The disadvantage of BB84 is its assumptions for ideal quantum sources and detectors, which makes it vulnerable to photon number splitting and detector noise attacks (Bennett, 1992). The weakness of the BB84 protocol against photon number splitting attacks is due to the fact that whenever Eve can keep one photon, she gets all the information, because after the sifting phase, she has to discriminate between two eigenstates of a known Hermitian operator. One possible solution to photon number splitting attack has been proposed by Scarani et al., in 2004, so so-called SARG04 protocol (Scarani et al., 2004). One change with respect BB84 protocol is in *sifting* process. The bases used are non-orthogonal states as in figure 6.5, which cannot be discriminated deterministically.

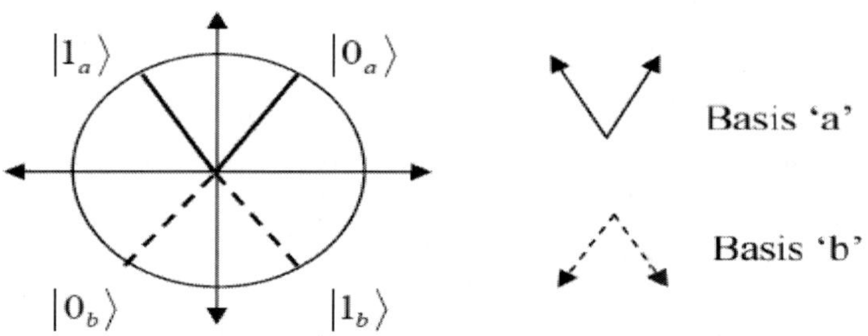

Figure 6.5. Example of two pairs of non-orthogonal states used in the SARG04 protocol. (Reproduced from (Lopes and Sarwade, 2014), with permission).

The protocol using non-orthogonal states can be described as follows: Alice sends randomly one of the four states (see the spin-1/2 notation mentioned in section 6.1) $|\pm x\rangle$ or $|\pm z\rangle$; Bob measures either σ_x or σ_z. At quantum level, the SARG04 protocol is identical to BB84, the difference between the two protocols is at *classical* sifting procedure: instead of revealing the basis, Alice announces publicly one of the four pairs of non-orthogonal states $A_{\omega,\omega'}=\{|\omega x\rangle, |\omega' z\rangle\}$, with $\omega,\omega' \in \{+,-\}$ and with the convention that $|\pm x\rangle$ code for 0 and $|\pm z\rangle$ code for 1. Within each set, the overlap of the two states is $1/\sqrt{2}$. Due to the peculiar choice of states, the usual procedure of choosing randomly between σ_x or σ_z turns out to implement the most effective unambiguous discrimination. For example, suppose that for a given qubit Alice has sent $|+x\rangle$, and that she has announced the set $A_{+,+}$. If Bob has measured σ_x, which happens with probability 1/2, he has certainly got the result +1, but since this result is possible for both states in the set $A_{+,+}$, he must discard it. If Bob measures σ_z and got +1, again he cannot discriminate. But if he has measured σ_z and got -1, then he knows that Alice has sent $|+x\rangle$ and adds a 0 to his key. After this sifting procedure Bob is left with ¼ of the raw list of bits, compared to the ½ of the original BB84 protocol. In any of the states if Bob gets the negative result, it indicates that Alice certainly has sent the opposite state. In terms of photon transmitted between Alice and bob, also if SARG04 has sifted key rate of 25% as compared to 50% for BB84, SARG04 increases the attenuation for pulses with one and two photons, thus indicating the presence of eavesdropping in case of weak coherent pulses. This makes it robust against photon number splitting attacks (Scarani et al., 2004).

Other protocols for QC are based on quantum entanglement. As mentioned, entanglement is one of the most puzzling phenomena in quantum mechanics. It states that, if two particles are entangled, measuring the properties of one particle instantly determines instantaneously the state of the second, independently by the distance between the two particles. Since it is possible of generating the pairs of such entangled photons, where each photon will always have a polarization orthogonal to the other photon, the polarization is indeterminate until a measurement is made, consequently, at the instant the measurement is made the polarization of the second photon becomes orthogonal to that of the first (Altepeter et al., 2005). Firstly, Ekert used this phenomenon for quantum cryptography by considering an un-trusted source of entangled photons between Alice and Bob (Ekert, 1991). Basically, if there is no information carried by photons during transit, thus no eavesdropping. But if eavesdropped injects extra photons in the communications, then their detection can be made by testing the Bell's Inequality at either ends (for a review on Bell's Inequality, see (Sakurai, 1985)). Here, we define a EPR source (so named from the Gedanken experiment suggested by Einstein, Podolsky and Rosen in the 1935, (Einstein et al., 1935)) as the source that emits pairs (qubits) of spin-1/2 particles in a singlet state and the Bell's Inequality as (Clauser et al., 1969)

$$S = E(a,b) + E(a,b') + E(a',b) - E(a',b') \text{ with } S \leq 2 \qquad (6.11)$$

where, a and a' are the detector settings on side Alice, b and b' are the detector settings on side Bob. The four combinations of these settings are tested in separate sub-experiments. The terms $E(\cdot,\cdot)$ denote the quantum correlations defined as the expectation value of the product of the outcomes of the experiment. The mathematical formalism of quantum mechanics predicts a maximum value for S as $2^{3/2}$, which is greater than 2, and Bell inequalities violations are predicted is the correlations are purely quantum. This property is utilized to check if Eve interacts with quantum transmission. Consider, for instance, that an EPR source *sends* to Alice and Bob n pairs of qubits (as in figure 6.6) in a Bell states represented as (Nielsen and Chuang, 2006)

$$\left|\psi^{+}\right\rangle = \frac{1}{\sqrt{2}}\left(|0\rangle_{A}|1\rangle_{B} + |1\rangle_{A}|0\rangle_{B}\right) \tag{6.12}$$

Eq. (6.12) represents entangled state particles, and that such qubits can be prepared to have spin components along one of the three directions (x,y,z) given by unit vectors $\theta_1^A = 0$, $\theta_2^A = \pi/4$, $\theta_3^A = \pi/2$ and $\theta_1^B = \pi/4$, $\theta_2^B = \pi/2$, $\theta_3^B = 3\pi/4$, where A and B refer to Alice and Bob respectively.

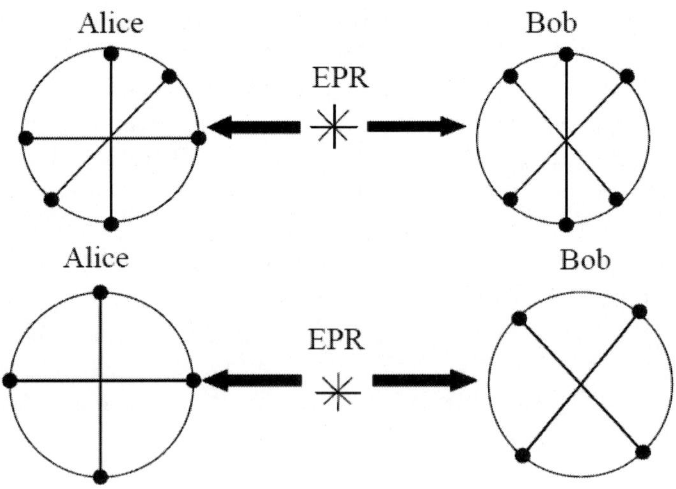

Figure 6.6. Basis used by Alice and Bob in normal phase, above, or in checking phase, below.

For any i=1,2..,n, each user randomly and independently chooses the basis to perform the measurements and only those cases where Alice and Bob's measurements match are used, while the others are discarded. However, among the matched cases, Alice and Bob agree on some results to be used for *checking phase* while remaining cases being used for the so-called *normal phase* (Fung et al., 2006). In normal phase, each user performs $S(z)$ measurements. The outcomes of these measurements are perfectly correlated and thus used as a key later. In the checking phase, each user performs the measurements for Bell's inequality violation of the state by using only two basis as shown in figure 6.6 (right). Alice (Bob) can randomly and independently decide one between the two directions (and analogously for Bob) for measurements. Then Alice (or Bob) performs spin-measurements in the chosen direction α (β). The probability that Alice gest a result ±1 in spin-measurement, say $S(\alpha)$, and Bob gest a result ±1 in spin-measurement $S(\beta)$ is denoted as $P_{\pm\pm}(\alpha, \beta)$. The correlation function $E(\alpha, \beta)$ is given by

$$E(\alpha,\beta)=P_{++}(\alpha,\beta)+P_{--}(\alpha,\beta)-P_{+-}(\alpha,\beta)-P_{-+}(\alpha,\beta) \quad (6.13)$$

and the Bell's inequality is given by Eq. 6.11. If the particles are perfectly entangled then this inequality will produce the value $2^{3/2}$, which is greater than 2, violating the inequality. If Eve provides separable states (not entangled) to Alice and Bob she will get detected in checking phase. If she provides perfectly entangled states, she may pass the checking phase but will not have any information about the key demonstrating the practical application of Bell's Inequality in cryptography as a tool for checking the safety of quantum key distribution.

One limiting aspect of quantum cryptography is that sources and detectors have an efficiency less than 100% so that such protocols are still vulnerable. For example photon number splitting exploits the replacement of single photon sources by weak coherent pulses source. In addition, dark count rate of detectors further leads to reduced detection efficiency which is analogous to the losses in the quantum channel. To overcome all these limitations, new protocols work as Device-Independent Quantum Key Distribution (DIQKD). The idea of a device-independent protocol is based on the property of a source to be untrusted and violation of Bell's inequality is used to decide the security of the protocol (Barrett et al., 2005). Since it is proved that the violation of Bell's inequality can be faked by using classical light and utilizing the detection loophole in single photon detector (Acin et al., 2006; Acin et al., 2007; Pironio et al., 2009), then to achieve total device independence Alice and Bob should not only distrust the source, but should also assume that their measuring apparatus are untrusted and controlled by Eve. Protocols of fully DIQKD provide that (Huang et al., 2013): (i) Alice and Bob's physical locations are secure; (ii) they have trusted random number generators. (iii) They have trusted classical devices to store and process the classical data. (iv) They share an open authenticated classical channel. (v) The quantum physics is correct.

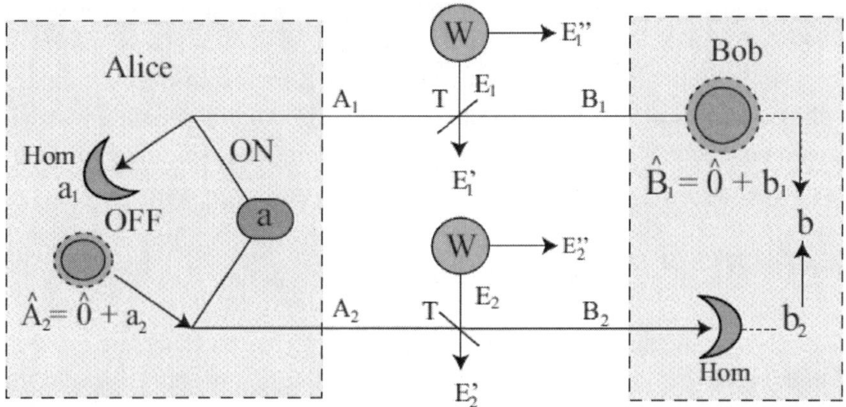

Figure 6.7. Schematic sketch of the two-way thermal QKD protocol under a collective-cloner attack by Eve, who is using two beam splitters with transmission T and two EPR states with variance W. The output modes E_1', E_1'', E_2', E_2'' are collected in a quantum memory which is coherently measured at the end of the protocol. (Reproduced from (Weedbrook et al., 2014), with permission).

However, from a practical point of view, QKD must consider realistic effects, in particular unknown preparation noise on Alice's signal states, for examples noise generated by a thermal source. Weedbrook et al. considered the security of continuous-variable quantum cryptography as approaching the classical limit, i.e., when the unknown noise at the sender's station becomes significantly noisy or thermal (Weedbrook et al., 2010). Subsequently, Weedbrook et al., (Weedbrook et al., 2014), suggested the possibility of using different wavelengths of the electromagnetic field to generate secure keys. They used the so-called two-way quantum communication, a scheme which is already known to tolerate higher levels of loss and noise (Pirandola et al., 2008). Figure 6.7 synthesizes the innovative approach used by Weedbrook et al., to generate secure communication in thermal QKD regime using two-way quantum communication.

The use of two-way quantum communication protocol suggested by Weedbrook et al. and based on Gaussian modulated thermal states, random Gaussian displacements, and homodyne detections should enable two parties to improve the security of thermal QKD, where (inaccessible) preparation noise is added to the signal states (Weedbrook et al., 2014).

6.3. QUANTUM MACHINE LEARNING

One possible application of quantum computer is in machine learning (Murphy, 2012; Lloyd et al., 2013). Due to the ability of quantum computation of manipulating vectors and matrices, quantum computers could provide an exponential speed-up over their classical counterparts in performing some machine learning tasks involving large vectors. One basic advantage of machine learning methods is the ability to learn from past experience to make more accurate predictions in the future, where the experience generally refers to past information or example data that the learner has known (Mackay, 2003; Bishop, 2006). In supervised machine learning, the learner is provided a set of training examples with features presented in the form of high-dimensional vectors and with corresponding labels to mark its category. Based on these training sets, the machine learner infers a mapping function from the features to the labels, and users it to classify new samples by analyzing the features (Cai et al., 2014). Recently, Lloyd et al. have demonstrated that the task of assigning N-dimensional vectors to one of k clusters, each with M representative samples, a quantum computer would take time $O(k\log(MN))$ (Lloyd et al., 2013). An example of supervised machine learning is reported in the experimental setup for quantum machine learning with photonic qubits in figure 6.8 (Cai et al., 2014).

Here, we present the proposal of quantum machine learning essentially as suggested by Lloyd et al., (Loyd et al., 2013), and recently developed by Cai et al. (Cai et al., 2014).

Classically, data sets are typically presented as array of symbols and numbers. The data sets generally consist of arrays of numbers (vectors), and array of arrays (collections of vectors), that are stored in random access memory (RAM) in the classical case, or in quantum random access memory (qRAM) in the quantum case. The key feature of quantum machine learning is that quantum random access memory allows us to access the data in quantum parallel. This procedure can be described as follows. Let us consider a vector $N=2^n$ dimensional complex vector $\boldsymbol{a}$ with components $\{a_i=|a_i|\exp(i\phi_i\}$ and assume that $\{|a_i|, \phi_i\}$ being stored as floating point numbers in quantum random access memory. The construction of the $\log_2 N$ qubit quantum state $|a\rangle = \mathbf{a}/\sqrt{|\mathbf{a}|}$ requires $O(\log_2 N)$ steps. One the exponentially compressed quantum versions of the vectors have been created, we can post-process them using quantum Fourier transforms, matrix version, etc. The post-processing takes time O(poly(log$N$)) or, at the best, O(poly$N$).

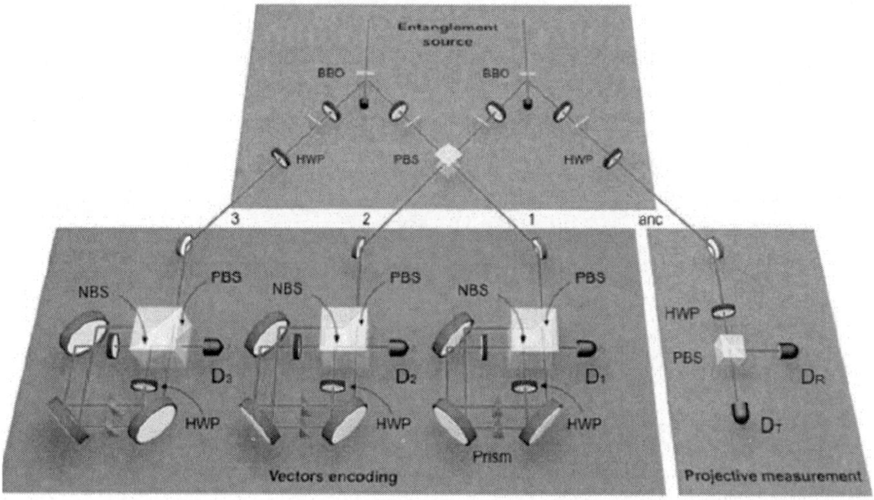

Figure 6.8. An optical system based on quantum machine learning used as spam filter that sorts incoming emails into spam and non-spam messages. (Reprinted from (Cai et al., 2014), with permission).

In a supervised quantum learning procedure, the working principle can be explained as follows (Cai et al., 2014). Let us consider to implement simple supervised machine learning tasks, assigning 2-, 4- and 8- dimensional vectors to two different clusters. The two clusters are labelled as A and B, each with one reference sample vector, $\boldsymbol{v}_A$ and $\boldsymbol{v}_B$, respectively. The classification of a new sample, here represented by the vector $\boldsymbol{u}$, can be made calculating and comparing the distance from A and B: $|\boldsymbol{u}\text{-}\boldsymbol{v}_A|$ and $|\mathbf{u}\text{-}\boldsymbol{v}_B|$, and the new sample is assigned to the cluster to which the distance is smaller. Since the vectors can be represented with quantum states, a key step in the quantum machine the evaluation of the distance $|\boldsymbol{u}\text{-}\boldsymbol{v}|$is to adjoin an ancillary qubit to the states of the reference and new vectors, creating an entangled state in the form (Cai et al., 2014)

$$|\varphi\rangle = \left(|0\rangle_{anc}|u\rangle_{new} + |1\rangle_{anc}|v\rangle_{ref}\right)/\sqrt{2} \tag{6.14}$$

A single-qubit measurement is made on the ancillary qubit alone whose success probability p is recorded. One p is known, the inner product between $|u\rangle$ and $|v\rangle$ can be estimated: $\langle u|v\rangle = (0.5 - p)\left(|u|^2 + |v|^2\right)/|u||v|$ and the distance, δ, between $\boldsymbol{u}$ and $\boldsymbol{v}$ is easily obtained, $\delta = \sqrt{2p\left(|u|^2 + |v|^2\right)}$. If $|u\rangle$ and $|v\rangle$ are identical, then the ancillary qubit is in the state $\left(|0\rangle + |1\rangle\right)/\sqrt{2}$, separable from the vector qubits, so that p=0 and δ=0. If $|u\rangle$ and $|v\rangle$ are orthogonal, then the Eq. (6.14) is maximally entangled, and p=0.5 and $\delta = \sqrt{\left(|u|^2 + |v|^2\right)}$. In a recent experiment proposed by Cai et al., they use single photons as qubits, where $|0\rangle$ and $|1\rangle$ are encoded with photon horizontal (H) and vertical (V) polarization, respectively, figure 6.8. In the experimental setup depicted in figure 6.8, four photons are produced, where one photon is used as the ancillary qubit, and the others are used to encode the vectors. The 2^n-dimensional vectors are encoded with the polarization state of n photonic qubits. The 2-, 4- and 8- dimensional vectors can be classified creating 2-, 3- and 4-photon entangled states

$$|\varphi_2\rangle = \left(|H\rangle_{anc}|u_1\rangle_{new} + |V\rangle_{anc}|v_1\rangle_{ref}\right)/\sqrt{2}$$
$$|\varphi_2\rangle = \left(|H\rangle_{anc}|u_2u_1\rangle_{new} + |V\rangle_{anc}|v_2v_1\rangle_{ref}\right)/\sqrt{2}$$
$$|\varphi_2\rangle = \left(|H\rangle_{anc}|u_3u_2u_1\rangle_{new} + |V\rangle_{anc}|v_3v_2v_1\rangle_{ref}\right)/\sqrt{2} \tag{6.15}$$

for classifying 2-, 4-, and 8-dimensional vectors, respectively. Cai et al. applied the system displayed in figure 6.8 to the classification of 2-dimensional vectors (Cai et al., 2014), but similar approaches can be used to classify 4- or 8-dimensional vectors based on the construction of three- and four-photon entanglement. The precision of such classifications is affected by the state fidelity (~75%) of the multi-photon entangled state, which is lower compared to that of two-photon entangled state (~94%). The method proposed by Cai et al. can be, almost in principle, extended to other physical systems such as trapped ions and superconducting qubits (Liebfried et al., 2003; Clarke and Wilhelm, 2008). Encoding higher (2^n) dimensional vectors would only need a logarithmic increase of the number (n+1) of qubits. For example, to encode the data of one exabytes (1018 bits), about the total size of the world's generated data every day in 2012, about 60 qubits could be necessary. Scaling to 60 photons could be optimistic given recent progress in on-demand generation of single photons on chip with near-unity indistinguishability, photon collection and detection, and high-performance quantum memories (He et al., 2013; Lee et al., 2011; Marsili et al., 2013, Bao et al., 2012).

The experiment supplied by Cai et al., is the first experimental implementation of supervised machine learning on a photonic quantum computer. They have shown that the manipulation of high-dimensional vectors and the estimation of the distance and inner product between two vectors, a ubiquitous task in machine learning, can be naturally and efficiently done with quantum computers, thus proved the suitability and potential power of quantum machine learning, and may provide a useful quantum toolkit for dealing with the *big data*.

References

Acin A., Gisin N., Masanes L., 2006, From Bell's Theorem to Secure Quantum Key Distribution, *Physical Review Letters*, 97(12), 120405.

Acin A., Brunner N., Gisin N., Massar S., Pironio S., Scarani V., 2007, Device-independent security of quantum cryptography against collective attacks, *Physical Review Letters*, 98(23), 230501.

Altepeter J., Jeffrey E., Kwiat P., 2005, Phase-compensated ultra-bright source of entangled photons, *Optics Express*, 13, 8951-8959.

Bao X.H., Reingruber A., Dietrich P., Rui J., Dück A., Strassel T., Li L., Liu N-L., Zhao B., Pan J-W., 2012, Efficient and long-lived quantum memory with cold atoms inside a ring cavity, *Nature Physics*, 8, 517-21.

Barrett J., Hardy L., Kent A., 2005, No Signaling and Quantum Key Distribution, *Physical Review Letters*, 95(1), 010503.

Bell J.S., 1964, On the Einstein Podolsky Rosen Paradox, *Physics*, 1, 195-200.

Benioff P., 1982A, Quantum Mechanical Hamiltonian Models of Turing Machines, *J. Stat. Phys.*, 29, 515-46.

Benioff P., 1982B, Quantum Mechanical Models of Turing Machines that Dissipate No Energy, *Physical Review Letters*, 48, 1581-85.

Bennett C.H., Brassard G., 1984, Quantum Cryptography: Public key distribution and coin tossing, in *Proceedings of the IEEE International Conference on Computers, Systems and Signal Processing*, Bangalore, India, pp. 175-179.

Bennett C., 1992, Quantum cryptography using any two non-orthogonal states, *Physical Review Letters*, 68, 3121-24.

Bishop C.M., 2006, Pattern Recognition and Machine Learning, Springer.

Cai X.D., Wu D., Su Z.E., Chen M.C., Wang X.L., Li L., Liu N.L., Lu C.Y., Pan J.W., 2014, Entanglement-Based Quantum Machine Learning, http://arxiv.org/abs/1409.770.

Clarke J., Wilhelm F.K., 2008, Superconducting quantum bits, *Nature*, 453, 1031-42.

Clauser J.F., Horne M.A., Shimony A., Holt R.A., 1969, Proposed experiment to test local hidden-variable theories, *Physical Review Letters*, 23, 880-4.

de Castro L.N., 2007, Fundamentals of natural computing: an overview, *Physics of Life Reviews*, 4, 1-36.

Dirac, P.A.M., 1982, The Principles of Quantum Mechanics, Oxford Science Publishing, UK.

Einstein A., Podolsky B., Rosen N., 1935, Can Quantum-Mechanical Description of Physically Reality be Considered Complete?, *Physical Review*, 47, 777-780.

Ekert A.K., 1991, Quantum cryptography based on Bell's theorem, *Physical Review Letters*, 67, 661-3.

Fung C., Tamaki K., Lo H., 2006, On the performance of two protocols: SARG04 and BB84, *Physical Review A*, 73, 012337.

He Y.M., He Y., Wei Y.J., Wu D., Atatüre M., Schneider C., Höfling S., Kamp M., Lu C.Y., Pan J.W., 2013, On-demand semiconductor single-photon source with near-unity indistinguishability, *Nature Nanotechnology*, 8, 231-17.

Hirvensalo M., 2000, Quantum Computing, Springer, Heidelberg-Berlin.

Huang J., Yin Z., Chen W., Wang S., Li H., Guo G., Han Z., 2013, A Survey on Device-Independent Quantum Communications, *China Communications*, 10.2, 1-10.

Lee K.G., Chen X.W., Eghlidi H., Kukura P., Lettow R., Renn A., Sandoghdar V., S. Götzinger S., 2011, A planar dielectric antenna for directional single-photon emission and near-unity collection efficiency, *Nature Photonics*, 5, 166-69.

Liebfried D., Blatt R., Monroe C., Wineland D., 2003, Quantum dynamics of single trapped ions, *Reviews of Modern Physics*, 75, 281-324.

Lloyd S., Mohseni M., Rebentrost P, 2013, Quantum algorithms for supervised and unsupervised machine learning, http://arxiv.org/abs/1307.0411

Lopes M., Sarwade N., 2014, Cryptography from Quantum Mechanical Viewpoint, *International Journal on Cryptography and Information Security*, 4(2), 13-25.

Lütkenhaus N., 1999, Estimates for practical quantum cryptography, *Physical Review A*, 59, 3301-19.

Mackay D., 2003, Information Theory, Inference and Learning Algorithms, Cambridge University Press, Cambridge, UK.

Marand C., Townsend P.D., 1995, Quantum key distribution over distances as long as 30km, *Optics Letter*, 20(16), 1695-97.

Marsili F., Verma V.B., Stern J.A., Harrington S., Lita A.E., Gerrits T., Vayshenker I., Baek B., Shaw M.D., Mirin R.P., Nam S.W., 2013, Detecting single infrared photons with 93% systems efficiency, *Nature Photonics*, 7, 210-14.

Murphy K.P., 2012, Machine Learning: A Probabilistic Perspective, MIT Press, USA.

Nielsen M.A., Chuang I.L., 2010, Quantum Computation and Quantum Information, 10th edition, Cambridge University Press, Cambridge, UK.

Pirandola S., Mancini S., Lloyd S., Braunstein S., 2008, Continous-variable quantum cryptography using two-way quantum communication, *Nature Physics*, 4, 726-730.

Pironio S., Acin A., Brunner N., Gisin N., massar S., Scarani V., 2009, Device-independent quantum key distribution secure against collective attacks, *New Journal of Physics*, 11(4), 045021

Pittenger A.O., 2000, An introduction to quantum computing algorithms, Birkhäuser, Ch.

Sakurai J.J., 1985, Modern Quantum Mechanics, The Benjamin/Cummings Publishing Company, Menlo Park, California.

Scarani V., Acin A., Ribordy G., Gisin N., 2004, Quantum cryptography protocols robust against photon number splitting attacks, *Physical Review Letters*, 92, 057901.

Shor P., 1994, Algorithms for Quantum Computation: Discrete Logarithms and Factoring, in *Proceedings of the 35th Annual Symposium on Foundations of Computer Science, Santa Fe*, IEEE Computer Society Press, pp. 124-134.

Weedbrook C., Pirandola S., Lloyd S., Ralph T.C., 2010, Quantum Cryptography Approaching the Classical limit, *Physical Review Letters*, 105, 110501.

Weedbrook C., Ottaviani C., Pirandola S., 2014, Two-way quantum cryptography at different wavelengths, *Physical Review A,* 89, 012309.

Analogously, the use of coupling functions, as well as noise or chaotic systems, is a common procedure for the development of encryption methods (Stankovski et al., 2012; Stankovski et al., 2014; Goel and Negi, 2008; Li et al., 2012; Kocarev and Parlitz, 1995; Hung and Hu, 2008). However, the use of coupling functions brings great freedom in the encryption process without changing the qualitative state of the system, and thereby without increases security (Kralemann et al., 2007; Hlaváčkováá-Schindler et al., 2007). The recent advances in the understanding of time-variable, non-autonomous, dynamics in geophysics, biology, and astrophysics is used to upgrade methods for secure communications (Stankovski et al., 2014). In such systems, the decryption receiver takes advantage of Bayesian inference. Its ability to infer multidimensional, time-evolving and coupled dynamical systems makes it ideally matched to such applications (D'Agostini, 2003; von Toussaint 2011). In addition, coupled systems generally span a large volume of state space gaining easier, faster and higher precision. The characteristic that has raised large interest in the community of cryptographers is that dynamical systems in nature mutually interact, exerting influence and transferring energy, and/or matter between each other. The interaction between two such systems is described by their coupling function and coupling amplitude. Coupling functions capture all the physical rules specifying how the interactions occur and defining also the possible transitions between systems. Coupling functions define many basic description of interaction between systems in many areas other than physics, such as chemistry (Kiss et al., 2007), geophysics (Murayama, 1982), biology (Winfree, 1967), and cosmology (Cai and Wang, 2005). The recent developments in such areas have unexpectedly opened the door to a novel class of secure communications strategies (Stankovski et al., 2014).

A dynamical systems can be classified as chaotic, when it has the following properties: (i) it is sensitive to initial conditions; (ii) it must be topologically mixing, and (iii) it must have dense periodic orbits (Lichtenberg and Lieberman, 1983, Reichl, 2004). The first condition, sensitivity to initial conditions, means that each point in a chaotic system is arbitrarily closely approximated by other points with significantly different future paths or trajectories. The condition of topologically mixing implies that the system evolves over time so that any given region or open set of its phase space will eventually overlap with any other given region. Finally, the third conditions, the property of dense periodic orbits, means that every point in the space is approached arbitrarily closely by periodic orbits. Generally, dynamical systems are chaotic everywhere in the phase space, but in many cases chaotic behavior can be found only in a subset of the phase space. The cases of most interest arise when the chaotic behavior takes place on an attractor, since then a large set of initial conditions will lead to orbits that converge to this chaotic region. The Lorenz system has chaotic solutions for certain parameter values and initial conditions. In particular, the Lorenz attractor is a set of chaotic solutions of the Lorenz system which, when plotted, resemble a butterfly or figure eight (Lorenz, 1963). Similarly to the Lorenz attractor, but easier to analyze qualitatively, the Rössler attractor from the Rössler systems of three non-linear ordinary differential equations presents many typical manifestations of chaos behavior (Rössler, 1976). Lorenz and Rössler systems are the physical base of the secure communication system described in section 7.2. Another concept commonly found in nonlinear nature of the world and extremely useful in secure communication systems is the synchronization (Pikovsky et al., 2004). First recognized in 1665 by Christian Huygens, synchronization phenomena are abundant in science, nature, engineering, and social life. Systems as diverse as clocks, cardiac pacemakers, singing crickets, firing neurons, and applauding audiences exhibit a tendency to operate in synchrony. These phenomena are universal and can be understood within a common framework based on modern nonlinear dynamics.

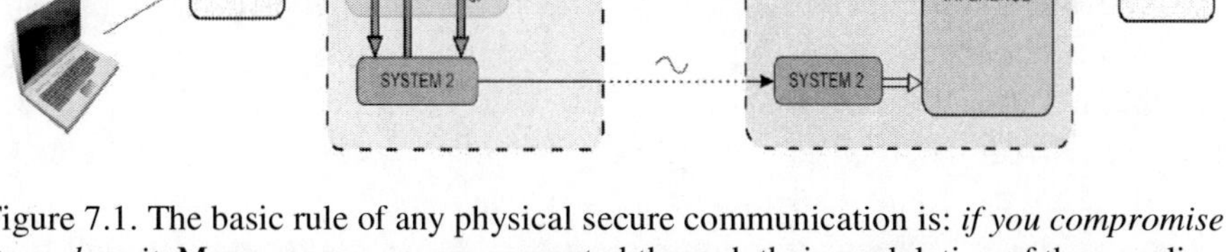

Figure 7.1. The basic rule of any physical secure communication is: *if you compromise it you lose it.* Messages $s_1,\ldots,s_n$ are encrypted through their modulation of the coupling functions connecting the two oscillators of the transmitter. Only two signals are transmitted through the public domain. For the particular realization of the cipher discussed in the 7.2, Eqs. (x) and (y), they are x1 and y2. The receiver consists of the same kind of oscillators and the same coupling functions (effectively forming the privately shared key) as the transmitter and uses time-evolving Bayesian inference to reconstruct $s_1,\ldots,s_n$. (Reproduced from (Stankovski et al., 2014), with permission).

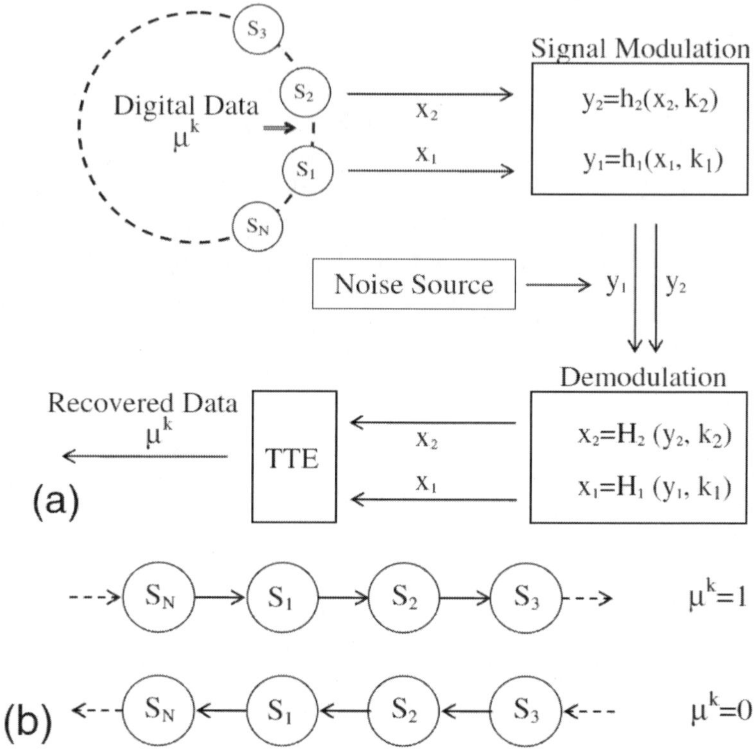

Figure 7.2. (a) Communication scheme based on temporal causality of the coupled maps ring, as proposed by Huang and Hu. (b) Correspondent encoding process of the binary information. (Reproduced from (Hung and Hu, 2008), with permission).

Some important schemes based on chaotic systems and synchronization for secure communication have been recently proposed (Cuomo and Oppenheim, 1993; Wu, 2006; Wagemakers et al., 2008; Hung and Hu, 2008; Banerjee, 2010; Thampi et al., 2013). Chaotic systems are particularly convenient to be coupled and one main advantage it is the possibility to include inference within a communications framework and confer the additional security associated with conventional chaotic communication by exploiting the unpredictable, random-like but deterministic nature of chaotic signals to encrypt the transmitted information. The basic common idea of such schemes is to take advantage from the chaotic nature of a system to encrypt a sequence of messages. Two typical techniques include the chaotic masking approach and the chaotic modulation method (Banerjee, 2010; Thampi et al., 2013), with several variants and refinements of the two methods containing the use of different levels of synchronization, different portraits of chaotic carriers, different techniques of chaos control, and different expressions of communications schemes. Anyway, the common point of these methods is the reliance on synchronization. One interest scheme using chaos has been proposed by Hung and Hu (Hung and Hu, 2008). Their model is a counterintuitive scheme which hides binary messages in causal relationships on a couple-map ring (CMR) consisting of chaotic elements. The clockwise or counterclockwise coupling on the ring indicates the bipolar data μ^k=1 or μ^k=0, see figure 7.2. The time series of two adjacent maps are used as transmitting signals through public channels. At the receiver, encrypted messages are recovered by a proposed measure, the temporal transfer entropy (TTE), based on information theory. One main advantage of such system is that the scheme is robust against external noise and some traditional attacks.

In the scheme proposed by Hung and Hu, the temporal causality of coupled chaotic systems is used for messages encryption and transmission. In details, as pictured in figure 7.2, an one-dimensional uni-directionally *CMR* of *N* nodes is chosen as the chaotic generator to encrypt transmitted messages, figure 7.2(a). The dynamics of the subsystems S_n at the nth node of the CMR is given by the relation (Hung and Hu, 2008)

$$x_n(t+1) = f\big((1-\varepsilon)x_n(t) + \varepsilon X_n(t)\big) \tag{7.1}$$

where n=1,2,…,N, t is the time index, Xn(t) is the driving force from the nearest systems Sn±1, and ε is the coupling strength. To encode a series of K binary information μk (k=1,…,K) into the instantaneous causal relations of the CMR, a possible choice suggested by Hung and Hu is

$$X_n(t) = \begin{cases} x_{n-1}(t) & \text{if } \mu^k = 1 \\ x_{n+1}(t) & \text{if } \mu^k = 0 \end{cases} \tag{7.2}$$

as reported in figure 7.1(b). The role of the CMR is to keep the phase portraits of subsystems invariant under every reversion of the coupling direction. The invariability prohibits intruders from mining the message by the technique of return maps. Hence, the output of the CMR containing message information are communicated to the receiver over public channels. If, for example, the iterations selected as carriers are $x_1(t)$ and $x_2(t)$, they can be further modulated by specific functions $h_1(x_1(t), k_1)$ and $h_2(x_2(t), k_2)$, where $k_{1,2}$ are security keys, which are pre-known by the receiver. Modified signals $y_1(t)$ and $y_2(t)$ are then transmitted to the receiver and demodulated by inverse functions $H_{1,2}=(h_{1,2})^{-1}$, figure 7.1 (a). In turn, the cipher messages can be retrieved by monitoring the temporal causality between the series $x_1(t)$ and $x_2(t)$. One basic problem in the chaos-based schemes for secure communications is the method of assessing causality. Transfer entropy (TE) is the most reliable one because of its solid mathematical foundation of information theory. Shannon entropy has been already described in the introduction, here, we have to connect such concept to nonlinear characteristic or the couplings of the systems of interest under consideration. To do this, we start considering that for a physical process I with probability distribution $\{p(i)\}$ visiting the state $\{i\}$, following Hung and Hu, we introduce another process J with probability $\{p(j)\}$ and joint probability $\{p(i,j)\}$, the average information gained about I by the knowledge of J is given by the mutual information where asymmetry is incorporated using Markov chains properties

$$TE_{J,I} = \sum p(i_{\tau+1}, i_\tau, j_\tau) \log \frac{p(i_{\tau+1} | i_\tau, j_\tau)}{p(i_{\tau+1} | i_\tau)} \tag{7.3}$$

where τ denotes time. It should be noted that the probability expressed in Eq. (7.3) must be considered under the concept of causal entropy (Ziebart et al., 2013), i.e., the probability distribution is updated once a new event is generated and evolves with time. After every update, the appropriate distribution is

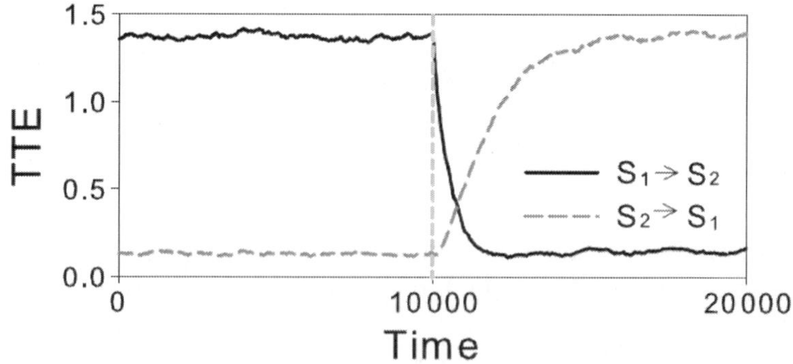

Figure 7.3. (Continued).

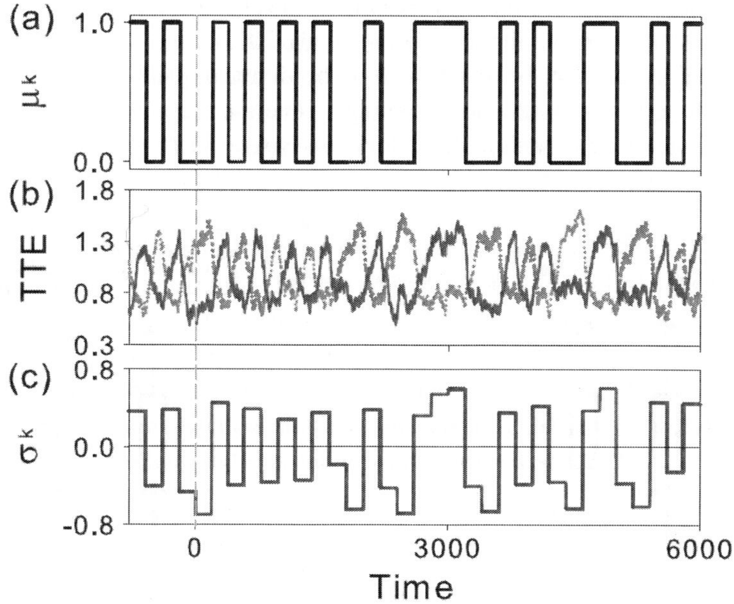

Figure 7.3. Top image, Temporal transfer entropies Tet S1;S2 and Tet S1;S1 as functions of time for a CMR of Ulam maps. At t ¼ 104, the coupling direction is reversed. The two qualities of TTE clearly reflect the variation of the causality. (a) A sequence of binary messages _k with the length of each information bit T_ ¼ 200. (b) The evolution of TTE in the directions of S1 ! S2 (blue solid line) and S2 ! S1 (red dotted line). (c) The sequence of _k: _k > 0 indicates _k ¼ 1, while _k < 0 indicates _k ¼ 0. (Adapted from (Hung and Hu, 2008), with permission).

$$p(i)_{\tau+1} = \begin{cases} \dfrac{p(i)+\Delta p}{1+\Delta p} & \text{if } i_{\tau+1} = i_\tau \\ \dfrac{p(i)}{1+\Delta p} & \text{otherwis e} \end{cases} \tag{7.4}$$

7.1. Secure Communication Form Noise

Very recently, it has been shown that noise can be utilized to carry secure information (Goel and Negi, 2005; Kish, 2006a; Mingesz et al., 2008; Li et al., 2012). Noise can be thermal source (in a special way in its artificial version,

The other application of noise to secure communication is through artificial noise (Goel and Negi, 2008). Goel and Negi proposed two different schemes to generate secure communication using artificial noise, figure 7.5. The common framework of such schemes is as follows: the transmitter can use some of the available power to transmit artificially generated noise. Since the noise is generated by the transmitter, then the transmitter can design it such that only the eavesdropper's channel is degraded. Thus, secret communication can be guaranteed by selectively degrading the eavesdropper's channel, because secret communication is possible if the eavesdropper's channel has a smaller capacity than the receiver's channel.

In the first scheme, the transmitter can use multiple transmit antennas to generate artificial noise. The scenario provides a base station wanting to communicate a secret message to a mobile handset. The second scheme provides that even if the transmitter does not have multiple transmit antennas, but helper nodes are present, the effect of multiple antennas can be simulated and artificial noise can be produced. This second scheme models a mobile handset, with a single antenna, wanting to communicate a secret message to another mobile handset or the base station.

Both the two secure communication systems employing noise indicate unrivalled fidelity and security levels among existing physical secure communicators and there are straightforward ways to further improve security, fidelity and distance range.

7.2. Encryption by Coupling Functions

A recent communication framework for secure communication has been proposed by Stankovski et al. (Stankovski et al., 2014). In such framework, a number of information signals coming from different channels or communications devices (mobile phone, sensor networks, etc.) are to be transmitted simultaneously. Each of signals s_i (see figure 7.1 for the notation) is encrypted in a coupling function. They serve as coupling scale parameters in the nonlinear coupling functions between two self-sustained systems in the transmitter. Two signal, one from each system, are transmitted through the public channel. At the receiving end, two similar systems are completely synchronized by the two transmitted signals. When a time-evolving Bayesian inference is applied to the reconstructed systems, one can infer the model parameters and decrypt the information signals s_i. The physical system describing the synchronization process consists of two noisy M-dimensional interacting systems given by the following stochastic differential equation (Stankovski et al., 2014):

$$\dot{\mathbf{x}}_i = \mathbf{f}(\mathbf{x}_i, \mathbf{x}_j | \mathbf{c}) + \sqrt{\mathbf{D}}\xi_i = \mathbf{g}(\mathbf{x}_i | \mathbf{c}_1) + \mathbf{q}(\mathbf{x}_i, \mathbf{x}_j | \mathbf{c}_2) + \sqrt{\mathbf{D}}\xi_i \tag{7.5}$$

where $i \neq j = 1$ or 2, **c** is the parameter vector, and $\mathbf{f}(\mathbf{x}_i, \mathbf{x}_j | \mathbf{c})$ are base functions that include both the autonomous dynamics $\mathbf{g}(\mathbf{x}_i)$ and the coupling functions $\mathbf{q}(\mathbf{x}_i, \mathbf{x}_j)$. The noise is assumed to be white, Gaussian, and parametrized by a noise diffusion matrix **D**. The system described by Eq. (7.5) gives the possibility to include inference inside the communication framework (Stankovski et al., 2012). Inferential methods are conventionally used to treat problems where the model (i.e., its base functions) is hidden or unknown. Stankovski et al., suggested to consider the inference to be performed in state space, and the base functions as well the model are known *a priori*, this is a special case of inferential problems, but give a great advantage to the model the a posterior information, as demonstrated for example in image analysis (D'Acunto et al., 2014). The mathematical development given by Stankovsky et al. is particularly interesting and it deserves to be presented in detail (Stankosvki et al., 2014).

Let us consider a 2×M time series $\chi = \{\mathbf{x}_n \equiv \mathbf{x}(t_n)\}$ provided as inputs, ($t_n = nh$), the fundamental task for the Bayesian dynamical inference is to reveal the unknown model parameters $\varphi = \{\mathbf{c}, \mathbf{D}\}$. The inference consist on the application of the Bayes theorem, which is used to calculate the so-called posterior density $p_\chi(\varphi|\chi)$ of the unknown parameters φ, given a prior density $p_{prior}(\varphi)$ that encloses previous knowledge of the unknown parameters based on observations, and the likelihood function $l(\chi|\varphi)$, that corresponds to the conditional probability density to observe χ given choice φ of the dynamical model. The system described by Eq. (7.5) can be usefully managed discretizing in time, if the sampling is enough dense,

$$\mathbf{x}_{i,n+1} = \mathbf{x}_{i,n} + hf(\overset{*}{\mathbf{x}}_{i,n}, \overset{*}{\mathbf{x}}_{j,n} | \mathbf{c}) + h\sqrt{\mathbf{D}}\mathbf{z}_n \tag{7.6}$$

where $\overset{*}{\mathbf{x}}_n = (\overset{*}{\mathbf{x}}_{n+1} + \overset{*}{\mathbf{x}}_n)/2$, where $\mathbf{z}_n$ is the stochastic integral of the noise term over time. The noise under consideration is statistically independent and the likelihood is given by a product over *n* of the probability of observing $\mathbf{x}_{n+1}$ at each time. The joint probability density of $\mathbf{z}_n$ is used to find the joint probability density of the process in respect to $\mathbf{x}_{n+1}$-$\mathbf{x}_n$. The system described above lends itself to some algebraic manipulations and to some important assumptions. One is that the prior probability is assumed to be a multivariate normal distribution. This ensures that the posterior probability will be a multivariate normal distribution when the likelihood function obeys to some properties and the base functions can be linearly parametrized as $\mathbf{f}(\mathbf{x}|\mathbf{c})=\mathbf{cf}(\mathbf{x})$. The main idea of the proposed model for secure communications by Stankovsky et al. is to encrypt the information in a specific time evolution of the parameters. Therefore, the inferential procedure must to follow the time evolution of the parameter set **c** while separating these effects from the unavoidable noise. The example suggested by Stankovsky et al., of a nature system for secure communication is composed by a transmitter consisting of a Rössler oscillator coupled to a Lorenz system.

The transmitting system is described by the equations (Stankovski et al., 2014):

$$\begin{aligned}
&\dot{x}_1 = 2 + x_1(x_2 - 4) + \xi_1 \quad \dot{y}_1 = 10y_2 - 10y_1 + \xi_2 \\
&\dot{x}_2 = -x_1 - x_3 \quad \dot{y}_2 = -y_1y_3 - y_2 + s_0(t)y_1 \\
&\qquad\qquad\qquad + s_1(t)x_2x_3 + s_2(t)x_3^2 \\
&\dot{x}_3 = x_2 + 0.45x_3 \quad \dot{y}_3 = y_1y_2 - 2.67y_3 + \xi_3
\end{aligned} \tag{7.7}$$

Only the signals x_1 and y_2 are transmitted and they synchronize the Rössler and Lorenz systems at the receiver described as follows (Stankovsky et al., 2014)

$$\begin{aligned}
&u_1 = x_1 \quad \dot{w}_1 = 10y_2 - 10w_1 + \xi_4 \\
&\dot{u}_2 = -x_1 - u_3 \quad w_2 = y_2 \\
&\dot{u}_3 = u_2 + 0.45u_3 \quad \dot{w}_3 = w_1y_2 - 2.67w_3 + \xi_5
\end{aligned} \tag{7.8}$$

The information signals acting as time-dependent non-autonomous terms are given by binary pseudorandom sequence signals $s_{0,1,2}(t)$, and the noise sources $\xi_1,\ldots,\xi_5$ are assumed to be white, Gaussian, and of the same intensity, defined by diffusion coefficient D. The Rössler and Lorenz oscillators are unidirectionally coupled through the information signals s_1 and s_2 and they can be either synchronized or nonsynchronized depending on signal s_0. Figure 7.6, shows such communication procedure based on coupled chaotic oscillators.

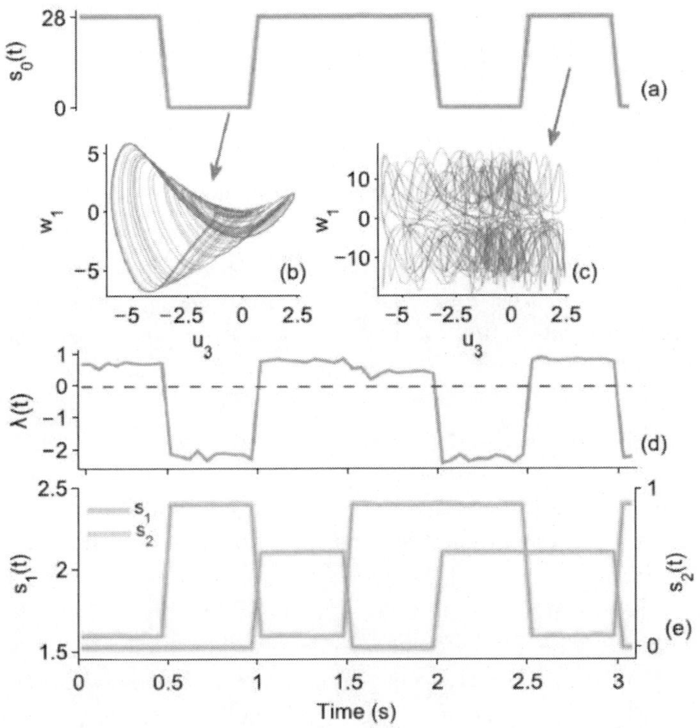

Figure 7.6. The communication procedure based on coupled chaotic oscillators as given by Eqs.7.7 and 7.8 . (a) The transmitted binary signal $s_0(t)$ acting as a ρ variable in the Lorenz oscillator. Lissajous curves qualitatively indicating the existence of generalized synchronization during (b) synchronized and (c) nonsynchronized intervals. The gray arrows point to synchronization intervals in the $s_0(t)$ signal. (d) The largest Lyapunov exponent detected from the driven Lorenz oscillator serves as an index of time-evolving generalized synchronization. (e) Simultaneously transmitted signals $s_1(t)$ and $s_2(t)$. For comparison, the original signals $s_0(t)$, $s_1(t)$, and $s_2(t)$ are presented in dark color below the received ones shown in light transparent color in (a) and (e)—note that in some intervals they are indistinguishable. (Reproduced from (Stankovski et al., 2014), with permission).

Two crucial advantages on the reliability can be outlined from the system described by Eqs (7.7-8). The first one is the security gained by the signals $s(t)$. The binary information signal $s_0(t)$ acts on and changes the attractor properties of the Lorenz oscillator alone. In this way, the signal $s_0(t)$ works more as decoy information and a control signal that takes the two oscillators through qualitative transitions of generalized synchronization. However, the two information signals $s_1(t)$ and $s_2(t)$ are encrypted through the weak and nonlinear interactions, providing a complicated dynamical mixing that is highly resistant to the standard attacks. In addition, the system can transmit more than one information signal simultaneously providing a higher level of security.

The second crucial advantage is the fact that an intruder being ignorant of the form and number of the coupling functions is unable to decrypt the signals in any simple way. Since the choice of the form of coupling functions comes from a set of functions that, almost in principle, is not bounded, this property is fundamental for constructing a private encryption key. Such two advantages enable the communication framework to resist to brute-force attacks and allow for the use of dynamical keys or dynamical physical unclonable functions.

Simulations with 10-bit binary transmission is shown in figure 7.7 (Stankovski et al., 2014). Four pseudorandom 10-bit messages (m_1=00110111010; m_2=1000010101; m_3=1111101010; m_4=0100100111) are sent and for any message ten signals $s_1(t),\ldots,s_{10}(t)$ are sent simultaneously. The detected signal after transmission indicate that the communication is accurate as well, with precisely detected messages demonstrating that the communication technique is able to transmit more than one information signals simultaneously. This simultaneity is possible thanks to the Bayesian inference that is able to separate in the same time the sent signal at the receiver end, as inspired and demonstrated in cardiorespiratory interactions (Smelyanskiy et al., 2005; Shiogai et al., 2010; Stankovski et al., 2012; Iatsenko et al., 2013).

The scheme presented in figure 7.7 is able to transmit more than one information signals simultaneously, in this case 10 signals. This property is very beneficial for any real applications because it allows multiplexing, being multiplexing the conventional method of sharing an expensive resource by sending multiple information signals simultaneously. This scheme can take advantage from the simultaneity thanks to Bayesian inference that is able to separate the simultaneously sent signals $s_i(t)$ to the receiver end. The scheme presented in figure has another useful property for practical applications, i.e., the speed of communication. This property depends on the time scales of the coupled systems and the speed of the Bayesian inference. Bayesian technique infers dynamical mechanisms and requires less data than other statistical methods. With each sequential block, the Bayesian inference exploits the dynamical model and the acquired prior knowledge, allowing the use of smaller blocks of data and better time resolution. The only basic requirement is that the time scale of the carrier signal should be longer than the time scales of the information signals. Unfortunately, the relationship between them has to be determined on a case-by case basis (Duggento et al., 2012).

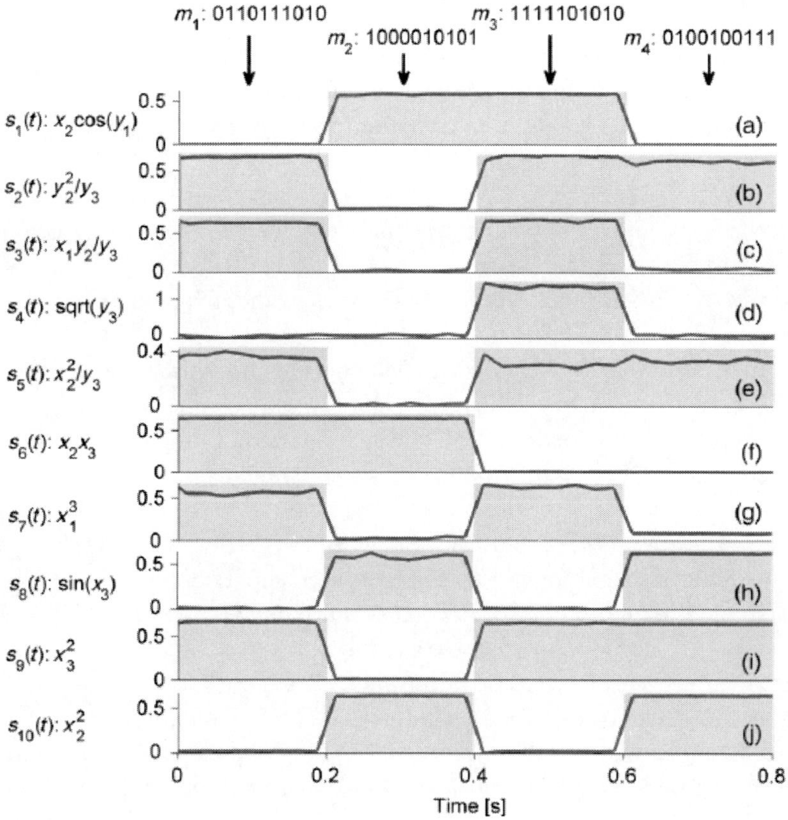

Figure 7.7. Transmission of ten pseudorandom binary signals encrypted in different coupling functions as proposed by Stankovski et al. The high values (binary '1') at the transmitter, prior to encrypting, are indicated by grey shading. The received signals, after decrypting, are shown by thick lines, each of which (a-j) represents one information signal $s_i(t)$. The particular coupling functions that were used for encrypting each signal are indicated on the ordinate axis. Each bit is transmitted during an interval of 0.2*s*, and four bits are transmitted in total for each signal e.g., $s_7(t) \rightarrow 1010$. The information could correspond either to ten separate serially-encoded messages, or to a single 10-bit parallel-encoded message, but all of it is being transmitted simultaneously. The bits are indicated by m_1–m_4 on the top of the figure. (Reproduced from (Stanskovski et al., 2014), with permission).

REFERENCES

Argyris A., Syvridis D., Larger L., Annovazzi-Lodi V., Colet P., Fischer I., garcia_ojalvo J., Mirasso C.R., Pesquera L., Shore K.A., 2005, Chaos-based communications at high bit rates using commercial fibre-optics links, *Nature*, 438, 343-46.

Banerjee S., 2010, *Chaos Synchronization and Cryptography for Secure Communications,* Information Science Reference.

Bennett C.H., 2000, Quantum Information and Computation, *Nature*, 404, 247-55.

Cai R.G., Wang A.Z., 2005, Cosmology with Interaction between Phantom Dark Energy and Dark matter and the Coincidence Problem, *J. Cosmol. Astropart. Phys.*, 3, 002(1-16).

Cho A., 2005, Simple noise may stymie spies without quantum weirdness, *Science*, 309, 2148-51.

Csiszar I., Korner J., 1978, Broadcast channels with confidential messages, *IEEE Trans. Inf. Theory*, 24(3), 339-348.

Cuomo K.M., Oppenheim A.V., 1993, Circuit Implementation of Synchronized Chaos with Applications to Communications, *Phys. Review Letters*, 71, 65-68.

D'Acunto M., Pieri G., Righi M., Salvetti O., 2014, A Methodological Approach for Combining Super-Resolution and Pattern-Recognition to Image Identification, *Pattern Recognition and Image Analysis*, 4, 209-217.

D'Agostini G., 2003, Bayesian reasoning in data analysis. A critical introduction, World Scientific Publishing, Singapore.

Duggento A., Stankovski T., McClintock P.V.E., Stefanovska A., 2012, Dynamical Bayesian Inference of Time-Evolving Interactions: From a Pair of Coupled Oscillators to Networks of Oscillators, *Phys. Rev. E*, 86, 061126.

Goel S., Negi R., 2008, Guaranteeing Secrecy using Artificial Noise, *IEEE Transactions on Wireless Communications*, 7(6), 2180-89.

Hlaváčkováá-Schindler K., Paluš M., Vejmelka M., Bhattacharya J., 2007, Causality Detection Based on Information-Theoretic Approaches in Time Series Analysis, *Physics Report*, 441, 1

Hung Y.-C., Hu C.-K., 2008, Chaotic Communication via Temporal Transfer Entropy, *Physical Review Letters*, 101, 244102(1-4).

Iatsenko D., Bernjak A., Stankovski T., Shiogai Y., Owen-Lynch P.J., Clarkson P.B.M., McClintock P.V.E., Stefanovska A., 2013, Evolution of

Cardio-Respiratory Interactions with age, *Phil. Trans. R. Soc.*, 371, 20110622.

Kish L.B., 2006a, Totally Secure Classical communications utilizing Johnson(-like) Noise and Kirchoff's Law, *Phys. Lett. A*, 352, 178-82.

Kish L.B., 2006b, Protection against the man-in-the-middle-attack for the Kirchhoff-loop-Johnson(-like)-noise cipher and expansion by voltage-based security, *Fluctuation Noise Lett.*, 6, L57-63. Addendum: http://www.ece.tamu.edu/~noise/C29_Kish_preprint.pdf

Kish L.B., 2006c, Methods of Using Existing and currently used Wise Lines (Power Lines, phone Lines, Internet lines) for totally secure classical communication utilizing Kirchhoff's Law and Johnson-like Noise, http://arxiv.org/ftp/physics/papers/0610/0610014.pdf

L.B. Kish and R. Mingesz, 2006, Totally secure classical networks with multipoint telecloning (teleportation) of classical bits through loops with Johnson-like noise, *Fluctuation and Noise Letters*, 6, C9-21.

Kiss I.Z., Rusin C.G., Kori H., Hudson J.L., 2007, Engineering Complex Dynamical Structures: sequential Patterns and Desynchronization, *Science*, 316, 1886-89.

Kittel C., Kroemer H., 1980, Thermal Physics, 2nd Ed., W.H. Freeman, USA.

Kocarev L., Parlitz U., 1995, General Approach for Chaotic Synchronization with Applications to Communication, *Physical Review Letters*, 74, 5028-31.

Kralemann B., Cimponeriu L., Rosenblum M., Pikovsky A., Mroka R., 2007, Uncovering Interaction of Coupled Oscillators from Data, *Phys. Rev. E*, 76, 055021(1-4)

Li W., Ghogho M., Chen B., Xiong C., 2012, Secure Communication via Sending Artificial Noise by the Receiver: Outage Secrecy Capacity/ Region Analysis, *IEEE Communications Letters*, 16(10), 1628- 31.

Lichtenberg A.J., Lieberman M.A., 1983, Regular and Stochastic Motion, Springer, Berlin.

Liu X., Chandrasekhar S., Winzer P.J., Chraplyvy A.R., Tkach R.W., Zhu B., Taunay T.F., Fishteyn M., DiGiovanni D.J., 2012, Scrambled Coherent Superposition for Enhanced Optical Fiber Communication in the Nonlinear Transmission Regime, *Optics Express*, 20, 19088-95.

Lorenz E.N., 1963, Deterministic nonperiodic flow, *J. Atmospheric Sciences*, 20(2), 130-141.

Mingesz R., Gingl Z., Kish L.B., 2008, Johnson(like)-Noise-Kirchhoff-loop based secure classical communicator characteristics, for rages of two to two thousand kilometers, via model-line, *Physics Letters* A, 372, 978-84.

Chapter 8

NATURE-INSPIRED COMPUTATION FOR IMAGE ANALYSIS AND VISION SYSTEMS

There are several interesting approaches to image processing and vision computing taking inspiration from the natural science. For example, the human eye and brain are biological systems that have the capability to act as sensors to record visual data and are able to enhance, segment, and recognize features of visions and images. In general, computer vision attempts to emulate these capabilities. Image enhancement, feature extraction, and segmentation play a fundamental role in analyzing images in field as medical (Toennies, 2012; Carvalho, 2012), geosciences (Heilbronner and Barrett, 2014), remote sensing (Prost 2013), facial extraction (Bartlett, 2001), biometrics (Yanushkevich et al., 2007; Dunstone and Yager, 2009) and more others. As described in the preview chapters, biological systems have natural capability to adapt to changes by learning promoting bio-inspired algorithms which have become useful in solving problems in any area of computer science, and in particular, image processing and vision systems. Evolutionary algorithms, swarm intelligence and bacterial foraging algorithms are very popular as bio-inspired algorithms, see chapter 4. However, other natural phenomena are inspiring algorithms as well as biological systems. Reaction-diffusion processes are such phenomena. In this chapter, we will focus the attention on genetic and evolutionary computation, as well as reaction-diffusion inspired algorithms.

The application of genetic algorithms to image analysis has an old and long history (Cagnoni et al., 2007; Melin et al., 2009). These methods have focused each topics inherent the image investigation, here, we focus only on two prevalent problems: the image segmentation and Hough transformation. Image segmentation consists of subdividing an image into its constituent regions or objects. The final result of a segmentation procedure is the labeling of the pixels in the image with a small number of labels of homogeneous regions characterized by one or more features (brightness, texture, color, just to cite some examples) sharing the same label. Regions of pixels with significantly different features have different labels. Many segmentation approaches have been proposed in the literature (Parker, 1996; Sonka et al., 1999; Gonzalez and Woods, 2002), and genetic algorithms have been successful applied to segment different kinds of images (Cagnoni et al., 1999; Fan et al., 2002; Mishra et al., 2003). Another successful application of genetic algorithms to image analysis is the Hough transform (Gonzalez and Woods, 2002; Louchet, 2007). The Hough transform is a feature extraction technique, able to find different instances of objects within a certain class of shapes by a voting procedure. This voting procedure is carried out in a parameter space, from which objects candidates are obtained as local maxima in the parameter space explicitly constructed by the algorithm for computing the Hough transform. One each feature has voted, this parameter set getting the highest number of votes is elected (local maxima), being considered as the best possible model parameterization. Unfortunately, the Hough transform and its extensions suffer from a computational complexity which increases with the complexity of patterns in the parameters space and the number of unknowns. Genetic and evolutionary strategies give an interesting opportunity to calculate only values in the part of the parameter space where population individuals actually are, rather than on the whole parameters space. In these genetic and evolutionary strategies the evolutionary procedure applied to the Hough transform follows generally some steps (for general details see chapter 4): (i) the population is a set of points in the parameters space; (ii) the fitness function measures the match quality of the individual to be evaluated, with the features of the given image; (iii) selection and mutation properties (Rachenberg, 1994).

Reaction-diffusion systems are mathematical models which explains how the concentration of one or more substances distributed in space changes under the influence of two processes: local chemical reaction in which the substances are transformed into each other, and diffusion which causes the substances to spread out over a surface in space. Reaction-diffusion systems find generally application in chemistry. However, the system can also describe processes that can be found in a variety of natural systems, just as an example, the FitzHugh-Nagumo equations are typical reaction-diffusion equations (FitzHugh, 1961; Nagumo et al., 1962). They simulate an information transmission phenomenon along a nerve axon. Other examples can be found in geology, physics and ecology.

Kuhnert et al. were the firsts to demonstrate that a chemical reaction system solves the typical image processing tasks of edge detection and segmentation (Kuhnert, 1986, Kuhnert et al., 1989). Their mathematical model was based on chemical reaction, specifically, a type of reaction-diffusion system, which consists of non-linear reaction terms combined with diffusion equations. Their successful demonstration showing the capability of the reaction-diffusion system to process images strongly motivated a wide number of algorithms and computing strategies. Asai and co-workers proposed reaction-diffusion devices for image processing realized utilizing large-scale integrated circuits and applied them for realistic applications (Asai et al., 2005; Adamatzky et al., 2005).

8.1. Genetic and Evolutionary Computation for Image Processing and Analysis

As mentioned in the introduction, the basic two problems of image analysis successful solved using genetic and evolutionary algorithms focused in this section are the segmentation problem and Hough transform.

Image segmentation into regions and active contour segmentation are the most widely requested procedures for a general segmentation problem (Kass et al., 1988; Ballerini 2007). Segmentation of regions in a 3D scene, for example, regards a portion of surface that is considered the only simple quantity which actually supports a physical process involved in the formation of a natural image, for example reflection and diffusion of light in optical source imaging. When light interacts with an object will naturally lead to introduce color, brightness values, complex reflection and diffusion properties, and texture as parameters attached to the physical surfaces to objects. In spite of all the instrumental artefacts that can appear when the digital image has been generated (noise, geometrical distortion, optical aberrations), these physical properties will have to be translated into object properties at the image level. Since in many cases, we have no specific knowledge on the scene, it is reasonable to suppose that two points in the image, if they belong to the same object, will be more likely made from the same material than if they appertain to the different objects. At a level of an image, the correspondent pixels of the two points will probably look more closely each other than is they belonged to two different objects. This pixel similarity (*homogeneity criterion*) may be evaluated on a photometric level, for example having the same color or gray-scale intensity, or on a geometrical level, for example havening the same texture, or on more elaborate levels. Once the homogeneity criterion has been established, the problem is then to find which is the best way to divide the image into regions so that a homogeneous region is fulfilled by all the points and sub-regions detected as homogenous by the criterion. A segmentation algorithm should to do this (D'Acunto and Salvetti, 2010). A segmentation algorithm should ideally consists of two parts. The first part consists of listing the properties one would expect from the result of segmentation, this is done by translating into image plane the general physical properties we already know about the scene. This first part can be denoted as *problem-specific knowledge* (Smola and Vishwanathan, 2008). The second part consists of writing or readapting an algorithm able to solve the problem. This is the common requirement of all knowledge-based systems and the basic requirement of artificial intelligence. Inside segmentation procedures, active contour problems play a fundamental role in many scientific applications, primarily in medicine (Gonzalez and Woods, 2002; Shen et al., 2011; Xu et al., 2014), to detect object boundaries in an image. However, the applications of active contour models (or snakes) to extract regions of interest suffers from the limitations. Active contour model operates as an energy minimizing spline and the classical model employs the variational calculus to iteratively minimize energy. Although different procedures have been proposed for the minimization, such methods are limited by the exhaustive searches for the admissible solutions and complicated parameters control and by accurate initialization. On the contrary, genetic algorithms have been found to overcome some of such limitations (Davis, 1991). Genetic algorithms offer a global search procedure that has shown its robustness in many applications, see chapter 4, and in pattern recognition and image processing (Cagnoni et al., 2007, Melin et al., 2009).

Active contour model (here, we simply name it as snake model) is a planar deformable contour. A snake is often useful to approximate location and shape of object boundaries on the basis of the reasonable assumption that boundaries are continuous and smooth. Considering the position of a snake parametrically by $\mathbf{v}(s)=(x(s), y(s))$, with $s\in[0,1]$, its energy can be written as (Ballerini, 2007)

$$E_{snake} = \int_0^1 E_{\text{int}}[\mathbf{v}(s)]ds + \int_0^1 E_{ext}[\mathbf{v}(s)]ds \tag{8.1}$$

where E_{int} represents the internal energy of the snake due to bending and it is associated with a priori constraints, while E_{ext} is an external potential energy which depends on the image and accounts for a posteriori information, and the final shape of the contour corresponds to the minimum of this energy. The internal energy can be defined as

$$E_{\text{int}}[\mathbf{v}(s)] = \frac{1}{2}\left[\alpha(s)\left|\frac{\partial \mathbf{v}(s)}{\partial s}\right|^2 + \beta(s)\left|\frac{\partial^2 \mathbf{v}(s)}{\partial s^2}\right|^2\right] \tag{8.2}$$

where the first-order term, dominated by $\alpha(s)$, simulates the physical characteristics of the contour that is be represented by the *tension*, and the second-order term, dominated by $\beta(s)$, that represents the *rigidity* of the contour (Ballerini, 2007). The external energy that couples the snake to the image *attracting* the snake toward the edges, can be defined as

$$E_{ext}[v(s)] = -\gamma\left|\nabla G_\sigma * I(x, y)\right|^2 \tag{8.3}$$

where $G_\sigma*I(x,y)$ denotes the image convolved by a Gaussian filter with a standard deviation σ, ∇ is the gradient operator, and γ a weight associated with image energies. In classical deformable contour models, the internal energy constraints of snakes can limit their geometric flexibility and the topology of the structure of interest must be known in advance since classical deformable contour are parametric and are unable of topological transformations without additional model adjustments. These drawbacks can be overcome using genetic algorithms for snake definition (Ballerini, 2007). The basic elements of genetic snakes are solution representation, fitness definition, and initialization. The parameters that undergo genetic optimization are the positions of the snake in the image plane $\mathbf{v}(s) = (x(s), y(s))$. The coordinates x and y are encoded in the chromosomes as well as the snake points and optimized using the genetic algorithm. The fitness function to be minimized is the total snake energy (8.1). The genetic optimization requires the definition of a region of interest given two radii, r and R, as in figure 8.1, that represent the minimum and maximum magnitude allowed for each v(s). The initial population is randomly chosen in such a region, and each solution is constrained to be in the region. Mutation randomly moves one snake point (x,y) to another point in the image plane, while crossover separates two parent snakes and recombines them to create two children snakes.

Another advantage of generic algorithm is given by the choice of the functional. The classical optimization techniques impose different restrictions on the type of image functional that can be employed, for example, explicitly requires the existence of derivatives, the use of genetic algorithm offers more freedom on the choice of such functionals giving the opportunity to experiment new energy terms ( ). Interesting is the application of genetic snakes to ocular fundus images, where snakes are used in the segmentation of the foveal avascular zone (Ballerini, 2007). Diabetic retinopathy is the leading cause of new adult blindness, and early detection of diabetic retinopathy is based on the study of the foveal avascular zone, figure 8.2.

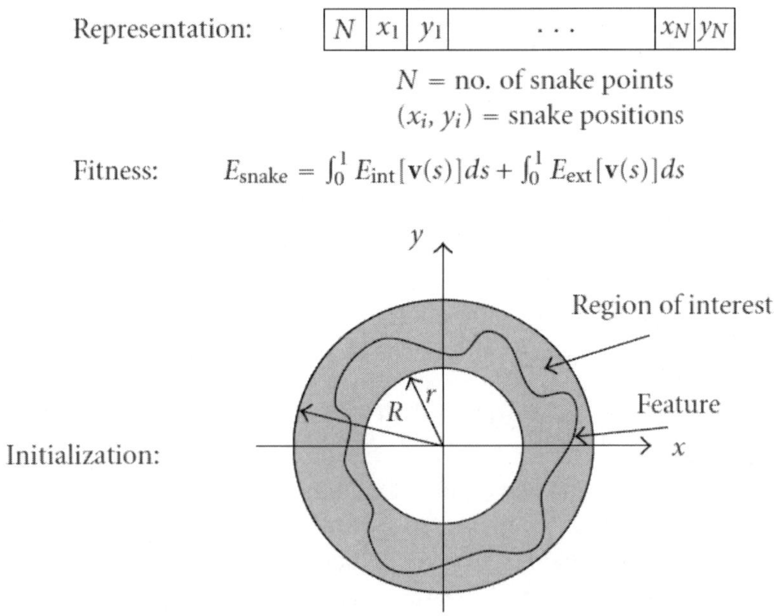

Figure 8.1. Basic elements of the genetic snakes. (Reproduced from (Ballerini, 2007), with permission).

Evolution strategies can actually amplify the field of application of Hough transform and its generalizations to solve real-time computer vison and image processing. Hough's technique leads to calculate vote values over the whole parameter space than explore it exhaustively in order to detect the best solutions. In a non-evolutionary context of the Hough transform, one method for detecting straight lines in images, for example, is that each point (x,y) in the images votes for the set of the (θ,ρ) in the parameter space such that $\rho=x\cos\theta+x\sin\theta$, so requiring memory consuming. The evolutionary version of such method, thanks to shared operator, enables to detect several solutions remaining reasonable in terms of memory and computing effort (Louchet, 2007). Consider the detection of unknown diameters (for example a moving ball) in a image sequence, the triplet (a,b,r) contains the parameters of the circles

$$(x-a)^2+(y-b)^2=r^2 \qquad (8.4)$$

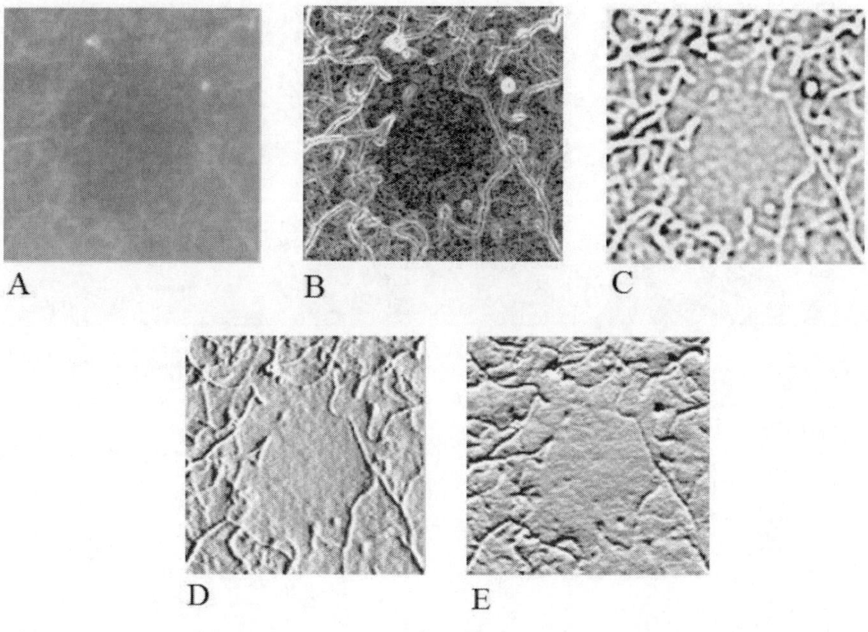

Figure 8.2. A, retinal image recorded by a scanning laser ophthalmoscope, with a frequency of 25 frames per second following the injection of a bolus of fluorescein. This images is digitized into 512×512 pixel matrices with 256 gray levels per pixel. The region of interest is the floveal avascular zone that is approximately the center of the image A. B, the previous image convolved by gradient of a Gaussian (σ=2), C, image convolved by Laplacian of Gaussian (σ=2). D, E, image segmentation with genetic snakes, the intensity of each pixel is proportional to the gradient component in that point. (Reproduced from (Ballerini, 2007), with permission).

If the object's motion small enough between two consecutive frames, the evolutionary Hough transform is able to track the object's movement, unlike the deterministic version which has to begin calculations from scratch at every new frame looking at the degree of consistency between consecutive images. The same result is obtained with recognizing an ellipse in an image, figure 8.3, using the same algorithm and parameters but with a larger genome (a,b,r_x,r_y,α) corresponding to the parametric equation of an ellipse:

$$x = a + r_x \cos\alpha\cos\theta + r_y \sin\alpha\sin\theta;$$
$$y = b - r_x \cos\alpha\sin\theta + r_y \sin\alpha\cos\theta.$$

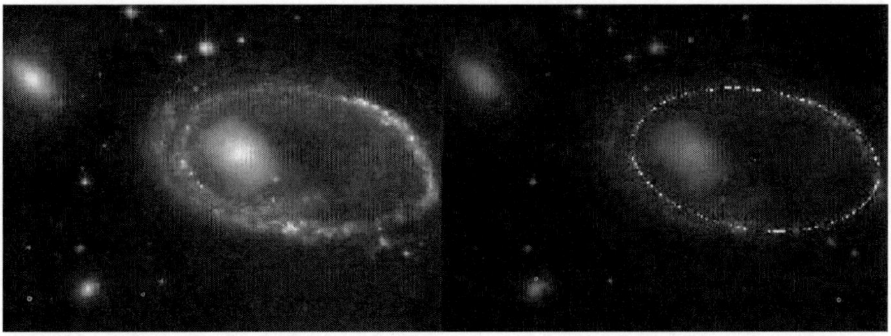

Figure 8.3. Image of galaxy AM 0644-741 taken by Hubble telescope (left) and the result of the evolutionary Hough ellipse detection (right). (Reproduced from (Louchet, 2007), with permission).

8.2. Reaction-Diffusion Processes for Image Analysis and Vision Systems

A reaction-diffusion system with two variables (u,v) consists of

$$\partial_t u = D_u \nabla^2 u + f(u,v);\ \partial_t v = D_v \nabla^2 v + g(u,v). \tag{8.5}$$

The operator ∂_t denotes the temporal partial derivative $\partial/\partial t$, and the Laplacian operator ∇^2 denotes $\partial^2/\partial x^2+\partial^2/\partial y^2$ in the two-dimensional coordinate system of (x,y), D_u is the diffusion coefficient of the variable u and, analogously, D_v is that of v. The functions $f(u,v)$ and $g(u,v)$ are the reaction

where a_0 is a constant and N is the number of groups. The additional contribution of Eq. (8.14) contains both the two constrains requirements. It works as the mutual inhibition mechanism by increasing the threshold value of others sets, and the mutual-sets of equations exclusively become the excited state having the high value of un, uniqueness constrain. While the continuity constraint is already built into the reaction-diffusion system, because the system originally has the spatial information propagation effect for its adjacent area. The results of the reaction-diffusion approach to grouping problem are impressive, figure 8.4.

8.2.1. Reaction-Diffusion System for Stereo Disparity Detection

Stereo camera project a target point located in a three-dimensional world onto two points on their left and right images planes, stereo disparity refers to the difference of such two points.

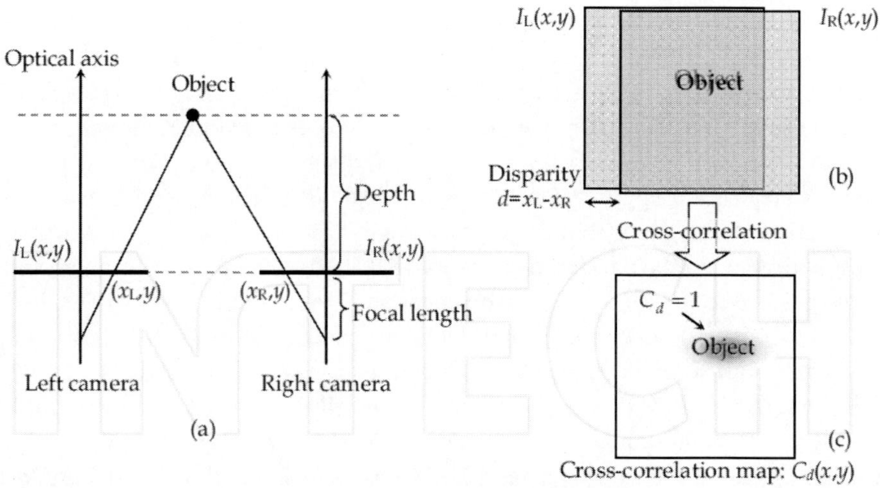

Figure 8.5. Schematic sketch of stereo vision geometry and cross relation map. (a) An object point is projected both onto the image plane $I_L(x,y)$ of the left camera and image plane $I_R(x,y)$ of the right one. (b) Stereo images overlapping generates a stereo disparity level d. (c) Cross-correlation map $C_d(x,y)$ obtained between the stereo images with a disparity level d. The condition $d= x_L-x_R$, implies $C_d=1$. (Reproduced from (Nomura et al., 2007), with permission).

Figure 8.5 reproduces the basic characteristic of a stereo system generating disparity. The left camera projects the object point onto a position (x_L,y) on its image plane $I_L(x,y)$; the right one does it onto (x_R,y) on $I_R(x,y)$. The stereo disparity that can be generates is $d= x_L-x_R$ that can be used to obtain the depth of the object. The key question is to find the correspondence between the two points (x_L,y) and (x_R,y) from only the two image brightness distribution functions $I_L(x,y)$ and $I_R(x,y)$, when such correspondence is known it is possible to obtain stereo disparity, that correspond to the depth of the object. A good strategy to find the correspondence is to overlap the two image distributions functions $I_L(x,y)$ and $I_R(x,y)$ at every possible disparity level d. A cross-correlation map $C_d(x,y)$ is computed for $I_L(x,y)$ and $I_R(x+d,y)$. By finding the highest value of $C_d(x,y)$ for all of the possible disparity levels, we can obtain a disparity map. For a binary stereo image pair, a simple logic operation provides the cross-correlation map as (Nomura et al., 1999)

$$C_d(x,y) = \neg[I_L(x,y) \oplus I_R(x+d,y)] \tag{8.15}$$

where – [·⊕·] is the XNOR logic operation that gives 1 for matched pair and 0 for an unmatched one. Since images have many similar brightness patterns, causing many miss matched pairs in $C_d(x,y)$, there is much uncertainty in finding correct match pairs in the cross-correlation map. Additional constraints must be addressed to solve the uncertainty and detect a reliable stereo disparity map. Marr and Poggio proposed biological inspired algorithm, i.e., a cooperative stereo algorithm (Marr and Poggio, 1976). They suggested two important constraints on stereo disparity distribution such as continuity and uniqueness. According to such two constraints and the biologically-inspired idea of a cell network, they formulated a modified cross-correlation map involving a cell state of the disparity level d, at various iteration steps. Zitnick and Kanade improved the cooperative algorithm modifying the cross-correlation map (Zitnick and Kanade, 2000). Nomura et al. proposed a reaction-diffusion algorithm as described by Eqs. (8.12) and (8.13), where the cross correlation map $C_d(x,y)$ as given by Eq. (8.15) is substituted to s_n in Eq. (8.12) and the disparity level d corresponds to the number n. Following the suggestion of Zitnick and Kanade, since the local support area in the stereo disparity detection is not only over space but also across the disparity direction, thus, it is necessary to modify the function $a(U_d)$ in Eq.(8.14) representing the uniqueness constraint, by taking into account the distance between the current disparity level d and the level having the largest value of

$u_{d'}$ in the so-called inhibition area. One formulation for eq. (8.14) for stereo disparity detection can be (Nomura et al., 2007)

$$a(U_d) = a_0 + U_d \cdot \frac{1}{2}[1 + \tanh(|d| - a_1)]$$
$$U_d = \max_{(x,y,d')\in\Omega} u_{d'}(x,y,t)$$
$$|d| = \left| d - \arg\max_{(x,y,d')\in\Omega} u_{d'}(x,y,t) \right| \quad (8.16)$$

where Ω is the inhibition area. An example of stereo disparity detection for image pairs using reaction-diffusion approach is reported in figure 8.6.

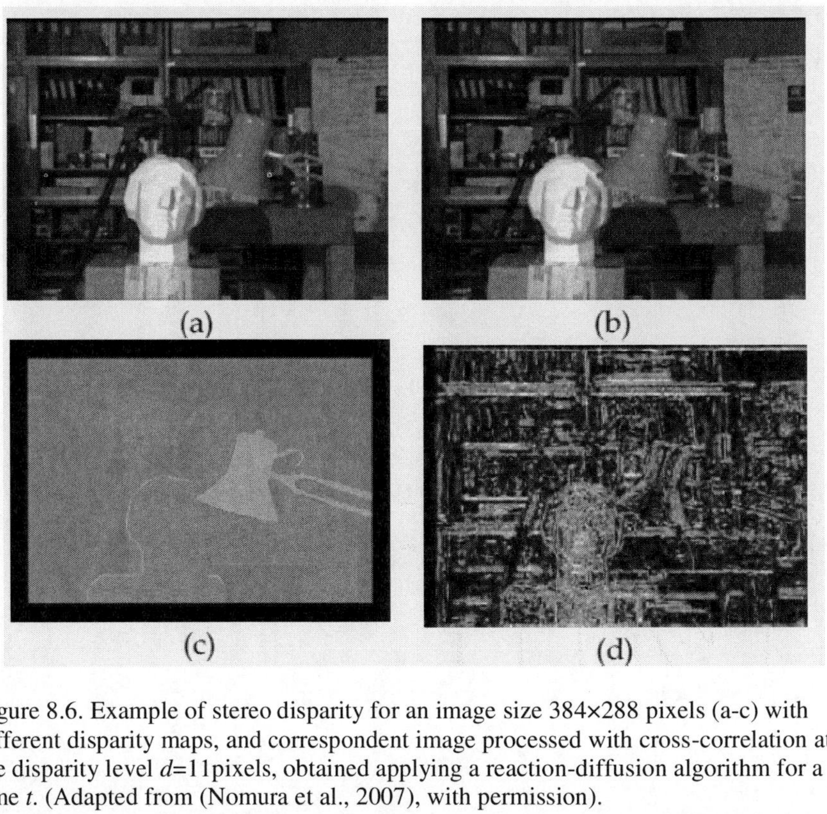

Figure 8.6. Example of stereo disparity for an image size 384×288 pixels (a-c) with different disparity maps, and correspondent image processed with cross-correlation at the disparity level d=11pixels, obtained applying a reaction-diffusion algorithm for a time t. (Adapted from (Nomura et al., 2007), with permission).

8.3. DIFFUSION-BASED PROCESS IMAGE ANALYSIS ALGORITHMS

Diffusion based algorithm are commonly used to remove noise from an image. Diffusion algorithms can be classified as isotropic or anisotropic. Isotropic diffusion is equivalent to using a Gaussian filter on the image, which blurs not only the noise or texture components, but the main edges as well. Perona and Malik first proposed an Anisotropic Diffusion (AD) functions that, according to scale-space theory allows diffusion along the edges or in edge-free territories, but penalizes diffusion orthogonal to the edge direction (Perona and Malik, 1990). Denoted an original image as $I(x,y,0)$, where (x,y) are the spatial coordinates, and $I(x,y,t)$:$\Re^2 \rightarrow \Re^+$ as the continuous variation due to the artificial time parameter t, the AD process can be described by the equation (Perona and Malik, 1990; Yu and Acton, 2002):

$$\frac{\partial I(x,y,t)}{\partial t} = div\left(g(\|\nabla I\|)\nabla I\right) \tag{8.17}$$

where ∇I is the image gradient, and $||\nabla I||$ is the magnitude of the gradient and $g(\cdot)$ is the weighting function that controls diffusion along and across edges. In the original paper, Perona and Malik proposed a g function accounting AD as

$$g(x,y,t) = \left(1 + \frac{|\nabla I|^2}{k^2}\right)^{-1} \tag{8.18}$$

Useful is the discretized form of the Eq. (8.17) that can be written

$$I(x,y,t+1) = I(x,y,t) + \frac{\lambda}{|\eta(x,y)|} \sum_{(x',y') \in \eta(x,y)} \nabla$$

$$\nabla^{(x',y')} g\left(\left\|\nabla^{(x',y')} I(x,y,t)\right\|\right) \nabla^{(x',y')} I(x,y,t) \tag{8.19}$$

where I is the processed image, (x,y) is the pixel position, t now denotes discrete time steps (iterations). The constant $\lambda \in \Re^{+}$ is a scalar that determines the rate of diffusion, $\eta(x,y)$ is the spatial neighborhood of (x,y), $|\eta(x,y)|$ is the number of neighboring pixels. $\nabla^{(x',y')}I(x,y,t)$ is an approximation of the image gradient at a particular direction (Yu and Acton, 2002):

$$\nabla^{(x',y')}I(x,y,t) = I(x',y',t) - I(x,y,t),\ (x',y') \in \eta(x,y) \tag{8.20}$$

AD belongs to a theoretically sound scale-space class of differential processes ensuring the denoising of an image along with the enhancement of its main structure (Jin et al., 2000). Recently, Sziranyi and Szolgay suggested a Perina-Malik AD algorithm with modified weights: instead of using $||\nabla^{(x',y')}I(x,y,t)||$ as the parameter of the weighting function, they use the edges of the Gaussian filtered image, $\nabla(G_\sigma * I)$:

$$\left\|\nabla^{(x',y')}(G_\sigma * I)(x',y',0) - (G_\sigma * I)(x,y,0)\right\|,$$
$$(x',y') \in \eta(x,y) \tag{8.21}$$

where G_σ is a Gaussian filter with σ bandwidth and * denotes the convolution operation. Since in many cartoon/texture decomposition, the texture part might contain high magnitude edges, which would inhibit the diffusion. Using a blurred image to control diffusion directions will give better results, so texture edges will not hinder the diffusion, but the strong main edges will do. In addition, the quality of the solution relies heavily on the σ parameter. Small σ implies that some texture might remain on the cartoon, while with greater σ, some of the carton edges will disappear.

Interestingly, there exists a relation between the Eq. (8.17) and the neural dynamics of brightness perception. For example, in 1984, Cohen and Grossberg proposed a model of the primary visual cortex with similar inhibition effects as in the Perona-Malik model (Cohen and Grossberg, 1984, Malik and Perona, 1990).

REFERENCES

Adamatzky A., Costello B.D.L., Asai T., 2005, Reaction-Diffusion Computers, Elsevier, Amsterdam.

Asai T., Costello B.D.L., Adamatzky A., 2005, Silicon implementation of a chemical reaction-diffusion processor for computation of Voronoi diagram, *International Journal of Bifurcation and Chaos*, 15, 3307-20.

Ballerini L., 2007, Genetic Snakes: active contour models by genetic algorithms, in *Genetic and Evolutionary Computation for Image Processing and Analysis*, Cagnoni S., Lutton E., Olague G., Eds. pp. 177-194, Hindawi Publishing Corporation, NY, USA.

Bartlett M.S., 2001, Face Image Analysis by Unsupervised Learning, Springer, Berlin.

Beck J., 1966, Effect of orientation and of shape similarity on perceptual grouping, *Perception & Psychophysics*, 1, 300-2.

Cagnoni S., Dobrzeniecki A.B., Poli R., Yanch J.C., 1999, Genetic algorithms-based intercative segmentation of 3D medical images, *Image and Vision Computing*, 17(12), 881-95.

Cagnoni S., Lutton E., Olague G., 2007, Genetic and Evolutionary Computation for Image Processing and Analysis, EURASIP Book Series on Signal Processing and Communications, Vol. 8, Hindawi Publishing Corporation, NY, USA.

Carvalho V.H., 2012, Image Processing: Methods, Applications and Challenges, Nova Science Publishers.

Cohen M., Grossberg S., 1984, Neural dynamics of brightness perception: Features, boundaries and resonance, *Perception and Psychophysics*, 36, 428-456.

Cottet G.H., Germain L., 1993, Image Processing through Reaction combined with Nonlinear Diffusion, *Mathematics of Computation*, 61, 659-673.

D'Acunto M., Salvetti O., 2010, Image analysis aided by Segmentation algorithms for techniques ranging from Scanning Probe Microscopy to Optical Microscopy, in Microscopy: Science, Tecnology, Applications and Education, A. Mendez-Vilas, J. Diaz, eds., pp. 1445-66, Formatex, Spain.

Davis L., 1991, Handbook of Genetic Algorithms, Van Nostrand Reinhold, NY, USA.

Dunstone T., Yager N., 2009, Biometric System and Data Analysis, Springer, Berlin.

Fan Y., Jiang T., Evans D.J., 2002, Volumetric segmentation of brain images using parallel genetic algorithms, *IEEE Transactions on Medical Imaging*, 21(8), 904-9.

FitzHugh R., 1961, Impulses and physiological states in theoretical models of nerve membrane, *Biophysical Journal*, 1, 445-466.

Gonzalez R.C., Woods R.E., 2002, Digital Image Processing, Prentice-Hall, Upper Saddle River, NJ, USA, 2nd edition.

Heilbronner R., Barrett S., 2014, Image Analysis in Earth Sciences, Springer, Berlin.

Jin J.S., Wang Y., Hiller J., 2000, An adaptive nonlinear diffusion algorithm for filtering medical images, *IEEE Transactions on Information Technology in Biomedicine*, 4, 298-305.

Kaplan D.T., Clay J.R., Manning T., Glass L., Guevara M.R., Shrier A., 1996, Subthreshold Dynamics in Periodically Stimulated Squid Giant Axons, *Physical Review Letters*, 76, 4074-77

Kass M., Witkin A., Terzopoulos D., 1988, Snakes: active contour models, *International Journal of Computer Vision*, 1(4), 321-331.

Kunhert L., 1986, A new optical photochemical memory device in a light-sensitive chemical active medium, *Nature,* 319, 393-94.

Kuhnert L., Agladze K.I., Krinsky V.I., 1989, Image processing using light-sensitive chemical waves, *Nature*, 337, 244-47.

Louchet J., 2007, Model-based image analysis using evolutionary computation, in Cagnoni et al., 2007, pp. 283-306.

Malik J., Perona P., 1990, Preattentive texture discrimination with early vision mechanisms, *J. of the Optical Society of America A*, 7, 923-932.

Marr D., Hildreth E., 1980, Theory of edge detection, *Proceedings of the Royal Society of London, Series B, Biological Sciences*, 207, 187-217.

Marr D., Poggio T., 1976, Cooperative computation of stereo disparity, *Science*, 194, 283-87.

Melin P., Kacprzyk J., Pedrycz W., 2009, Bio-inspired Hybrid Intelligent Systems for Image Analysis and Pattern Recognition, Springer, Heidelberg-Berlin.

Mishra A., Dutta P.K., Ghosh M.K., 2003, A GA based approach for boundary detection of left ventricle with echocardiographoic image sequences, *Image and Vision Computing*, 21(11), 967-76.

Nagumo J., Arimoto S., Yoshizawa S., 1962, An active pulse transmission line simulating nerve axon, *Proceedings of the I.R.E.*, 50, 2061-2070.

Nomura A., Ichikawa M., Miike H., 1999, Solving random-dot stereograms with a reaction-diffusion model under the Turing instability, *Proceedings of the 10th International DAAAM Symposium*, pp.385-86, Wien, Austria.

Nomura A., Ichikawa M., Sianipar R.H., Miike H., 2007, in *Vision Systems: Segmentation and Pattern Recognition*, Obinata G., Dutta A., Eds. pp. 61-80, I-Tech, Vienna, Austria

Parker J.R., 1996, Algorithms for Image Processing and Computer Vision, John Wiley& Sons, New York, NY, USA.

Perona P., Malik J., 1990, Scale-space and edge detection using anisotropic diffusion, *IEEE Transactions Pattern Anal. Machine Intelligence*, 12, 161-192.

Prost, G.L., 2013, Remote Sensing for Geoscientists: Image Analysis and Integration, 3rd ed., CRC Press.

Rechenberg I., 1994, Evolution strategy, in Computational Intelligence: Imitation Life, Zurada J.M., Marks II J., Robinson C., Eds., pp. 147-159, IEEE Press, Piscataway, NJ, USA.

Schnakenberg J., 1979, Simple Chemical Reaction Systems with Limit Cycle Behavior, *Journal of Theoretical Biology*, 81, 389-400.

Shen T., Li H., Huang X., 2011, Active Volume Models for Medical Image Segmentation, *IEEE Trans. on Medical Imaging*, 30(3), 774-91.

Smola A., Vishwanathan S.V.N., 2008, Introduction to Machine Learning, Cambridge University Press, Cambridge, UK.

Sonka M., Hlavac V., Boyle R., 1999, Image processing: Analysis and Machine Vision, PWS, Pacific Grove, CA, USA, 2nd edition.

Toennies, K.D., 2012, Guide to Medical Image Analysis, Springer, Berlin.

Weickert J., 1998, Anisotropic Diffusion in Image Processing, ECMI Series. Teuber Verlag, Stuttgart, Germany.

Xu T., Vavylonis D., Huang X., 2014, 3D Actin Network Centerline Extraction with Multiple Active Contours, *Medical Image Analysis*, 18(2), 272-84.

Yanushkevich S.N., Wang P.S.P., Gavrilova M.L., Srihari S.N., 2007, Image Pattern Recognition, Synthesis and Analysis in Biometrics, Series in machine Perception and Artificial Intelligence, 67, World Scientific Publishing, Singapore.

Yu Y., Acton S.T., 2002, Speckle Reducing Anisotropic Diffusion, *IEEE Transaction on Image Processing*, 11, 1260-70.

Zitnick C.L., Kanade T., 2000, A cooperative algorithm for stereo matching and occlusion detection, *IEEE Transaction on Pattern Analysis and Machine Intelligence*, 22, 675-84.

Chapter 9

NANO-OPTICS AND NANOPHOTONICS INFORMATION: COMPUTATION INSPIRED BY LIGHT-MATTER INTERACTION AT NANOSCALE

The possible connections between photonics and computation are significant both from the point of view of the scientific and technological challenges. There are points in time at which a well-known technology, which has been used and gradually improved for decades, reaches its physical limitations, forcing in many cases a shift towards drastic different technology. The point at which these massive shifts in technology occur is often decades after the initial invention. The supercomputing based on optics, the solution of NP-problems with optical tools and the advent of nanophotonic computing paradigms are opening the doors to new exciting technological jumps in computer science both by an hardware and software point of view (Andrews and Gaburro, 2007; Ohtsu, 2009). For decades, optics have demonstrated to be the best means of conveying information between two points, as can clearly be seen by the growth of the massive fiber optics communications industry. The fact that light beams can be easily transmitted in parallel in free space, and do not suffer from crosstalk, is of fundamental importance. However, optical technology also has the opportunity to go beyond being just a convenient pipe for ultrafast data transmission, and actually perform data processing. Given that the basic computing element of a computer is a transistor, that is an electronic switching element, and that great progress has been made in all-optical switching and logic, there is an opportunity to avoid light-to-electronics and electronics-to-light conversions in the design of all all-optical computers. So, today the question is: could optical technology offer a solution to the heat generation and bandwidth limitations that the computing industry is starting to face? The benefits of energy-efficient passive component, low crosstalk and parallel suggest that the answer may be yes. The design of optical computers does not necessarily have to mimic the design of electronic computer, just as the design of electronic computers did not mimic the design of mechanical computing devices. In fact, optics implies a new means for the application of parallelism, with many beams in space representing individual computations. As we have seen in the introduction, the widely accepted Church-Turing thesis asserts that anything can be computed by a digital computer. Under such assumption, the optics offers no new computational capability. To be useful, the best that optics can do is to accomplish the same goals as digital electronics, but in a more efficient manner.

Another example of technological shift using light is in computational complexity. In computational complexity theory, a decision problem is NP (that refers to nondeterministic polynomial time) if the set of all decision problems for which the instances where the answer is *yes* have efficiently verifiable proofs of the fact that the answer is *yes*. Analogously, a NP-complete problem is when the problem is both NP and NP-hard. NP-hard (Non-deterministic Polynomial-time hard) denotes a class of problems *that are at least hard as the hardest problems* in NP (Karp, 2010; Wu et al., 2014). A class of famous complexity problems known as NP-complete problems consists are well-known as the traveling salesman problem that aims to find the shortest possible route on a map (Cook, 1971). Another example of NP-complete problem is the real-world clique problem of graph theory for finding the largest subset of people who all know each other (Aaronson, 2005). A NP-hard problem is the decision *subset sum problem*, which is defined as follows: given a set of integers, does any non-empty subset of them add up to zero?

After many years of research, no improved algorithm has been found to solve these problems within a polynomial time using a deterministic Turing machine. This has generated the idea commonly recognized by many researchers that such an algorithm does not exist in principle. As a reaction to such failure of conventional computers, a wide number of physics approaches have been considered for NP problems (Aaronson, 2005). These approaches include the use of soap bubbles, DNA computation, protein folding, quantum and optical computation (Adleman, 1994; Ezziane, 2006; Liu et al., 2000; Kiu, 2003; O'Brien, 2007; Shaked et al., 2007; Oltean, 2008; Caulfield and Dolev, 2010; Woods and Naughton, 2012). Unfortunately, not one of them reduces the complexity of the problem or offers technologically efficient solutions without exponentially increasing the demand of physical resources. However, recently, Wu et al. demonstrated that an NP-complete problem may be solved using an optical telecommunication fiber network as the information carrier (Wu et al., 2014). The demonstration uses the directed Hamiltonian path problem of deciding whether a map can be traveled in a unidirectional manner such that each town is visited exactly once by exploiting the network for supporting decision on the existence of the Hamiltonian path rather than for finding the exact path itself. The solution does not remove the fundamental mathematical complexity, it provides a robust and fast decision that could be scaled to analyze maps of considerable maps. The importance of such method is that the realization and demonstration of a fast-working solution for NP-complete problems within telecommunication networks may have a significant potential impact in applications such as secure communications, routing optimization and optical data processing. The details of the methods proposed by Wu et al., as well as other similar proposals are described in section 9.2

Another example of light inspired computation is the nanophotonic computation paradigm using spatiotemporal photoexcitation transfer dynamics proposed by Naruse et al. (Naruse, 2014). They demonstrated that the photoexcitation transfer phenomena in certain quantum nanostructures mediated by optical near-field interactions mimic the spatiotemporal dynamics of the single-celled amoeba (a plasmodial smile mold). The amoeba exhibits complex spatiotemporal oscillatory dynamics and sophisticated computing capabilities (Aono et al., 2010; Aono et al., 2013; Zhu et al., 2013). The representation of amoeba complex dynamics with spatiotemporal photoexcitation transfer dynamics could in principle be used to solve two highly complex problems: (i) the satisfiability problem, which is one of the most difficult combinatorial optimization problems, to determine whether a given logical proposition is self-consistent, and (ii) the multi–armed bandit problem, which is a decision-making problem in finding the most profitable option from among a number of options that provide rewards with different unknown probabilities. The new computation paradigm introduced by Naruse et al. is an innovative and suitable problem-solving and decision-making model exhibiting better performances than conventionally known best algorithms. In such model, both coherent and dissipative processes are exploited for performing powerful solution searching and efficient decision making with low energy consumption. The details about such methods are described in section 9.3.

9.1. Optics and Supercomputing

Compared to electronics, optics has a supplemental advantage: many independent beams may be modified by a single pixel in an optical processor. In principle, supercomputers based on optical technology may help to mitigate the heat generation that plagues electronic computers. The heat problem of electronic devices becomes much worse as speed increases and density decreases, both of which are scaling rapidly according to Moore's law (which provides a nearly two-year doubling in the number of transistors on a silicon chip). Faster operations require more power, while smaller components provide less are through which to remove the resulting heat from each element. The use of optical components involves little or no heat dissipation. Such use depends on the special approaches for exploiting the features of light for information processing.

One approach is the so-called vector matrix optical multiplier (Tamir et al., 2009). It uses a lens to split the light received from each entry of an input vector to the corresponding entries of the vectors of the matrix. When a beam crosses the matrix, the intensity of the beam is changed according to the value of the entry that the beam reached. Thus, another lens is used to sum the resulting light intensity of each resulting vector. An optical digital signal processor (ODSP) could work as follows (Tamir et al., 2009): the input is a vector of light sources that are projected in parallel by lenses on the rows of a slide or on a spatial light modulator, and the output that encodes the multiplication product is obtained by gathering light from each row to a sensitive detector. Loading data in parallel to the input vector, the spatial light modulator leads to a great improvement in computing speed. In addition, the architecture supports principal DSP primitives such as vector-by-matrix and matrix-by-matrix multiplications, convolution, correlation and discrete Fourier transforms. In turn, functioning as a co-processor of a legacy processor, the architecture can efficiently process integers as well as complex numbers and perform extended-precision arithmetic.

Another approach for information processing with light is the zero-energy logic, figure 9.1 (Hardy and Shamir, 2007; Caulfield et al., 2007). This is an idea coming from the 1960s. As described in the introductive chapter, Landauer showed that the energy needed to operate such a gate stems from the need to erase one of the output bits, as the Boolean logic gates have two binary inputs but only one binary output, see the Introduction chapter of this book for further details. If the extra bit is kept, there would be no minimum energy for gate operation. Unless the energy needed to input data and readout results, the logic itself could be free. Recently, there has been a renewed interest on the logic systems that consume zero energy. In figure 9.1, two designs for optical implementation of an energy-free logical gate are described. Both designs are zero-energy devices. Figure 9.1a shows a new kind of logic that gives the same result as conventional Boolean logic but does so in a way that is optics-friendly (Caulfield and Dolev, 2010). The device produces both A AND B and also its complement A NAND B. Figure 9.1b presents a generalized optical logic element. It is essentially a physically embodied lookup table that computes A AND B, with the NAND obtained using a supplemental Rochon prisms (a Rochon prism is a type of polarizer, made from two prisms of a birifrangent material cemented together). By choosing the beams to deflect or not to deflect, we can implement any Boolean logic gate using only passive components.

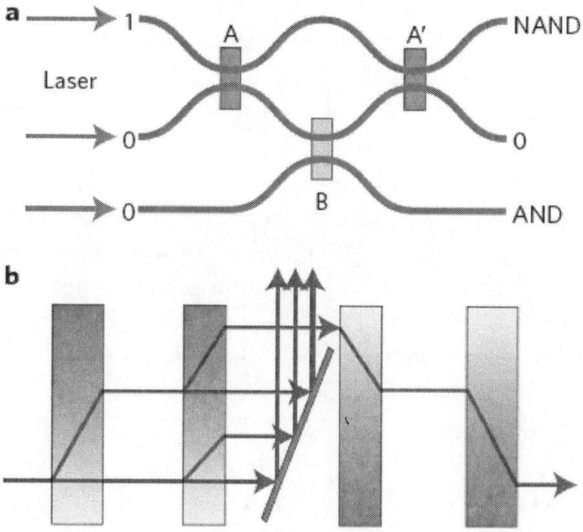

Figure 9.1. Schematic example of zero-energy logic gates using optical passive elements. **a**, Powered electronic elements to perform AND and NAND Boolean functions, A, A′ and B are the inputs of the device. **b**, Example of Rochon prisms. (Reproduced from (Caulfield and Dolev, 2010), with permission).

Another possibility for information processing with light is given by an optical pre-processing procedure. Designs based on optical pre-processing yield an exponential growth in the number of results with the number of iterations. The basic idea consists to record an intermediate result as an optical pattern on a film and then projected and optically modified to gain the next multiplicative step over a larger film, thus gaining exponential size results within a linear number of steps (Dolev and Fitoussi, 2007). The doubling process can be executed once, as a pre-processing stage, to support any future input. For instance, all the Hamiltonian paths in a clique can be represented in a very large matrix, with the transparent points in each line of the matrix representing a single Hamiltonian path. If a current weighted graph is given, the weight vector of the graph is multiplied in parallel by the pre-processed matrix to obtain the best Hamiltonian path.

It has been proved that pre-processing by modifying and copying previously obtained results are useful procedures in architectures that are based on the representation of Turing machine configurations as a location in three-dimensional space (Dolev and Fitoussi, 2007; Dolev and Nir, 2009). Traditional microprocessors support a set of computation primitives, such as addition and multiplication. In addition, a new set of primitives that fits the optics capabilities, and is based on the Turing machine mapping to configurations has been proposed by Dolev and Fitoussi (Dolev and Fitoussi, 2007). One such configuration is designed to solve the Hamiltonian path problem. The basic procedure consists to allow many light beams to traverse all possible Hamiltonian paths in parallel, and design the traversal length to be proportional to the edges' weights, the beam that succeeds in doing so first must have traversed the shortest Hamiltonian. In some cases, the number of beams that arrive simultaneously at a location representing a city may grow exponentially with a number of cities, creating a number that can overwhelm any physical device (Bozhevolnyi, 2008). The next section is dedicated to the Hamiltonian path problem solved with optics.

9.2. Solving Hamiltonian Paths with Optical Computation

Several computational devices which use light rays for solving the Hamiltonian path problem on a directed graph has been recently proposed (Oltean 2008; Woods and Naughton, 2012; Wu et al., 2014). These devices have a graph-like representation and the light is traversing it by following the routes given by the connections between nodes. At the destination node, it is enough only to search for particular rays that have passed only once through each node. Hamiltonian path problems for a directed graph can be described as follows. Given a directed graph $G=(V,E)$ with $|V|=n$ nodes and a start node (v_{start}) and a stop node (v_{stop}), the problem asks to compute is there is a simple path, beginning with node v_{start} and ending with node v_{stop}, containing all nodes exactly once. The output for this decision problem is either YES and NO depending on whether the Hamiltonian path does exist or not. The idea of using light is based on two basic properties. One property is that the light speed has a limit. The second one the light ray can be easily divided into multiple rays of smaller intensity/power by using some beam-splitters. Commonly, such devices work as follows: initially a light ray is sent to the start node. When a ray passes through a node there are two operations: (i) the light ray is marked uniquely so that we know that it has passed through the node; (ii) the ray is divided into a number of rays equal to the external degree of that node. Each obtained ray is directed toward one of the nodes connected to the current node. At the destination node it is enough to search only for particular rays that have passed only once through each node. To be sure about a single passage, it is necessary to mark all rays which pass through a particular node with a unique label, such that Hamiltonian path is uniquely identified at the destination node. Oltean suggested to mark the rays passing through a node by delaying them with a certain amount of time (Oltean, 2008). This delay can be easily obtained by forcing the rays to pass through an optical fiber of a certain length. The delays, introduced at any node, cannot take any value. In this case, if a certain ray has traversed a Hamiltonian path only it its delay is equal to the sum of delays of all nodes in that graph. Roughly speaking, we need only the ray, which has traversed a Hamiltonian path, to arrive in the destination node at the moment equal to the sum of delays of each node, and the moment when the ray has entered in the start node is considered moment 0. If the delays introduced by each node of the graph is denoted $d_1, d_2, .. d_n$, a correct set of valûes for a systems should satisfy the condition: $d_1+d_2+\ldots+d_n \neq a_1 \cdot d_1+a_2 \cdot d_2+\ldots+a_n \cdot d_n$; where $a_i=1,\ldots,n$ ($a_i>0$) and cannot be all 1 in the same time. Thus, if value a_k is strictly greater than 1 it means that the ray has passed at least twice through node k.

A schematic example of a graph-like system as proposed by Oltean is represented in figure 9.2. In such scheme, the light will enter in node 0. Its will be delayed with a certain amount of time and then it will be divided into three rays which will be sent to nodes 1, 3 and 6. In node 1, the ray will be delayed with the amount of time corresponding to node 1. Thus, it will be sent to nodes 2 and 3. One of the rays will be able to generate a Hamiltonian path (0, 1, 2, 3, 4, 5, 6). The rays which have passed one through the previously described cycle cannot be considered Hamiltonian path because the moments when they arrive, at the destination node, are different from the sum of delays introduced by each node. Since the signal is continuous, in output the arrival of rays is notified by fluctuations in the intensity of the light. These fluctuations will be transformed in fluctuations of electric power making use of a photodiode and then read by an oscilloscope.

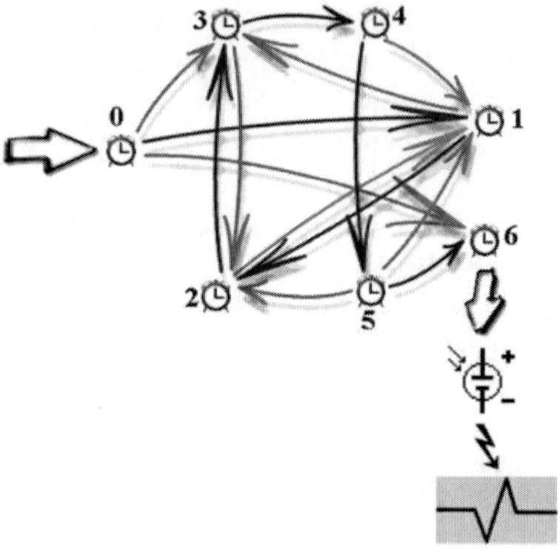

Figure 9.2. A schematic representation of the device as proposed by Oltean. Here, it is considered a graph with seven nodes. Start node is 0 and the destination node is 6. The list of arcs is: (0, 1), (0, 3), (0, 6), (1,2), (1, 3), (2, 1), (2, 3), (3, 2), (3,4), (4, 1), (4, 5), (5, 2), (5, 6). In each node the rays are delayed with a certain amount of time. The destination node is represented by a photodiode and an oscilloscope. When a ray will arrive in the destination node there will be a fluctuation, in the light intensity, which could be measured by the oscilloscope. (Reproduced from (Oltean, 2008), with permission).

One critical aspect in the Oltean proposal for a solution of Hamiltonian path problem is if the solution proposed is polynomial-time. It could seem that given the ability of the proposed device to provide output to any instance by traversing only once all nodes (O(n) complexity), then this could mean that we have found a polynomial-time algorithm for the Hamiltonian path problem. However, this is not the case, essentially because the delay time increases exponentially with the number of nodes. Even if the ray has the transverse only n nodes, the total time required by the ray to reach the destination node increases exponentially with the number of nodes. It should be noted that the device proposed by Oltean cannot find the Hamiltonian path. It can only say if this path exist or not. If there are multiple paths the device is not able to distinguish among them. However, the fascinating research on such topics is open, and surely it will reserve interesting developments in the next future.

A similar optical fiber network device for the Hamiltonian path has been proposed by Wu et al. (We et al., 2014), figure 9.3. The proof-of-principle demonstration is performed on a fiber network representing a graph with five towns in which the decision is successfully obtained in only a few tend of nanoseconds, figure 9.3. Although this result does not break the limitation of exponential solution of this NP-complete problem at a rate that is hundreds of times faster than that of brute-force computation and my already find applications in routing a secure communications. In fact, for making less severe scaling issues typical of physical method and to realize more complex cognitive photonic functions, the optical device can readily be implemented in integrated optical networks, such as silicon photonics or plasmonics networks. The details of the optical device are summarized in figures 9.3 and 9.4.

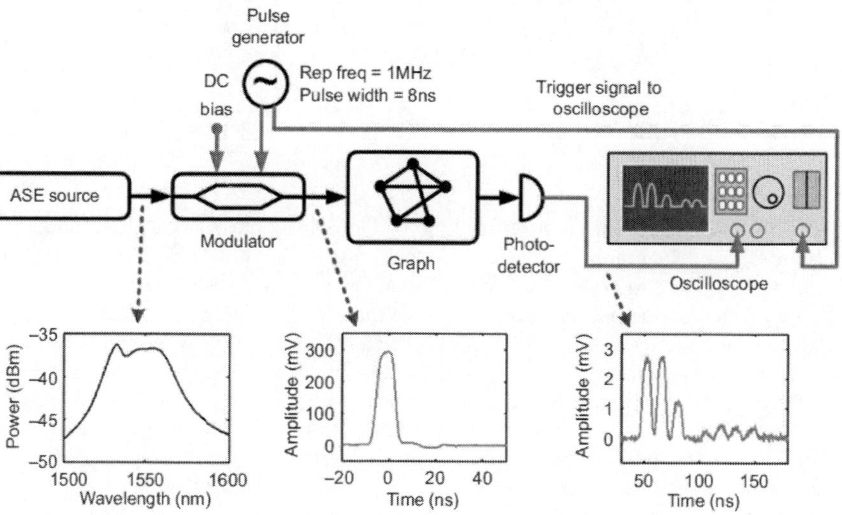

Figure 9.3. Experimental setup for solving the Hamiltonian path problem with on optical device. Light from a low-coherence ASE (amplified spontaneous emission) source is fed into an optical intensity modulator driven by an electrical pulse generator. The pulse train after the modulator has a pulse energy of 48pJ, a pulse width of 8ns and a repetition rate of 1MHz. The pulse train is injected into the target graph built from an optical fiber network. The pulses generated by the graph are monitored by a photodetector and an oscilloscope for detection of the pulse, thus indicating the existence of a Hamiltonian path. (Reproduced from (Wu et al., 2014), with permission).

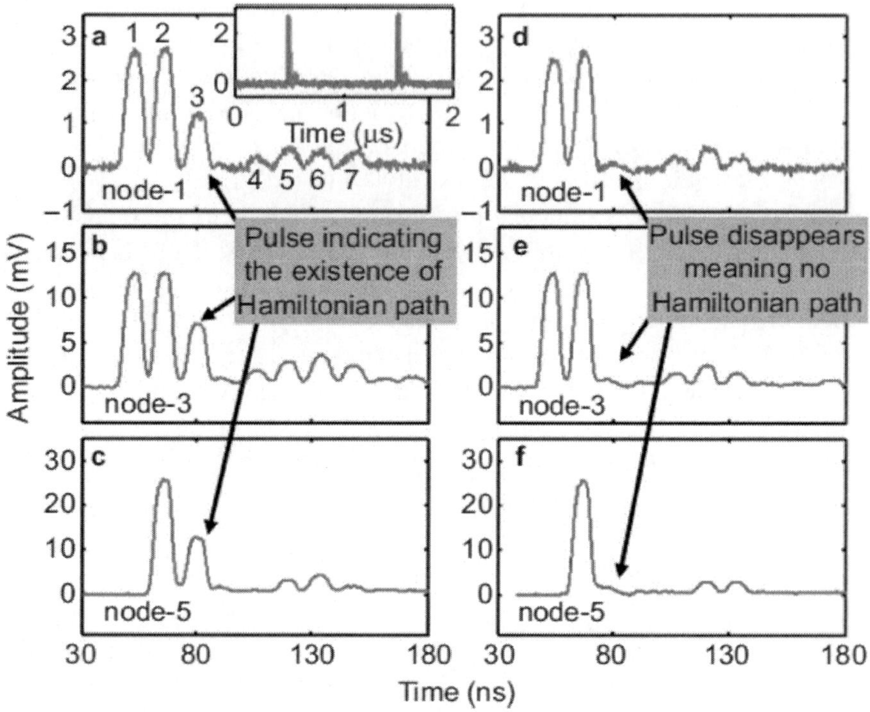

Figure 9.4. Pulse train outputs from the graphs. Outputs from (**a**) node 1, (**b**) node 3, and (**c**) node 5 of the graph and outputs from (**d**) node 1, (**e**) node 3 and (**f**) node 5 after the path from node 2 to node 5 is disconnected. The inset of (**a**) shows the pulse outputs from node 1 on a larger time scale. All the time axes are referenced to the pulse injected into the graph. In (**a**)-(**c**) the third pulse has a delay of 82ns, which is equal to the total delay of the graph demonstrating that this pulse indicates the existence of a Hamiltonian path. Analogously, in (**d**)-(**f**), because the path from node 2 to node 5 is disconnected, thee is not Hamiltonian path, and the third pulse disappears accordingly, confirming that the experimental setup is effective in indicating the existence of a Hamiltonian path. (Reproduced from (Wu et al., 2014), with permission).

9.3. Nanophotonic Computation Paradigm

Recently, Ohtsu, Naruse et al. showed that the spatiotemporal dynamics of photoexcitation transfer between quantum mechanical electronic states, which are represented by excitonic states in semiconductor nanostructures and are mediated by optical near-field interactions, could be used to solve constraint satisfaction problems (Ohtsu et al., 2009; Kawazoe et al., 2006; Yatsui et al.,

2007; Nomura et al., 2010, Naruse et al., 2014). As a consequence, they have been proposed a methodology to utilize photoexcitation transfer dynamics to solve satisfiability and bandit problem (Thompson, 1933, Robbins, 1952, Kim et al., 2010). Optical near-field interactions occur at scales far below the wavelength of light and enable photoexcitation transfer to dipole-forbidden energy levels, which cannot be realized by conventional optical far-fields. The system for photoexcitation transfer is pictured in figure 9.5(a), it consists of two spherical quantum dots (QDs) with two different radii (small and large $QD_{S,L}$, respectively). Under irradiation by input light, an exciton (electron-hole pair) is generated in QDs and the photoexcitation transfer process between the two QDs takes place with the transition of an excitation to two states, denoted q_1, q_2, where q_1 and q_2 are the orbital angular momentum quantum number and magnetic quantum number, respectively. The energy eigenvalues of the states are given by (Naruse et al., 2014)

$$E_{(q_1,q_2)} = E_g + E_{ex} + \frac{\hbar^2 \alpha^2_{(q_1,q_2)}}{2mr^2} \tag{9.1}$$

where E_g is the bandgap energy of the bulk semiconductor, E_{ex} is the exciton binding energy in the bulk system, m is the effective mass of the exciton, and α is determined from the boundary conditions. In general, there is a resonance between the level with quantum number (1,0) in QD_S, denoted by S, in figure, and that with number (1,1) in QD_L, if the ratio between the QD radii is 1.43π. These energy levels are in resonance and connected by a Yukawa-like potential (Ohstu et al., 2008). Transitions between such states are allowed only in near-field interactions due to large spatial inhomogeneity of the localized optical near fields at the surface of nanoscale materials, therefore, the exciton at level S in QD_S can be transferred to level L_2 in QD_L. Two basic properties are particularly considerable in the system represented in figure 9.5, i.e., first, the exciton transfer from QD_S to QD_L is unidirectional, where the unidirectionality of exciton transfer originates from the energy dissipation occurring in QD_L, and, second, exciton transfer can be blocked if the level L_1 is already filled with another exciton (Ohstu et al., 2009). The blocked exciton will bounce back and forth between QD_L and QD_S and will finally dissipate from QD_S according to the relaxation constant γ_S, figure 9.5(b).

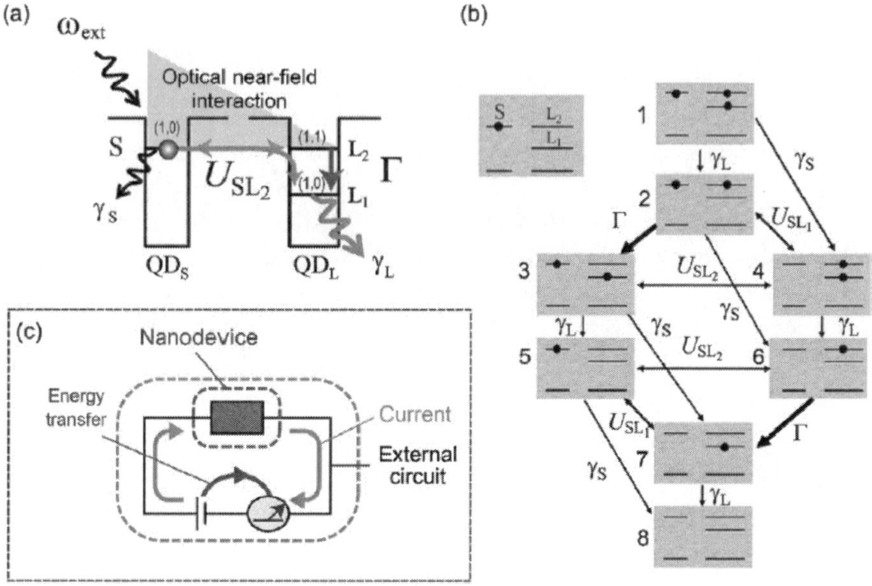

Figure 9.5. Schematic example of Optical excitation transfer mediated by optical near-field interactions. Optical excitation in the smaller quantum dot (*QD_S)* can be transferred to the larger one (*QD_L)*. Note that transition to the energy level L_2 in QD_L is conventionally dipole-forbidden. The optical near-field interaction, described by a Yukawa-type potential, allows such a transition on the nanoscale when QD_S and QD_L are located close to each other. The energy dissipation occurring at QD_L, or the relaxation from L_2 to L_1, guarantees uni-directionality. (*b*) State transition diagram for the purpose of modeling optical excitation transfer from QD_S to QD_L. (*c*) In contrast with nano-electric devices that require wiring, such as those based on single electron tunneling, a high-impedance circuit is necessary for achieving unidirectional signal transfer. (Reproduced from (Naruse et al. 2013), with permission).

Naruse et al. suggested the Nanophotonic Problem Solver (NPS) to simulate numerical calculation of satisfibility problem and multi-armed bandit problem (Naruse et al., 2014). Satisfiability problem can be described as follows: given a logical formula ϕ, which consists of *N* Boolean variables $x_i \in \{0(\textit{false}), 1(\textit{true})\}$ ($i \in I = \{1,2,\ldots, N\}$), the problem is to determine whether there exists at least one satisfying assignment of the truth values (0 or 1) to the variables represented by x_i such that it makes the formula evaluate to true (ϕ=1). Here, ϕ represents a logical proposition, and the existence of a satisfying assignment verifies that the proposition is self-consistent. For example, the formula $\phi_{ex}=(x_1 \vee \neg x_2) \wedge (\neg x_2 \vee x_3 \vee \neg x_4) \wedge (x_1 \vee x_3) \wedge (x_2 \vee \neg x_3) \wedge (x_3 \vee \neg x_4) \vee (\neg x_1 \vee x_4)$ has a satisfying assignment, $(x_1,x_2,x_3,x_4)=$

(1,1,1,1), which is a uniquely existing solution (Aono et al., 2013; Naruse et al., 2014). A schematic sketch of the NPS is shown in figure 9.6.

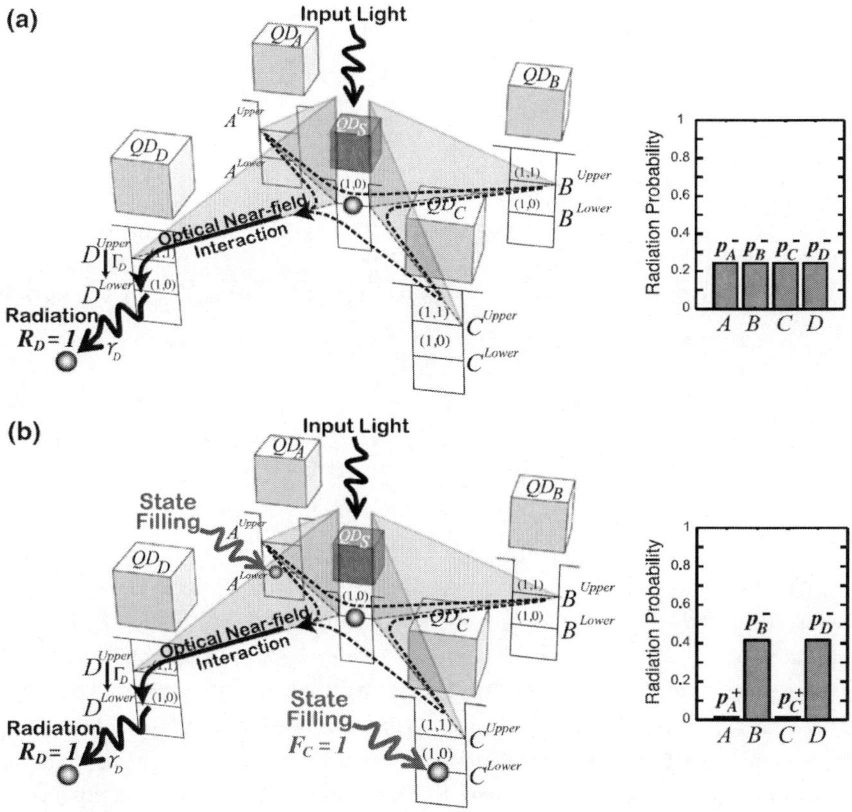

Figure 9.6. Nanophotonic problem solver with a *QDS* surrounded by four *QDLs*, *QDA*, *QDB*, *QDC*, and *QDD* (Aono et al., 2013). **a** In the absence of state-filling stimulation, radiation occurs in the four large dots with an equal probability, as shown in the *right panel.* **b** When *QDA* and *QDC* are state-filled, the exciton is likely to be transferred to either *QDB* or *QDD* from which it radiates with a higher probability. (Reproduced from (Naruse et al., 2014), with permission).

The NPS represented in figure 9.6 is a system where a QD_S is surrounded by four QD_L, each of which has the same energetic levels, upper and lower, and the same relaxation constants. If initially, the system has one exciton in *S*, the exciton can be transferred to any QD_L. This possibility is described by a quantum master equation using the density formalism:

$$\frac{d\rho(t)}{dt} = -\frac{i}{\hbar}[H_{\text{int}}, \rho(t)] - N_\Gamma \rho(t) - \rho(t) N_\Gamma \quad (9.2)$$

where $\rho(t)$ is the density matrix with respect to the five energy levels, $\hbar$ is the Planck's constant, N_Γ the is the relaxation matrix $N_\Gamma = diag(\gamma_S, \Gamma_A, \Gamma_B, \Gamma_C, \Gamma_D)$ and H_{int} is the interaction Hamiltonian given by

$$H_{\text{int}} = \begin{pmatrix} 0 & U_{S,A} & U_{S,B} & U_{S,C} & U_{S,D} \\ U_{S,A} & 0 & 0 & 0 & 0 \\ U_{S,B} & 0 & 0 & 0 & 0 \\ U_{S,C} & 0 & 0 & 0 & 0 \\ U_{S,D} & 0 & 0 & 0 & 0 \end{pmatrix} \quad (9.3)$$

typical experimental values are $\gamma_S^{-1} \cong 2.9\,\text{ns}$, $\Gamma_L^{-1} = 1\,\text{ps}$. The solution of the Liouville equation gives the time evolution of populations of the lower energy levels of the QD_Ls and the probabilities p_L that the exciton in QD_S is transferred in QD_L. The system shown in figure 9.6 uniformly grows the populations of A^{Lower}, B^{Lower}, C^{Lower}, D^{Lower} while reducing the population of S and finally reaches an equilibrium. Figure 9.6(b) shows the case where QD_A and QD_C are subjected to state filling by light stimulation. A way of describing such a state-filling effect is to induce a significant increase in the sublevel relaxation lifetime of the state-filled QD_A and QD_C, where lifetimes as $\Gamma_A^{-1} = \Gamma_C^{-1} = 5\,\text{ps}$ are assumed. Because of such changes in the parameters, the exciton is more likely to be transferred to QD_B or QD_D than to QD_A or QD_C, as shown in figure 9.6(b). As shown in figure, p_A and p_C decreased owing to state-filling stimulation, whereas $(p^-)_{B,D}$ increased as if they tried to compensate for the decrements in p_A and p_C. The reason for this is due to the fact that the radiation probability of each QD_L varied in response to the current state-filling stimulation applied to other distant QD_Ls. Since the stimulus response of each QD_L is not determined locally, the radiation probabilities of the state-filled and nonstate-filled increased nonlinearly as a function of the number of all state-filled of QD_Ls.

The question now is: how can the NanoPS solve a satisfiability problem (SAT)? A solution of a N-variable 3-SAT (a 3-SAT problem is when ϕ consists of M clauses that are connected by $\wedge$ (and), and each clause connects at most three literals by $\vee$ (or) as $(x_j \vee x_k \vee x_l)$, where each x can be either x or $\neg x$) can be supported by 2N $QD_L s$, $QD_{i,v}s$, which receive optical energy from QD_S. The label (i,v) indicates that values $v \in \{0,1\}$ is assigned to variable x_i $(i \in I = \{1,2,\ldots,N\}$. When the exciton in QD_S is transferred to $QD_{i,v}$ and subsequently radiation is observed at a discrete time step t, we write this status as $R_{i,v}(t)=1$, whereas $R_{i,v}(t)=0$ indicates that no radiation occurs (). If a new function $F_{i,v}(t)$ is introduced to quantify the state-filling stimulation applied to $QD_{i,v}$, $F_{i,v}(t)=1$ denotes a filled state and $F_{i,v}(t)=0$ denotes anon-filled state, thus radiation $R_{i,v}(t)=1$ occurs with a probability that depends on the state filling stimulation $F_{i,v}(t)$ as follows (): (i) $R_{i,v}(t)=1$ with probability $p^{+}_{i,v}(t)$ if $F_{i,v}(t)=1$; (ii) $R_{i,v}(t)=1$ with probability $p^{-}_{i,v}(t)$ if $F_{i,v}(t)=0$; (iii) $R_{i,v}(t)=0$, otherwise. Each radiation event $R_{i,v}$ is accumulated by a newly introduced variable $X_{i,v} \in \{-1,0,+1\}$ as follows (Naruse et al., 2014): (i) $X_{i,v}(t+1)= X_{i,v}(t)+1$ if $R_{i,v}(t)=1$ and $X_{i,v}(t)<1$; (ii) $X_{i,v}(t+1)= X_{i,v}(t)-1$ if $R_{i,v}(t)=0$ and $X_{i,v}(t)>-1$; (iii) $X_{i,v}(t+1)= X_{i,v}(t)$, otherwise. The values of $X_{i,v} \in$ can be stored either by some additional QDs or by some external control unit, respectively. At any step t, the system transforms a configuration $X=(X_{1,0},X_{1,1}, X_{2,0}, X_{2,1},\ldots,X_{N,0},X_{N,1})$ into an assignment $x=(x_1,x_2,\ldots,x_N)$ as follows: (i) $x_i(t)=0$, if $X_{i,0}(t)=1$ and $X_{i,1}(t)\leq 0$; $x_i(t)=1$, if $X_{i,0}(t) \leq 0$ and $X_{i,1}(t)=1$; (iii) $x_i(t)= x_i(t-1)$, otherwise; and $x_i(0)=$*undefined* for all i. The state-filling stimulations $F_{i,v}$s are updated synchronously according to the following dynamics:

$$F_{i,v}(t+1)=\begin{cases} 1 & \text{if} \quad \exists (P,Q) \in B(\forall (j,u) \in P(X_{j,u}(t)=1) \\ 0 & \text{otherwise} \end{cases}$$

$$\text{and} \quad (i,v) \in Q)$$

where B is a set of bounceback rules (Naruse et al., 2014). Each element (P,Q) in B implies the following statement: if all the $X_{i,u}$s specified by P are positive at t, the stimulate all $QD_{i,v}$s specified by Q to inhibit their radiation at $t+1$, with the constraint that if $x_j=u$, then x_i should not be v. The bounceback rule can defined as follows: let us consider the example formula ϕ_{ex}, to satisfy this formula for $\phi_{ex}=1$, for example, we should make every clause *true* because all clauses are connected by $\wedge$. Suppose, for instance, the system tried to assign $x_1=0$, i.e., $X_{1,0}(t)=1$, as indicated by the black broken circle as in figure 9.7, where the entire structure of the NanoPS is shown (Naruse et al., 2014). To make *true* the first clause in ϕ_{ex}, $(x_1 \vee \neg x_2)$, if $x_1=0$, then x_2 should not be 1. Therefore, it must be applied the state-filling $F_{2,1}(t+1)=1$ to inhibit the radiation $R_{2,1}(t+1)$ of $QD_{2,1}$ as indicated by the gray broken circle in figure 9.7(a). In addition, because x_3 in the third clause $(x_1 \vee x_3)$ should not be 0, $F_{3,0}(t+1)=1$ must be applied (the gray dotted circle). Therefore, $F_{1,1}(t+1)=1$ (solid circle) must be applied, because if $x_1=0$, consequently x_1 should not be 1. Likewise, the set of all bounceback rules B is determined by scanning all clauses in ϕ_{ex}. The computation starts at $X_{1,v}(0)=R_{i,v}(0)=F_{i,v}(0)=0$ for all (i,v) and the time evolution of the system is simulated by calculating the equations iteratively. Figure shows the overall system for the example formula ϕ_{ex} at $t=13$, figure 9.7(b).

The performance of NanoPS solver has been compared with that of the best studied stochastic local search algorithm, the WalkSAT, with excellent results (http://www.cs.rochester.edu/~kautz/walksat/). The performance was conducted on 500 trials consisting of MonteCarlo simulations to obtain the average number of iterations required to find a solution. NanoPS found a solution after a much smaller number of iterations than WalkSAT, and the advantage of NanoPS over WalkSAT increased as N increased.

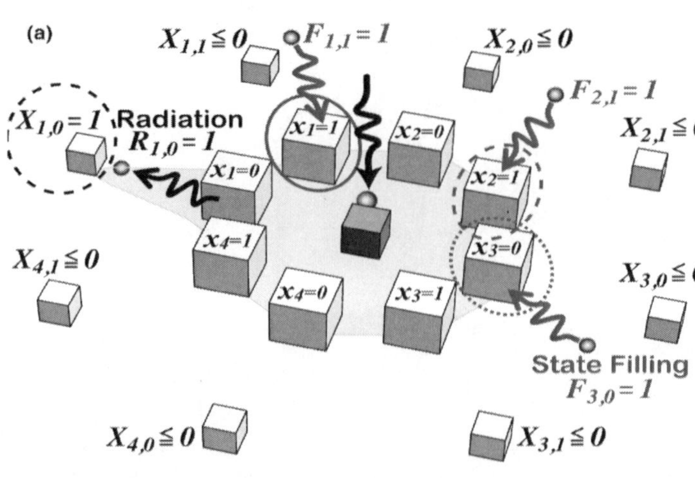

Figure 9.7. (Continued).

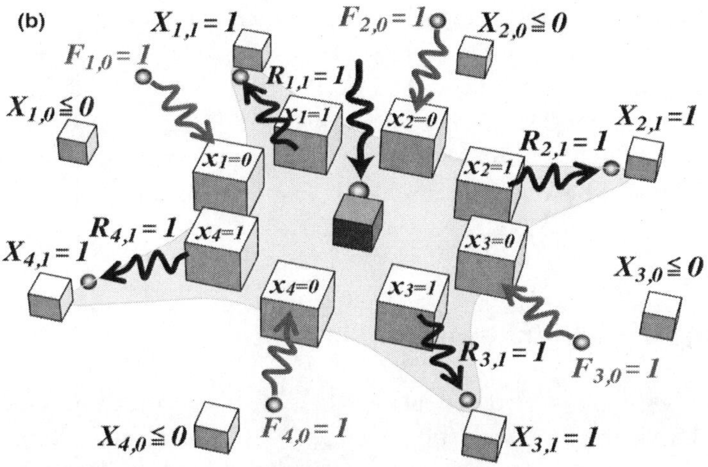

Figure 9.7. NanoPS solver for a four-variable satisfiability problem.
(a) Bounceback control applies state-filling stimulations $F_{1,1}(t+1)=F_{2,1}(t+1)=F_{3,0}(t+1)=1$, if $X_{1,0}=1$.
(b) Configuration X=(0,1,0,1,01,0,1), which represents a solution $(x_1,x_2,x_3,x_4)=(1,1,1,1)$. (Reproduced from (Naruse et al., 2014), with permission).

Photoexcitation transfer dynamics among *QD*s can be used as a nanophotonic decision maker (NanoDM) and applied to the multi-armed bandit problem (BP) (Kim et al., 2010; Aono et al., 2013). The BP can be defined as follows. Consider a number of slot machines, each of which rewards the player with a coin at a certain probability P_k ($k \in \{1,2,\ldots,N\}$ when played. To maximize the total amount of reward, it is necessary to make a quick and accurate judgment of which machine has the highest probability of giving a reward. To accomplish this, the player should gather information about many machines; however, in this process, the player should not fail to exploit the reward from the known best machine. These requirements are not easily met simultaneously, because there is a trade-off between *exploration* and *exploitation* (Naruse et al., 2014). Biological organisms commonly encounter this *exploration-exploitation dilemma* in their struggle to survive in an unknown world. This dilemma has not commonly recognized optimal solution. BP can be used to determine the optimal strategy for maximizing the total reward with incompatible demands, either by exploiting rewards obtained through already collected information or by exploring new information to acquire higher pay-offs through risk taking ( ). BP was originally proposed and applied by Thompson and Robbins (Thompson, 1933; Robbins, 1952), and the optimal strategy is known only for a limited class of problems where the reward distributions are assumed to be known *a priori* by the players. NanoDM is modeled using the density matrix formalism on a set of 11 energy levels plus a vacancy state for a total of 12 states (Naruse et al., 2014). The performance of NanoDM has been compared with Softmax algorithm, which is known to be the best-fitting algorithm for human decision-making behavior in the BP task, with excellent results in favor of NanoDM (Kuleshov and Precup, 2000; Bishop 2006; Naruse et al., 2014).

9.3.1. Hierarchical Information Photonics

Naruse et al. associated optical near-field interactions at various scales to different levels of the information hierarchy (Naruse et al., 2005). Optical near-field interactions between sub-wavelength-size objects allow the design of optical devices and systems at densities beyond those conventionally limited by the diffraction limit of light (Tate et al., 2009). One useful aspect of near-field systems that could be exploited in devices and systems is the physical hierarchy of optical near-fields, meaning that the system exhibits different physical behavior at different scales (Girard et al., 2000). A certain nanostructure may appear differently depending on how we observe it, for example, depending on the size of a fiber probe used to measure it. Naruse et al. have demonstrated that one of the simplest forms of such a hierarchy in optical-fields and associate it with an information hierarchy (Naruse et al., 2005).

Hierarchy of information can be found in terms of its meaning, quality, or level of importance, such as detailed and abstract information, high resolution and low-resolution information, high-security and less-critical information. A simple hierarchical system based on the scale-dependency of optical near-field interactions is presented in figure 9.8.

Let us consider the observation of an array of small particles distributed with sub-wavelength pitch using a probe whose diameter is substantially larger than that of observed particles, figure 9.8. The spatial distribution of the particles can be obtained by using a fiber probe of comparable size, this configuration can be defined as *near-mode* (Novotny and Hecht, 2006). On the contrary, the distribution cannot be resolved by a large fiber probe, and this configuration is defined as *far-field* (Novotny and Hecht, 2006). The electric field at position r in figure 9.8 is given by

$$E(r) = \sum_{\theta} \frac{E_\theta}{|r - s_\theta|} \exp(-i\omega t + ik|r - s_\theta|) \tag{9.4}$$

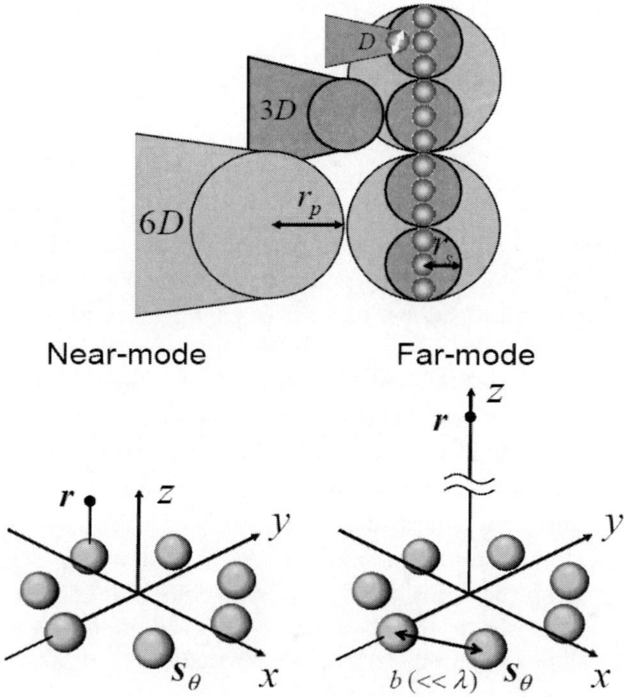

Figure 9.8. A simple spatial hierarchy observed in optical near-fields. (a) Dipole-dipole interaction. (b) Signal contrast as a function of the ratio of the radius of the sample and the probe. (c) Spatial resolution varies depending on the scale of the sample and the probe. (d) Array of dipole moments distributed on sub-wavelength scale and its observation in *near-mode* and *far-mode*. (Reproduced from (Naruse et al., 2005), with permission).

where ω is the operating frequency, k is the wave number, and s_θ represents the position of a dipole specified by θ (θ=1,2,…). The existence of a dipole at position s_θ is indicated by a near-code as follows: $E_\theta=0$ if *near-code*(θ)=0, or $E_\theta=E_0$, if *near-code*(θ)=1. The far-field configuration involves a probe located a great distance from the small particles, this means that the Eq. (9.4) is modified as follows:

$$E(r) = E_0 \frac{\exp(-i\omega t + ikr)}{r} \sum_{\theta} near - code(\theta) \tag{9.5}$$

which means that the electric field intensity at position r is proportional to the number of dipole moments given by the near-code. When the near-code is made of n bits, the number of dipole moments can range from zero to n. Therefore, n+1 different signal levels appear in the signal obtained in far-mode, since the total number of bit combinations in the near-code is 2^n.

Consider, now, a two-layer hierarchical memory based on concepts of far-codes and near-codes. The far-code depends on an array of bits distributed within a certain area and is determined logically to be either 0 or 1. Consider an (N+1)-bit digital code, where N is an even number and let the *far-code* be defined depending on the number of 1 (or 0) contained in the (N-1)-bit digital code according to the rule: *far-code*=1, if the number of 1>N/2, or *far-code*=0, otherwise. Therefore, (N+1) digits provide a total of 2N+1 possible permutations, or codes. Half of them, namely 2^N permutations, have more than N/2+1 the value 1 among the (N+1) digits (*far-code*=1) and the other half, always 2^N permutations, have more than N/2+1 the value 0 (*far-code*=0). This means that 2^N different codes could be assigned to two (N+1)-bit digital sequences so that their corresponding far-codes are 1 and 0, respectively. Such (N+1)-bit code can be considered the *near-code* (Naruse et al., 2005). Examples of *near-codes* for N=8 are listed in figure 9.9. Figure b schematically shows example of codes in which a 9-bit *near-code* is represented as a 3×3 array of circles, where black and white mean 1 or 0, respectively. In such example, if the number of 1 in the *near-code* is larger than five, then the *far-code* is 1, otherwise the *far-code* is 0. This computation scheme can be applied to text data, as well as to image data, in fact, as in figure c the *far-code* stores text data and the *near-code* stores 256-level (8-bit) image data (Naruse et al., 2005).

It is possible to define a series of rules for an encoding and decoding scheme, where the *near-codes* and *far-codes* could be respectively associated with image and text data for multimedia applications, or with high-security and less-critical verifications for security applications. To describe briefly such rules, consider a situation where the *far-code* should represent an ASCII code for the letter *A*, whose binary sequence is 0100001. It is possible to assume that the gray levels of the first two pixels, which will be coded in the *near-code*, are the same value, in this case *92*. However, the first two *far-codes* are different (0 followed by 1). As in the correspondence of figure a, and seeing that the first *far-code* is 0 and the *near-code* should represent *92*, thus, the first *near-code* should be 001101010. Analogously, the second *near-code* is 110001011, which represents 92, whereas its corresponding *far-code* is 1.

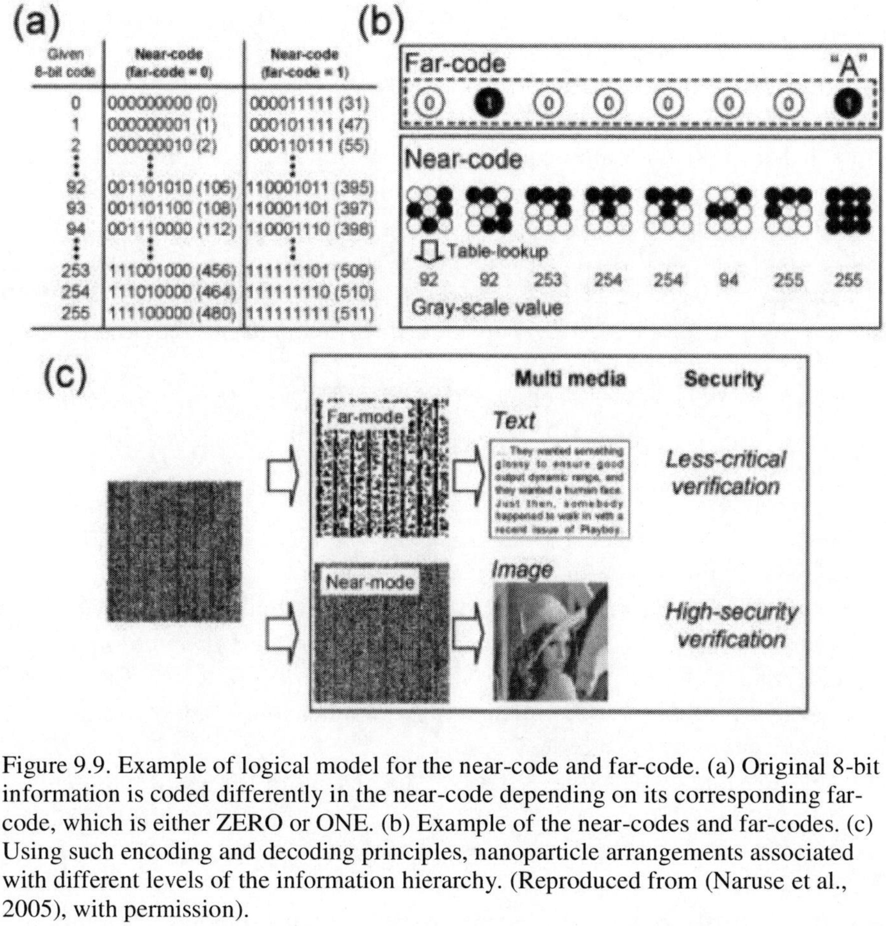

Figure 9.9. Example of logical model for the near-code and far-code. (a) Original 8-bit information is coded differently in the near-code depending on its corresponding far-code, which is either ZERO or ONE. (b) Example of the near-codes and far-codes. (c) Using such encoding and decoding principles, nanoparticle arrangements associated with different levels of the information hierarchy. (Reproduced from (Naruse et al., 2005), with permission).

REFERENCES

Aaronson, S., 2005, NP-complete problems and physical reality, *SIGACT News*, 36, 30-52.

Adleman L.M., 1994, Molecular computation of solutions to combinatorial problems, *Science*, 266, 1021-1024.

Andrews D.L., Gaburro Z., 2007, Frontiers in Surface Nanophotonics Principles and Applications, Springer, Berlin.

Aono M., Hirata Y., hara M., Aihara K., 2010, A model of amoeba-based neurocmpunter, *Journal of Computer Chemistry*, 9, 143-156.

Aono M., Naruse M., Kim S.J., Wakabayashi M., Hori H., Ohtsu M., Hara M., 2013, Amoeba-Inspired Nanoarchitectonic Computing: Solving Intractable Computational Problems Using Nanoscale Photoexcitation Transfer Dynamics, *Langmuir*, 29, 7557-7564.

Bishop C.M., 2006, Pattern Recognition and Machine Learning, Springer.

Bozhevolnyi S.I., 2008, Plasmonics Nanoguides and Circuits, World Scientific, Singapore.

Caulfield H.J., Soref R.A., Qian L., Zavalin A., Hardy J., 2007, Generalized optical logic elements- GOLEs, *Optics Communications*, 271, 365-376.

Caulfield H.J., Dolev S., 2010, Why future supercomputing requires optics, *Nature Photonics*, 4, 261-263.

Cook S.A., 1971, The complexity of theorem-proving procedures, *Proceedings of the third annual ACM Symposium on Theory of Computing*, pp.151-158, OH:ACM.

Dolev S., Fitoussi H., 2007, The Traveling Beams, Optical Solutions for Bounded NP-Complete Problems, *Proc. 4th Int. Conf. FUN 2007*, pp. 120-134, Springer, Berlin.

Dolev S., Nir Y., 2009, Optical Designs for Non-determinitic Turing Machines, *Proc. 2nd Int. Workshop on Optical SuperComputing*, pp. 47-55, Springer, Berlin.

Ezziane Z., 2006, DNA computing: applications and challenges, *Nanotechnology*, 17, R27-R39.

Girard C., Joachim C., Gauthier S., 2000, The physics of the near-field, *Report on Progress in Physics*, 63, 893-938.

Hardy J., Shamir J., 2007, Optics Inspired logic architecture, *Optics Express*, 15, 150-56.

Karp, R.M., 2010, Reducibility among combinatorial problems, *50 years of Integer Programming 1958-2008*, pp.219-241, Springer, Berlin.

Kawazoe T., Kobayashi K., Akahane K., Naruse M., Yamamoto N., Ohtsu M., 2006, Demonstration of nanophotonic NOT gat using near-field optically coupled quantum dots, *Applied Physics B*, 84(1-2), 243-46

Kieu T., 2003, Quantum algorithm for Hilbert's tenth problem, *Int. J. Theoretical Physics*, 42, 1461-1478.

Kim S.J., Aono M., Hara M., 2010, Tug-of-War model for the two-bandit problem: Nonlocally-correlated parallel exploration via resource conservation, *Biosystems*, 101, 29-36.

Kuleshov V., Precup D., 2000, Algorithms for the multi-armed bandit problem, *J. of Machine Learning Research*, 1, 1-48.

Liu Q., Wang L., Frutos A.G., Condon A.E., Corn R.M., Smith L.M., 2000, DNA computing on surfaces, *Nature*, 403, 175-179.

Naruse M., Yatsui T., Nomura W., Hirose N., Ohtsu M., 2005, Hierarchy in optical near-fields and its application to memory retrieval, *Optics Express*, 13,(23), 9265-71.

Naruse M., Tate N., Aono M., Ohtsu M., 2013, Information physics fundamentals of nanophonotonics, *Report Prog. Physics*, 76, 056401 (1-50)

Naruse M., 2014, Nanophotonic Information Physics, Springer-Verlag, Berlin Heidelberg.

Nomura W., Yatsui T., Kawazoe T., Naruse M., Ohstu M., 2010, Structural dependency of optical excitation transfer via optical near-field interactions between semiconductor quantum dots, *Applied Physics B*, 100(100), 181-87.

Novotny L., Hecht B., 2006, *Principles of Nano-Optics,* Cambridge University Press, UK.

O'Brien J.L., 2007, Optical quantum computing, *Science*, 318, 1567-70.

Ohstu M., Kobayashi K., Kawazoe T., Yatsui T., Naruse M., 2008, Principles of Nanophotonics, Taylor and Francis, Boca Raton.

Ohstu M., 2009, Nanophotonics and Nanofabrication, Wiley-VCH.

Ohtsu M., Kawazoe T., Yatsui T., Naruse M., 2009, Nanophotonics: Applications of Dressed Photons to Novel Photonic Devices and Systems, *IEEE J. Selected Topics in Quantum Electronics*, 14(6), 1404-17.

Oltean M., 2008, Solving the Hamiltonian path problem with a light-based computer, *Natural Computing*, 7, 57-70.

Robbins H., 1952, Some aspects of the sequential design of experiments, *Bulletin of the Amer. Mathematical Society*, 58, 527-536.

Shaked N.T., Messika S., Dolev S., Rosen J., 2007, Optical solution for bounded NP-complete problems, *Applied Optics*, 46, 711-24.

Tamir D., Shaked N., Wilson P., Dolev S. 2009, High-speed and low-power electro-optical DSP coprocessor, *J. Opt. Soc. Am. A*, 26, A11-A20.

Tate N., Nomura W., Yatsui T., Naruse M., Ohtsu M., 2009, Hierarchy in optical near-fileds absed on compositions of nanomaterials, *Applied Physics B*, 96, 1-4.

Thompson, W.R., 1933, On the likelihood that one unknown probability exceeds another in view of the evidence of two samples. *Biometrika,* 25(3–4), 285–294.

Woods D., Naughton T.J., 2012, Optical computing: photonic neural networks, *Nature Physics*, 8, 257-259.

Wu K., García de Abajo J., Soci C., Shum P.P., Zheludev N.I., 2014, An optical fiber network oracle for NP-complete problems, *Light: Science and Applications*, 3, e147.

Yatsui T., Sangu S., Kawazoe T., Ohstu M., An S.J., Yoo J., Yi G.C., 2007, Nanophotonic switch using ZnO nanorod double-quantum-well structures, *Applied Physics Letters*, 90(22), 223110(1-3).

Zhu L., Aono M., Kim S.-J., Hara M., 2013, Amoeba-based computing for traveling salesman problem: Long-term correlations between spatially separated individual cells of Physarum polycephalum, *BioSystems*, 112, 1-10.

INDEX

D

E

F

G

H

I

J

K

L

M

N

O

P

Q

R

S

T

U

V

W

Y

Z